Contesting Australian History

Contesting Australian History

Essays in Honour of Marilyn Lake

Edited by Joy Damousi and Judith Smart

Contesting Australian History: Essays in Honour of Marilyn Lake
© Copyright 2019
Copyright of this collection in its entirety is held by the editors, Joy Damousi and Judith Smart.
Copyright of the individual chapters is held by the respective author/s.

All rights reserved. Apart from any uses permitted by Australia's Copyright Act 1968, no part of this book may be reproduced by any process without prior written permission from the copyright owners. Inquiries should be directed to the publisher.

Monash University Publishing
Matheson Library and Information Services Building
40 Exhibition Walk
Monash University
Clayton, Victoria 3800, Australia
www.publishing.monash.edu

Monash University Publishing brings to the world publications which advance the best traditions of humane and enlightened thought.

Monash University Publishing titles pass through a rigorous process of independent peer review.

ISBN: 9781925835069 (paperback)

www.publishing.monash.edu/books/cah-9781925835069.html

Second printing, 2019.

Series: Australian History
Series Editor: Sean Scalmer

Design: Les Thomas

Cover image: Personal collection, Marilyn Lake

A catalogue record for this book is available from the National Library of Australia

Printed in Australia by Griffin Press an Accredited ISO AS/NZS 14001:2004 Environmental Management System printer.

The paper this book is printed on is certified against the Forest Stewardship Council ® Standards. Griffin Press holds FSC chain of custody certification SGS-COC-005088. FSC promotes environmentally responsible, socially beneficial and economically viable management of the world's forests.

TABLE OF CONTENTS

Introduction vii
    Joy Damousi and Judith Smart

1   From the Island 1
    Graeme Davison

2   Contesting 'Anzacery': Marilyn Lake and Envisioning
   Australian Nationalism 9
    Stephen Garton

3   Negotiating the Local and the Global: Marilyn Lake and
   the Writing of Australian Women's History 21
    Patricia Grimshaw

4   Radical Feminists and Respectable Radicals: Progressive
   Feminism and the Mainstream Women's Movement in
   Australia 37
    Judith Smart

5   Peace Politics and Women's Liberation 51
    Kate Laing

6   Scholarly Activism in Women's Studies 66
    Liz Conor

7   'My Work Does Not Wait for Revolutions': Elizabeth Reid
   and the Possibilities of State Feminism in Iran 80
    Roland Burke

8   Transforming Australian History: Humanitarianism and
   Transnationalism 94
    Joy Damousi

9   In Search of Emily 107
    Mark McKenna

10 'For the Record': A History of the New South Wales
    Aborigines Protection Board 121
    John Maynard and Victoria Haskins

11 Genealogies of Self-determination........................ 136
    Tim Rowse

12 Faith Bandler and the Politics of Race 152
    Henry Reynolds

13 Muslims in Australia: Beyond Narratives of Pioneers
    and Aliens.. 162
    Samia Khatun

14 Trouble in White Australia: Marilyn Lake, Australian History
    and Asian Exclusion................................... 175
    Sophie Loy-Wilson

15 Victor Selden Clark's *The Labour Movement in Australasia*:
    Comparative Colonialism and American Exceptionalism 190
    Ian Tyrrell

16 American Exceptionalism Subtracted: Taking on Transnational
    History from an Australian Stance....................... 204
    Warwick Anderson

17 Settler Colonialism and African American Historiography:
    Reflections on Marilyn Lake's Contribution to Transnational
    Histories of Race 217
    Clare Corbould

Tributes from Afar 229
About the Editors 245
List of Contributors 246
Index 247

INTRODUCTION

Joy Damousi and Judith Smart

In December 2016 a Festschrift was held over two days at the University of Melbourne to celebrate the outstanding career and achievements of Marilyn Lake, highly distinguished professor of history at, first, La Trobe University and then the University of Melbourne. This book contains seventeen chapters based on papers presented at the Festschrift. One of Australia's leading scholars, Marilyn forged a career that spanned several decades across a number of universities, including as Harvard Chair of Australian Studies in 2001–02. She also held Visiting Professorial Fellowships at Stockholm University, the Australian National University, the University of Sydney, the University of Western Australia, and the University of Maryland.

Marilyn's intellectual endeavours have encompassed many subjects and issues. She has made significant contributions to several fields including the impact of war and the history of Anzac, the history of feminism and women's history, gender, postcolonialism, race relations and racial identities, transnationalism and internationalism, human rights, biography, labour history, progressivist social reform, and settler colonialism. Her award-winning books have significantly advanced our understanding not only of Australian social, cultural and political history but also of the interdependence of that history with those of Britain, the US and the Asia–Pacific region. The chapters in this book span the breadth of Marilyn's scholarly influence on the directions historical research is taking today.

Marilyn's commitment to the history profession is evidenced through her contribution to the Australian Historical Association as a two-term president, and her input as a member of the Council of the Australian Academy of the Humanities, as well as her membership of several major and significant editorial boards including *Labour History*, *Journal of Women's History*, *Social Politics: International Studies in Gender, State & Society*, and *Australian Historical Studies*. She has also played an important role as a public intellectual on radio and television programs and in wide-ranging newspaper opinion pieces, as well as organising public lecture series such as 'Australia in the World' (2013), engaging in public policy such as the National History Curriculum, and in heritage and museum advocacy as a Museums Victoria councillor, a director of the Victorian Women's Trust, and a member of the Sullivan's Cove Waterfront Authority in Hobart, Tasmania.

These achievements have been recognised in a variety of awards and honours. In 2003 Marilyn was presented with the Governor General's Centenary Medal for Service to History and in 2006 was admitted to the Victorian Honour Roll of Women. Most recently, in 2018, she was appointed an Officer of the Order of Australia (AO) for 'distinguished service to higher education, particularly to the social sciences, as an academic, researcher and author, and through contributions to historical organisations'.

Significantly, amongst the contributors to this volume are several of her postgraduate students and she has inspired generations of students. Colleagues from around the globe have benefited from collaborating with Marilyn through publications and international conferences. Many messages of gratitude and admiration for Marilyn's work were sent from overseas colleagues and Australian scholars abroad, and we are delighted to be able to publish these tributes in a final chapter in this book.

Marilyn Lake has made an outstanding contribution to the history discipline, to the Australian academy, and to the community in promoting Australian history nationally and internationally. This volume is a tribute to her work and a recognition of her enduring influence and leadership in the profession.

Chapter 1

FROM THE ISLAND[*]

Graeme Davison

It is time someone wrote a history of the Tasmanian diaspora. The island has a population of only half a million, barely 3 per cent of the national total, but its contribution to the life of the nation far exceeds that proportion. In politics, think of Andrew Inglis Clark, Joe and Enid Lyons, Bob Brown, Neal Blewett, the Newmans and, now, Jacqui Lambie. In sport, think of Peter Hudson, Darrell Baldock, David Boon and Ricky Ponting. In literature, think of Christopher Koch and Richard Flanagan. In music, consider Peter Sculthorpe and Eileen Joyce. Other notable Tasmanian exports include the critic Peter Conrad and the political scientist and Gay activist Denis Altman. As for the historians, Tasmania has produced four of the finest—Lloyd Robson, Henry Reynolds, James Boyce and Marilyn Lake. What is it in the water, the climate or the culture of the island state that grows such prodigies?

Most of those Tasmanian high achievers eventually left the state for bigger places. Since the 1850s, Tasmania has had the highest rate of outward migration and the lowest rate of inward migration in the Commonwealth. Ambitious children growing up in Hobart and Launceston knew—or soon discovered—that, in all probability, they would have to move away to realise their ambitions. Marilyn reminded me of Peter Conrad's aphorism: If you are born in Tasmania, he says, you have only two choices: reinvent Tasmania or reinvent yourself. Only a few, like the admirable Richard Flanagan, stayed to reinvent Tasmania; some others, like Henry Reynolds,

---

[*] I am grateful to Marilyn's former teacher at the University of Tasmania, Michael Roe, for his recollections of her time here and to Marilyn herself for an informative exchange of emails that filled out her biography.

returned after spending most of their lives elsewhere; but most leave, never to return.

Marilyn was a member of this distinguished exodus. I did not really get to know Marilyn until the early 1980s when, as a newly arrived professor at Monash, I took over supervision of her PhD thesis from Alan Shaw. I don't recall us talking much about her Tasmanian origins and, in retrospect I'm sorry we didn't for I think they have a significant bearing on the kind of historian she has become.

Her family, the Calverts, are such prodigies of Tasmanian-nurtured national success that they have their own entry in the *Companion to Tasmanian History*.[1] Marilyn's distant forebear, Christopher Calvert, a free settler from Yorkshire, arrived in Van Diemen's Land in 1832, and later with his wife Hannah bought land at South Arm, south of Hobart, where he and his descendants grew apples and pears, ran coastal steamers, and provided postmistresses and teachers. There are almost fifty Calverts buried in the yard of St Barnabas Church in South Arm.[2] 'In the south of Tasmania there is no more respected name than that of the Calvert family', the *Hobart Mercury* declared when four generations of them gathered for a reunion in 1928.[3] Marilyn's own generation, however, has carried the Calvert name to a new peak. Her late elder brother Ashton, a Rhodes Scholar, became a distinguished diplomat and head of the Department of Foreign Affairs and Trade. Her sister Pamela became assistant director-general of the National Library. And then, of course, there is Marilyn herself. One day, when we read her autobiography, we may discover more about the mix of parentage, farm life, schooling, sibling rivalry and of the distinctive social and political culture of Tasmania that went into the making of the historian.

Like her siblings, Marilyn was educated in state schools in Kettering and Hobart. She credits a young teacher at Hobart High, Bruce Poulson, with kindling her interest in history and English.[4] At sixteen she won a Commonwealth scholarship. Her teachers had to plead that she was mature enough for university study, and the university had to waive its admission statute to permit her to begin undergraduate study in 1965. Like many of

---

1 Alison Alexander, *The Companion to Tasmanian History* (Hobart: Centre for Tasmanian Historical Studies, 2005), 63.

2 http://gravesoftas.com.au/municipalities/Clarence/South%20Arm%20St%20Barnaba%20Anglican.htm, accessed 10 December 2017.

3 *Mercury*, 6 January 1928.

4 Marilyn Lake, 'Taking Our Past with Us', in *Feminist Histories*, eds Bain Attwood and Joy Damousi (Melbourne: History Institute of Victoria, 1991), 40.

us, she began as a combined English and History student, but her interests quickly shifted towards history. Michael Roe, who was one of her teachers at the University of Tasmania, recalls: 'As an undergraduate Marilyn did as many History units as the rules allowed, ever proving a student of high calibre. That record continued as she moved into fourth-year Honours; she was the ideal seminar student, informed, questioning, fluent with both pen and tongue'.

The History Department at the University of Tasmania was one of the best for its size in Australia, and Marilyn was fortunate to be taught by three outstanding historians. Michael Roe, the only one of the three still alive, is one of Australia's most original historians. A quiet retiring scholar, he pioneered the study of Australian intellectual history in both the early colonial period and the early twentieth century. Against the nationalising tendencies that dominated Australian historical writing in the 1960s and 70s, he emphasised the American and European, as well as British, contexts. As his student in American history, Marilyn won the first of the many prizes that have marked a stellar career and later tutored for him in American history. Roe's important book *Nine Australian Progressives* (1984) anticipates some of the themes of *Drawing the Global Colour Line* and Marilyn's current project on 'the Progressive New World'.[5]

The second of Marilyn's influential teachers, Kay Daniels, was educated at the University of Adelaide and the University of Sussex before her arrival at the University of Tasmania at about the same time as Marilyn in 1967. She became one of the pioneers of Australian feminist history with her books *Women in Australia: An Annotated Guide to Records* (1977) and *Uphill all the Way* (1980).[6] Marilyn was a participant in the feminist history circle she began in the early 1970s and contributed to the archival research project for International Women's Year that led to Kay's two books. Not many Australian academic departments at that time had as formidable an

---

5   Michael Roe, *Nine Australian Progressives: Vitalism in Bourgeois Social Thought 1890–1960* (Brisbane: University of Queensland Press, 1984); compare Marilyn Lake and Henry Reynolds, *Drawing the Global Colour Line: White Men's Countries and the Question of Racial Equality* (Melbourne: Melbourne University Press, 2008); Marilyn Lake, '"This great America": H.B. Higgins and Transnational Progressivism', *Australian Historical Studies* 44 (2) (June 2013): 172–88; and Marilyn Lake, *Progressive New World: How Settler Colonialism and Trans-Pacific Exchange Shaped American Reform* (Cambridge, MA: Harvard University Press, forthcoming).

6   Kay Daniels, Mary Murnane and Anne Picot, *Women in Australia: An Annotated Guide to Records* (Canberra: AGPS, 1977); Kay Daniels and Mary Murnane (eds), *Uphill all the Way: A Documentary History of Women in Australia* (Brisbane: University of Queensland Press, 1980).

advocate of feminist history as Tasmania. From Kay, Marilyn acquired the conviction that women's history was not simply the recovery of something that had accidentally fallen through the cracks of orthodox history but that it had the potential to reconstitute the whole practice of the discipline.[7]

The third of the trio, Malcolm McRae, is now the least known of the three (he published very little beyond a few articles in local journals) but was probably the most influential on Marilyn at the time. Tasmanian born, he was educated at the famous Quaker school, 'Friends', and at the University of Tasmania. 'McRae', Michael Roe recalls, 'had distinguished qualities of mind ... Both his tongue and his pen were instruments of powerful exposition. As a teacher he could stir and spur in a remarkable way'. 'Handsome, passionate, extroverted' is how the adoring teenage Marilyn remembered him.[8] Of gentry background, McRae became a powerful advocate for the radical nationalism we associate with Russel Ward, Robin Gollan and Ian Turner. He suffered significant stress and ill-health in defending the philosopher Sydney Sparkes Orr in the notorious dismissal case that divided the university and Tasmanian society in the 1960s and died, aged only 49, in 1974, not long after Marilyn had completed a Master's thesis that bears marks of his influence.

Michael Roe recalls that he and Marilyn had a long discussion about the topic of the thesis. He inclined to a study of the Tasmanian press, but, as he now concedes, 'she judged better and so embarked on the project that was to culminate in *A Divided Society: Tasmania During World War One*.[9] What a Master's thesis that was, meriting publication by Melbourne University Press: in splendid prose Marilyn explored and illuminated a rich story. Thus were set the parameters for a phenomenal academic life'. It is indeed a fine thesis and today would easily meet the requirements for a PhD. (I will refrain from melancholy reflections on what this might say about changing academic standards.) Within the limited geographical scope of a single small state, Marilyn was able to encompass the several dimensions of a social and political crisis—often treated by other historians in tunnel-histories of conscription, sectarianism, labour relations and the like—to show, as her fellow Tasmanian Lloyd Robson noted, 'how middle-class fears and obsessions helped to turn one of the most democratic and

---

7   Lake, 'Taking Our Past with Us', 44; Marilyn Lake, 'Kay Daniels as Feminist Historian', *Women's History Review* 12 (2) (June 2003): 149–51.
8   Lake, 'Taking Our Past with Us', 42.
9   Marilyn Lake, *A Divided Society: Tasmania During World War One* (Melbourne: Melbourne University Press, 1975).

progressive countries into one of the most conservative'. 'The whole book', Robson concluded, 'is infinitely depressing and a grim example of how close Australia may always be to admiring the authoritarian and Fascist mentality'.[10] Looking back, Marilyn was critical of the limitations of the labourist paradigm in which the book was written, and of her failure not just to include women in the story but also to register the gendered dimension of that much-divided society. But, by the time it was published in 1975, her personal life, as well as the politics of the time, had brought those issues into sharper focus.

In 1968 nineteen-year-old Marilyn had married Sam Lake, then a senior lecturer in zoology at the University of Tasmania. Sam, who had grown up in Canberra and taken a PhD in Southhampton, would become an internationally distinguished freshwater ecologist. In the early 1970s, while completing her Master's thesis, Marilyn tutored in the History Department. In 1976 she and Sam decided to move to Melbourne, believing that the mainland offered them, and Marilyn especially, wider opportunities. She was offered scholarships at Melbourne, La Trobe and Monash but opted for the last, attracted by its strong team of Australian historians, who then included Alan Shaw, Geoffrey Serle, Ian Turner, Duncan Waterson, John Rickard and Richard White, soon to be joined by Marian Quartly, Stephen Foster and Graeme Davison. Sam joined the Monash Department of Zoology and Marilyn began doctoral studies on the history of soldier settlement in Victoria. Their first daughter, Kath, was born in 1977 and the second, Jess, in 1981.

Like many other women who had enjoyed early academic success, Marilyn suddenly found herself juggling childrearing, part-time work and further study. Among the opportunities to come her way was the task of co-editing a collection of women's biographies published to mark the sesquicentenary of Victoria in 1985. (The project was convened by Marian Quartly, then a member of the anniversary publications committee chaired by Marilyn's supervisor Alan Shaw.) Exactly who suggested the title of the volume, *Double Time*, I'm not sure, but it resonated strongly with Marilyn's personal situation. 'During the past six years', the biographical note on the flyleaf reads, 'she has struggled to meet a triple time table, combining full-time teaching at Monash University, then the University of Melbourne, writing a PhD thesis on soldier settlement and (together with her husband)

---

10 Review of *A Divided Society* in *Historical Studies* 17 (67) (October 1976): 272–3.

raising two daughters—all of which she feels has generated insights as well as exhaustion'.[11]

Supervising PhD theses is one of the most rewarding tasks of academic life, but the rewards are often unaccountably unequal to the effort expended. We bask in the reflected glory of students who largely supervised themselves and owe us little beyond words of encouragement. So it was, I think, with Marilyn who had already been working on her thesis for five years or so before Alan Shaw retired and handed her over to me. As a supervisor, as in his personal relations generally, Alan was understated: 'Good' was apparently about as much as Marilyn got in the way of comment on her drafts. I probably offered more words, but the message was much the same.

Soldier settlement was a logical extension of the project Marilyn had tackled in her first book, but it represented a marked advance in both theoretical sophistication (notably her Foucauldian analysis of the bureaucratic machinery of soldier settlement in the first half of the thesis) and especially in incorporating women's experience. As her supervisor, I was aware of the theoretical debates among feminist historians that framed Marilyn's analysis, especially those coming from the 'Women and Labour' conferences, but I knew less—at least then—of why she had been drawn to her subject. As a girl growing up on the orchard, she had witnessed at first hand her mother's struggle to accommodate the cross-pressured demands of respectability and economic survival. 'Twenty years labour in the orchard in addition to the domestic grind, in the dependent relationship sometimes glorified as a partnership, had taken its toll on my mother', she recalled in 1991.[12] She remembered the stained, scratched hands and personal penury that spoke, more eloquently than words, of her mother's situation. When Marilyn was about to begin her third year of university, the Calverts' house, workshop and much of their orchard were destroyed by the catastrophic 1967 bushfires: a blow from which, she says, her family never quite recovered. So, when she came to write about the wives and daughters of the soldier settlers, the experience of her own family, and her own experience of triple duty, were never too far from her mind. The standard feminist critique of Justice Higgins' 'living wage'—that it entrenched the sexual division of labour—had some validity, but, as she concluded in *The Limits of Hope*,

---

11 Marilyn Lake and Farley Kelly (eds), *Double Time: Women in Victoria, 150 Years* (Melbourne: Penguin, 1985), flyleaf.
12 Lake, 'Taking Our Past with Us', 45.

the book of her PhD thesis, 'it is nevertheless important also to recognise what the working day was for these exhausted women, for only then can we begin to comprehend how to many, being "just a housewife" came as blessed relief'.[13] The words 'masculinity' and 'femininity' do not appear in the index of *The Limits of Hope*, but an attentive reader can easily discern the paths of thought that were leading its author to broader reflections on their significance. Guided by theory but holding fast to the lessons of experience, Marilyn fashioned a history that was both analytically powerful and moving. One of her examiners, Ken Inglis, thought so highly of it that he invited Marilyn up to the ANU to share her experience with other PhD students, including the young Joy Damousi.

When *The Limits of Hope* was published by Oxford University Press in 1987, Marilyn kindly invited me to launch it. Big public book launches were a rarity in those days so we gathered convivially at the Lakes' house in Armadale. The other day, as I reached for the book, I found my speech tucked into the jacket. As I noted then, the research and writing had 'called heavily upon [Marilyn's] reserves of determination'. In the mid-1980s, however, her determination began to pay off. In the interval between the completion of the thesis and the launch of the book, she had published two important articles, one on William Lane, and the other focused on J.F. Archibald and the *Bulletin* writers, entitled 'The Politics of Respectability'.[14] As a primary source of Australian nationalist sentiment, the *Bulletin* had long been a target for historians with revisionist intentions. Some years earlier I had published an article, 'Sydney and the Bush', exploring the urban context of 'The Australian Legend'. Apart from a few lines about the feminism of Louisa Lawson, however, I largely overlooked what Marilyn called its 'masculinist context'. When I read her article, my first reaction was not so much to contest it—although there were soon critics aplenty—but to wonder why I had missed what seemed so obvious, once I had adjusted my spectacles. Marilyn herself later described the experience of writing the article as 'a moment of epiphany', when she moved beyond 'women's history', conceived in terms of 'women's role', to a broader study of

---

13   *The Limits of Hope: Soldier Settlement in Victoria 1915–38* (Melbourne: Oxford University Press, 1987), 194.
14   Marilyn Lake, 'Historical Reconsiderations IV: The Politics of Respectability: Identifying the Masculinist Context', *Historical Studies* 22 (86) (April 1986): 116–31; Marilyn Lake, 'Socialism and Manhood: The Case of William Lane', *Labour History*, no. 50 (May 1986): 54–62; compare Graeme Davison, 'Sydney and the Bush: An Urban Context for the Australian Legend', *Historical Studies* 18 (71) (October 1978): 191–209.

gender as a central category of historical analysis. Along with *Double Time* and *The Limits of Hope*, it marked a fresh departure in Australian historiography. Others in this volume will consider the fruitful consequences of that moment; but it is appropriate to begin by acknowledging the years of preparation and struggle that preceded it.

Once young Tasmanians left home, they often just kept travelling. Marilyn's scholarship has followed an arc of steadily growing breadth, depth and maturity. Her first book was about her home state, her second about her adopted one. In mid-career, much of her work was Australian in scope, while in the last decade or so she has worked within an explicitly transnational frame. One of the contexts in which our interests have intersected in recent years has been the Harvard Chair of Australian Studies. As the chair of the Australian Nominating Committee, I had a close perspective, not just on the appointment process, but also on how the appointees fared at Harvard and what they brought home. Marilyn's term in the chair in 2001–02 was one of the most fruitful in recent times, and she has continued to build on it. The scholarly links she made then and later, and the research she undertook during that year on the project that culminated in the book she wrote with Henry Reynolds, *Drawing the Global Colour Line*, was a striking demonstration of the value of placing Australian history—the history of race relations, in this instance—in an international perspective. It has been a long journey from the early 1960s when Marilyn won her first undergraduate prize at the University of Tasmania for work in American history, but it is not yet over. She may not have reinvented Tasmania, but she has gone some way towards re-imagining Australia.

Chapter 2

CONTESTING 'ANZACERY'

Marilyn Lake and Envisioning Australian Nationalism

Stephen Garton

Geoffrey Serle's famously acerbic 1967 indictment of Americanisation, 'Austerica', lamented not just cultural imperialism from across the Pacific but more importantly the shallow roots of Australian nationalism that made us so vulnerable to surrender: emaciated by 'Anzacery', materialism, hedonism and simplistic accounts of a bush tradition. Australian nationalism lacked deeper emotional bonds that would make us a more resilient culture. We were diverted by displays, rituals and confected ceremonies that manipulated sentiment, but there was no well-grounded spirit of patriotism to activate national life.[1] As the centenary of Anzac approached many feared that Australians, once again, would be dazzled by Anzacery—shallow, sentimental, politically motivated appeals to sacrifice and nation-making at Gallipoli that distorted the past and stifled alternative histories. Critics girded their loins for the onslaught of vacuous accounts of the Anzac legend as the founding moment of the nation: marches, flag waving and droning speeches about sacrifice, mateship, and the 'digger legend'. Journalist and historian Bruce Haigh lost little time, condemning then Prime Minister Tony Abbott's 2014 speech opening the National Anzac Centre in Albany: 'the substance was superficial and shallow ... Abbott was prepared to trot out hoary old chestnuts that Australian sacrifice ... shaped the future of the nation'.[2]

---

1   Geoffrey Serle, 'Austerica Unlimited', *Meanjin* 26 (3) (September 1967): 244–5.
2   Bruce Haigh, 'Australia and WWI: Proportion, Propaganda and the Nation-building Myth', *Sydney Morning Herald* (*SMH*), 5 November 2014.

Academics also prepared for what they feared would be an avalanche of trite mythologising: distorted, selective and simplistic jingoistic renderings of the 'founding' of the nation on the shores of Gallipoli. This was a past that needed to be contested and countered by more complex interpretations grounded in evidence rather than myth. Historians, such as Peter Stanley and Frank Bongiorno, and a host of others, established the 'Honest History' group and an accompanying website to counter Anzacery, and it has proved to be a lively site of debate.[3] The foreboding emerged well in advance of the celebrations. In 2010, some of our most distinguished contemporary historians, Marilyn Lake, Henry Reynolds, Joy Damousi and Mark McKenna, entered the fray with an important collection of essays, *What's Wrong with Anzac?*, bemoaning the militarisation of Australian history.[4]

A few years into the centenary program of events it might be argued that the worst fears of critics have not been realised. There have been commemorations aplenty, both here and overseas, and abundant opportunities for nationalist speechifying, as in Tony Abbott's speech in Albany. But the jingoism, and public support for excessive absorption in the legend, has been muted. Prominent businessman Lindsay Fox's efforts to raise over $100m in corporate donations to match government funding for Anzac celebrations proved to be a dismal failure.[5] Television efforts to capitalise on the centenary, such as *Anzac Girls* (ABC) and *Gallipoli* (Nine Network), produced only modest ratings.[6] When I was invited to join the NSW Government's Anzac Advisory Council, we were told by the then premier, Barry O'Farrell, that there was no public funding available and anything we proposed had to be funded from other sources. The Council was full of prominent veterans, members of the RSL, the War Widows Guild and local community representatives. I was part of a small committee that took charge of producing a history of NSW in the Great War, to be sent to all schools in the state. In the end the project was entirely funded by private sources. And

---

3   See http://honesthistory.net.au/wp/.

4   Marilyn Lake, Henry Reynolds, Joy Damousi, Mark McKenna, *What's Wrong with Anzac?: The Militarisation of Australian History* (Sydney: NewSouth Books, 2010).

5   Michael Brissenden, 'Anzac Centenary public fund for 2015 celebrations falling millions of dollars short', ABC News, 22 April 2014.

6   Craig Mathieson, 'Gallipoli Ratings Fail Highlights Australia's Inferiority Complex', *SMH*, 18 February 2015. I am not sure I agree with this journalist's conclusion that it represents the persistence of the cultural cringe. Far more plausible in my mind is Claire Wright's argument that it represents commemoration fatigue—we have seen and heard it all before. See Alice Matthews and Nick Grimm, '"Gallipoli fatigue" causes poor ratings for WWI TV shows as war weary Australians switch off', ABC News, 'The World Today', 24 April 2015.

the resulting book was hardly Anzacery, being largely a social history of the home front with vital accounts of the horrors as well as the heroism of the front line.[7] Nor were the authors uncritical promoters of 'the legend'. Even more important there was no official effort to tone down or censor the social history. The authors were given full rein by Air Vice-Marshall Bob Treloar, chair of the oversight committee, to undertake the social history approach, with sections on the peace movement, the 1917 General Strike, conscription, the Wobblies and much more. There was only one point of debate on the committee in four years—whether to title a section 'venereal disease' or 'public health' (the latter won). What also interested me was that discussions around the table of the larger Advisory Council were far more about commemoration than celebratory nationalism. Fears were expressed that overt jingoism might tarnish the centenary, making it vulnerable to criticism. Solemn commemoration was the preferred mood: an ethos that it seems to me has marked many of the commemorative occasions, much to the surprise of critics.

The failure of the Anzac centenary celebrations, on the whole, to unleash a torrent of simplistic nationalist bombast (although inevitably there has been some) says something about the growing sophistication of the general public when it comes to the Anzac legend. It is not that Australians are weary of Anzac, as the pilgrimages of young Australians to Gallipoli and the crowds at Anzac Day marches show, but, I would suggest, the sense of the tragedy of so many young Australians killed, the costs of their sacrifice, and the burden of their return on families and later generations are more appreciated than before.[8] This sombre, reflective strand in the culture of Anzac (although jingoism still thrives) owes a lot to the labours of many historians who have worked over recent decades to craft a more complex picture of the damage wrought by our participation in wars of the twentieth century; shattered lives, loss, grief and the long-term consequences and costs of war have become prominent themes in Australian historiography.[9]

---

7   Naomi Parry and Brad Manera, with Will Davies and Stephen Garton, *New South Wales and the Great War* (Sydney: Longueville Press, 2016).

8   See Bruce Scates, *Return to Gallipoli: Walking the Battlefields of the Great War* (Melbourne: Cambridge University Press, 2006).

9   The list of potential contributors here is considerable and, rather than giving a very long list of references, let me just give the names of a few of the more prominent contributors. In addition to Marilyn Lake others include, Joy Damousi, Raymond Evans, Marina Larsson, Bobbie Oliver, Melanie Oppenheimer, Bruce Scates, Judith Smart, Bart Ziino, Pat Jalland, Colin Bale and Kerry Neale.

Such is the power of these approaches, they are no longer the domain of the political left or critical school of Australian historiography, the much derided 'black arm-band' brigade. James Brown is certainly more to the right on the political spectrum than many contemporary historians of Anzac (a veteran himself, noted political commentator, and recently appointed president of the NSW RSL); yet his account of the Anzac myth is highly critical of the time and money spent on propagating the legend, and importantly he charts the deleterious consequences of the myth on the psychological health of current veterans.[10] Locked in our sheltered cloisters of scholarship we tend to lose sight of the fact that sometimes our ideas do catch hold, do have impact, do make a difference to the culture. They may take decades to percolate up but uncovering the past opens up the possibility of new ways of thinking. We could be a bit more optimistic about the potential of writing history, as the late Donald Horne often argued, for the work of small groups of committed thinkers often sows the seeds for the future. History can matter.[11]

One of the most significant contributors to this historiographical and, I would argue, cultural transformation has been Marilyn Lake. The rich corpus of her contribution to the discipline ranges very widely, especially in such fields as gender history, but Anzac, its meaning, significance and the way it impacted Australians, has been one of her major preoccupations over the years. It is a topic that she has returned to often, offering original and provocative perspectives to complicate our understanding of the importance of Anzac within Australian culture. In this collection in her honour, however, I do not propose to use the work of Marilyn as a departure point or methodological tool to write something more on the history of Anzac (as many, including myself, have done in the past). Rather I would like to hold up the mirror to the historian and use Anzac as a way into understanding some of the wellsprings of Marilyn's work more generally and even perhaps some of the underpinnings of the critical school of scholarship. My focus will be on highlighting some of the ideas and influences that have shaped her various interventions into the history of the Anzac legend.

---

10 James Brown, *Anzac's Long Shadow: The Cost of our National Obsession* (Melbourne: Black Inc. Press, 2014).

11 For a nice evocation and insightful argument about the sources of Horne's optimism (and let me note a conflict of interest here, Donald was my father-in-law), see Glyn Davis, 'A Public Intellectual: The Life and Times of Donald Horne', in *Donald Horne: Selected Writings*, ed. Nick Horne (Melbourne: La Trobe University Press, 2017), ix–xlv.

A divided culture

The impact of the Great War on Australian society was the launching pad for Marilyn's career: her first two monographs (products of her MA and her PhD respectively) were *A Divided Society* (1975), an exploration the social and political tensions in Tasmania during the war, and *The Limits of Hope* (1987), a path-breaking study of soldier settlement in Victoria between the wars.[12] Both approached Anzac from an oblique angle. Rather than confronting the legend through direct critique or tackling military history itself, they deployed elements of the new social history and, brilliantly in *The Limits of Hope*, feminist history, to pick away at the foundations of the legend. In *A Divided Society*, we see the fissures that erupted in Tasmanian society and politics during the course of the war, anger towards 'enemy aliens' and later Bolsheviks, and tensions over wages, prices and inevitably conscription. This became a story, familiar now but more radical when published, of a community 'more British than Australian', characterised by 'uniformity', disintegrating under the pressures of the war when 'class was set against class, creed against creed, district against district, soldier against civilian'.[13]

A Divided Society is inevitably a creature of its time—class, labour, religion, ethnicity and politics dominate the narrative. Nevertheless, it elucidates a number of themes and questions of continuing historiographical relevance today: the stresses and strains of return, the strengthening of Empire loyalism and its linkage to a newly invigorated nationalism, and the defeat of pre-war progressivism and the triumph of post-war conservatism.[14] For those familiar with Marilyn's later work the absence of women (it is not even a category in the index) may come as a surprise. Context is everything here. This is a thesis of the early 1970s, well before the founding texts of Australian women's history—by Anne Summers, Bev Kingston and Miriam Dixson—had been published.[15] It is work more grounded in social

---

12 Marilyn Lake, *A Divided Society: Tasmania During World War I* (Melbourne: Melbourne University Press, 1975), and *The Limits of Hope: Soldier Settlement in Victoria 1915–38* (Melbourne: Oxford University Press, 1987).
13 Lake, *A Divided Society*, 189.
14 Some of these themes have been a particular influence in my own work. See Stephen Garton, 'Demobilization and Empire: Empire Nationalism and Soldier Citizenship in Australia after the First World War—In Dominion Context', *Journal of Contemporary History* 50 (1) (January 2015): 121–43.
15 Anne Summers, *Damned Whores and God's Police* (1975), Miriam Dixson, *the Real Matilda* (1976), and Bev Kingston, *My Wife, My Daughter and Poor Mary Ann* (1975).

and labour history. But a closer reading of the text suggests that the seeds of the later Marilyn had been sown. The voices of a number of women—Marjorie Kearney, Helen Barton, Vida Goldstein and others—illuminate the argument, and organisations dominated by women, such as the Red Cross, temperance movements and housewives associations, find, unusually for the time, a place in the larger narrative.

The Limits of Hope is a more mature and iconoclastic work. Soldier settlement was an established, although little studied, theme in Australian history, commonly mentioned in passing in general histories and frequently a theme in local and regional histories (usually those that had their origin in settlement schemes). Important work by J.M. Powell and others on the political, economic, geographic and policy dimensions of soldier settlement was just beginning to put its historiography on a sounder scholarly footing.[16] Marilyn hurdled all this, landing in an original space that she carved out for herself—the fate of families, particularly the wives, mothers and children who accompanied veterans on the land, and the hardships that ensued as a result of policy failures, climate, inexperience, ill health, and misfortune. Soldier settlement was a vehicle for exploring gender and family dynamics under duress, a focus that allowed for deeper ruminations and insights into gender relations more generally. This was genuinely ground-breaking, both in the richness of the archival research that underpinned the analysis and in the conceptual and theoretical armoury she used to open out new questions about loss, grief, domestic tensions and the impact of war on families when men returned from war. They are ones that have been taken up by many historians, such as Joy Damousi, Marina Larsson, Bart Ziino, myself and many others since. This was pioneering feminist history and a fundamental transformation of the historiography of soldier settlement.

While Marilyn's first two books were grounded in an analysis of the impact of the Great War, her career took off in many other directions thereafter—including the history of feminism, sexuality and desire, masculinism, maternal citizenship, transnationalism, race and ethnicity, a biography of Faith Bandler and much more—a corpus of books and articles of significant impact and importance. The Great War, however, remained a noteworthy theme in her work, one that she would return to at various points in her career. In the late 1980s and early 1990s there were chapters

---

16   J.M. Powell, 'The Mapping of Soldier Settlement: A Note for Victoria, 1917–1929', *Journal of Australian Studies* 2 (3) (1978): 44–51. See also Ken Fry, 'Soldier Settlement and the Agrarian Myth after the First World War', *Labour History*, no. 48 (May 1985): 29–43.

and articles, notably on the 'Power of Anzac' and more importantly on the masculinisation of Australian nationalism, that focused on the idea of Anzac and its role in shaping Australian national identity.[17] In both these pieces the sense of a rupture in Australia's history is a powerful trope. For Marilyn, the Great War and its aftermath represented a triumph of conservatism in Australia, where mateship was appropriated to support 'industrial peace' and returned soldier discontent was focused on non-soldiers.[18] More radically, in her path-breaking article 'Mission Impossible', she explored in considerable detail how the Great War and the political divisions it unleashed stifled the more optimistic pre-war socialist, liberal and feminist nation-building enterprise that had promoted ideals of economic rights and broad-based citizenship. The war instead trumpeted notions of manhood, sacrifice and national birth that placed the citizen soldier at the centre of national discourses, pitting soldiers and their families against 'shirkers', trade unionists, Bolsheviks, Sinn Fein agitators and other radicals. Repatriation systems gave soldiers and their families special privileges and benefits far above those available to others. Commemoration of sacrifice placed loyalty to nation and Empire on a pedestal, marginalising women, radicals and liberals who had been central to nation-building before and after Federation: 'citizenship was constructed in terms of masculine attributes and privilege'.[19]

In the shadow of the Great War centenary celebrations, Marilyn returned to many of these themes giving them greater focus and force. Written in collaboration with other colleagues, the *What's Wrong with Anzac?* collection is a powerful critique of the militarisation of Australian history. This is both an indictment of the wider culture that perpetuates the 'myth' of Anzac as the founding of the nation and the politicians (and historians) who have bought into the myth, perpetuating it for later generations. It is a plea to move on from this obsession to build a more inclusive and embracing account of nation-building, one grounded in critical reflection on the violence inherent in colonisation but one that also recognises that out of these troubled beginnings Australians, from many walks of

---

17 See Marilyn Lake, 'The Power of Anzac', in *Australia: Two Centuries of War & Peace*, eds Michael McKernan and Margaret Browne (Canberra: Australian War Memorial, 1988): 194–222, and 'Mission Impossible: How Men Gave Birth to the Australian Nation—Nationalism, Gender and other Seminal Acts', *Gender & History* 4 (3) (Autumn 1992): 305–22.

18 Lake, 'Power of Anzac', 222.

19 Lake, 'Mission Impossible', 319.

life (and cultures), have contributed to a unique national story. It envisions accounts that embrace the full panoply of our history, accounts that are appropriately evidence based, unafraid to shirk critical narratives but equally alive to the positive dimensions of the Australian story, and ones that stretch back over our full history: thousands of years not frozen at a single moment of time.

Death of a nation

In her presidential address to the 2014 Australian Historical Association conference in Brisbane, '1914: Death of a Nation', Marilyn returned to these themes again and set out in greater detail her dismay at the perversion of Australia's national story through the lens of Anzac.[20] Here, in broad brush strokes, enlivened by close focus on key figures such as Henry Bournes Higgins and Alfred Deakin, Marilyn outlined a very different narrative of nation-building: the defeat of idealism, hope, radicalism, liberalism, a distinctive Australian democracy, and the values of equality and social justice, and the triumph, as a consequence of the Great War, of militarism, conservatism, Empire loyalism, repression, conformity and creeping inequality.[21] Gallipoli represented not the birth of the nation but its death, or more accurately the replacement of one national story by another, one that effectively erased the former.

Marilyn's aim is to craft an alternative genealogy of Australian nationalism, one that restores the early nation builders to a rightful place in the narrative. Her focus is on recovering the earlier (defeated) national tradition embodied in figures like Higgins and Deakin. This is a familiar story but one viewed now through a transnational lens, bringing to light important insights. Australia's radical and liberal reformers and our unique 'social experiments' of the late nineteenth and early twentieth centuries—the secret ballot, arbitration, old age pensions, the 'living wage', female suffrage and more—are placed in a wider international context, drawing on the views of visiting English, Canadian and American visitors and commentators. While British liberals and social democrats, like the Webbs and Charles

---

20 Marilyn Lake, '1914: Death of a Nation', *History Australia* 12 (1) (January 2015): 7–24.
21 And Australia was uniquely backward-looking in its post-war nationalism, in contrast to other Dominions in the British Empire as well as Ireland and India. This is a theme I have explored in 'The Dominions, Ireland and India', in *Empires at War: 1911–1923*, eds Robert Gerwarth and Erez Manela (Oxford: Oxford University Press, 2014), 152–78.

Dilke, viewed Australia's emerging democracy and state experiments with some disdain, North American and European commentators were far more appreciative (or, in the case of Lenin, alarmed lest workers think capitalism could work).[22] Some of Higgins' and Deakin's most important interlocutors and correspondents were American liberals, such as Josiah Royce and Felix Frankfurter, who saw Australian developments as a triumph of Idealism and liberal progressivism, state efforts to advance national well-being rather than serving the interests of a particular class. The contrast in these international perceptions is crucial. It propels Marilyn's argument that Australian democracy was not aping British ideas but consciously attempting to break from British class-bound traditions. Australia's radicals and liberals sought to craft measures to prevent the poverty and severe economic inequalities of Britain from emerging here. Australian democracy was a reaction against British culture, not an embrace of British ideals. Thus, Marilyn shapes a narrative that stands in marked contrast to the post-war conservative story of nationhood.

A radical nationalist?

This effort to link the familiar history of state experiments to a distinctive tradition of Australian political culture grounded in ideals of equality and social justice marks out Marilyn's argument as an important contribution to the historiography of Australian nationalism. While it echoes some earlier accounts of the Federation generation, its emphasis on the transnational context and the importance of the woman question within the larger reform tradition is distinctive. Moreover, she is far from an uncritical 'booster' of Australia and New Zealand's state experiments. Her collaborative work with Henry Reynolds on the blindness of radical and liberal reformers to questions of 'colour', and more importantly the way that racial inequality and regulation of non-white peoples became the glue that held this alliance of liberals and radicals together, is a vital contribution to our understanding of early Federation and the formation of 'whiteness' in Australian national identity.[23] There are some (me included) who might quibble about her sharp contrast between the liberal and radical

---

22   Jill Roe, 'Leading the World? 1910–1914', in *Social Policy in Australia: Some Perspectives 1901–1975*, ed. Jill Roe (Melbourne: Cassell, 1976), 5.

23   Marilyn Lake and Henry Reynolds, *Drawing the Global Colour Line: White Men's Countries and the Question of Racial Equality* (Melbourne: Melbourne University Press, 2008).

emphasis on peace and the militarisation that happened as a consequence of war. While these reformers did introduce, for their time, major and innovative social policy reforms that in many respects led the world in the pursuit of economic equality and social justice (as Marilyn argues), they were also mindful of the darkening clouds on the international horizon. In the years after Federation and before 1914, the Commonwealth built a military armaments factory in Lithgow, implemented compulsory military cadet training in Australian schools and established a program in military science at the University of Sydney to train an officer class for the future.[24]

Nonetheless, Marilyn's compelling account of the pre-war reform tradition within Australian political culture, bolstered by the transnational perspective in its praise of the 'worker's paradise', gives us an avenue into the deeper historiographical currents that have inspired some of her work. In its admiration for the confident, idealistic, colonial democratic tradition that had evolved by the end of the nineteenth century, Marilyn's presidential address echoes the views of an earlier generation of radical nationalist historians, although this is far from simply a return to an older tradition. This is not the radical nationalist tradition of Russel Ward. Marilyn has been a trenchant critic of the masculinist tradition in Australian culture that nurtured the 'Australian legend' and some of the key historians in the radical nationalist school who promoted its central tenets, notably its marginalisation of women, its glorification of manliness and 'bachelordom', and its antipathy to domesticity. It was a culture that sought to thwart the woman movement, denouncing feminists as 'wowsers' and 'killjoys' determined to hobble men. In this context, the Anzac celebration of masculinity and mateship was 'mythic reparation' for this older tradition of Australian manhood, born in the bush and now condemned to live in the cities.[25]

Instead Marilyn's argument is a vital affirmation of the radical liberal, democratic, demotic tradition of Australian politics—one where radicals, socialists, liberals, feminists and democrats differed on many issues but fed off each other, and sometimes collaborated, to craft a distinctive social contract for the benefit of both labour and capital, and even in a limited way for women. Their aim was to encourage a political culture different from that

---

24   See Parry and Manera, 14–17 and 36.
25   Marilyn Lake, 'The Politics of Respectability: Identifying the Masculinist Context', *Historical Studies* 22 (86) (April 1986): 116–31.

of Britain, one based on a sense of fairness, social justice and egalitarianism. This echoes the argument of Bob Gollan, in his influential *Radical and Working Class Politics* (1960), that we have underestimated the significance and the radical nature of these distinctive social experiments in Australia.[26] While Marilyn is alive to the fact that this was a 'white' compact, one that drew added strength from its racial and ethnic exclusiveness, and unlike Gollan is closely attuned to questions of gender, her presidential address, like her other work, makes a powerful case for this tradition as preferable, despite its flaws, to the masculinist militaristic tradition that followed. And importantly, she argues, this social justice and equality tradition is urgently in need of revival in the face of growing inequality and heightened international tensions.

It is possible to glimpse the early roots of some of these arguments and ideas in Marilyn's work on Tasmania during the Great War and in many of her subsequent articles and interventions in Anzac historiography. The sense that Australia came to a fork in the road in 1915—sustaining Australia's distinctive democratic tradition or embracing Empire loyalty, sustaining a tradition of egalitarianism or embracing a belief that soldier citizens deserved greater reward, remaining liberal or embracing conservatism—marks much of her work in this field. While she is too rigorous a historian to fall into nostalgia, there is an underlying echo of dismay at the fate of Australian nationalism since 1915 and a passionate commitment to what might have been had the egalitarian and democratic tradition survived and sunk deeper roots into the national consciousness. There is an underlying sense of tragedy in her work about opportunities lost. If only the democratic traditions that might have shaped the nation in a very different way had been nurtured rather than destroyed by militarisation. If only Australians had had the courage to defend our unique tradition. Despite her insightful critique of radical nationalism, there is also a powerful strand of radical nationalism that threads its way through her work. We can glimpse the influence of her early teachers in Tasmania in nurturing these perspectives: Michael Roe and his interest in the history of Australia's distinctive political culture and the importance of progressivism, and the ethical, egalitarian, radical nationalism of Malcolm McRae (an 'inspiring teacher' who sadly died just before the publication of her MA and to whom she dedicated *A Divided Society*). She has taken these influences in

---

26   Robin Gollan, *Radical and Working Class Politics: A Study of Eastern Australia 1850–1910* (Melbourne: Melbourne University Press, 1976, first published 1960).

very different directions, but in her work on Anzac we can see that she sits in an important lineage while making it more relevant for Australia in the twenty-first century. That is no mean achievement.

Chapter 3

NEGOTIATING THE LOCAL AND THE GLOBAL

Marilyn Lake and the Writing of Australian Women's History[*]

Patricia Grimshaw

Marilyn Lake played a significant role in the transformation of women's history as it emerged from the 1970s as a new field with a serious place in academia.[1] Originating in the upsurge of feminism that accompanied the worldwide radical movements of the post-war decades, women's history began in Australia with a determined focus on the past lives of women and gender at the local level but swiftly enlarged these insights through the double lens of internationalism and transnationalism. Marilyn assumed a prominent place among those who built and broadened its outreach and scope as an energetic advocate for the transformative role of women's history.[2]

Marilyn is one of several historians who showed that the radicalism of the women's movement had a formative impact on the new women's history

---

[*] I thank Rosemary Francis, Jackie Dickenson, Shurlee Swain, Charles Sowerwine and Judith Smart for reading and commenting on this chapter.

[1] See 'Lake, Marilyn', in *The Encyclopedia of Women and Leadership in Twentieth-Century Australia*, eds Judith Smart and Shurlee Swain (Melbourne: Australian Women's Archive Project, 2014), http://www.womenaustralia.info/leaders. See also Marilyn Lake, 'In and Out of Empire: Old Labels and New Histories', in *How Empire Shaped Us*, eds Antoinette Burton and Dane Kennedy (London: Bloomsbury, 2016), chapter 7, and 'Women's and Gender History in Australia: A Transformative Practice', *Journal of Women's History* 25 (4) (Winter 2013): 190–211.

[2] This chapter draws on Patricia Grimshaw, 'Transnationalism and the Writing of Australian Women's History', in *Transnationalism, Nationalism and Australian*

that emerged globally and locally.[3] A new history was a key component of activists' agendas, reflecting the left-wing political orientation of their feminism nurtured in international social movements such as black civil rights, opposition to the Vietnam war and decolonisation. In Australia, participants in women's liberation groups and the Women's Electoral Lobby voiced radical demands for change, combined in the latter case with challenges to formal discrimination. Women attracted to feminism expressed their views through demonstrations, protests, meetings and conferences. A distinguishing feature of this radical feminist activism was a keen interest in history, often understood as the source of women's oppression. Feminists, labour activists and students recovered neglected figures and events to highlight the persistence of women's second-class status.

There had not of course been a dearth of women's history before this date. From the early twentieth century, educated women, influenced by first-wave feminism, had lodged their papers in national archives and recorded women's achievements in their efforts to close the glaring gaps in Australia's historical narratives. By and large they had accepted existing accounts of a white nation's progress towards a progressive society but strove to insert women within it. There is little evidence that male historians in universities who had assumed responsibility for defining the watersheds in Australia's past took any notice of their publications.[4] But those who practised the new women's history in the early 1970s sustained a confrontational stance that demanded and received wider attention, exemplified in Anne Summers' *Damned Whores and God's Police*, which appeared in 1975—International Women's Year—followed by Miriam Dixson's *The Real Matilda* in 1976.

History, eds Anna Clark, Anne Rees and Alecia Simmonds (London: Palgrave, 2017), 69–85; and Patricia Grimshaw, Sharon Harrison and Shurlee Swain, 'History', in Smart and Swain (eds).

3   Marilyn Lake, 'A History of Feminism in Australia', in *Australian Feminism: A Companion*, ed. Barbara Caine (Melbourne: Oxford University Press, 1998), 132–42; *Getting Equal: The History of Australian Feminism* (Sydney: Allen & Unwin, 1999); and 'Nationalist Historiography, Feminist Scholarship and the Promise and Problems of New Transnational Histories: The Australian Case', *Journal of Women's History* 19 (1) (March 2007): 180–6. See also Marian Sawer, *Making Women Count: A History of the Women's Electoral Lobby* (Sydney: UNSW Press, 2008).

4   See Patricia Grimshaw and Shurlee Swain, 'Dominion Women Writers', in *Companion to Women's Historical Writing*, eds Mary Spongberg, Ann Curthoys and Barbara Caine (New York: Palgrave Macmillan, 2005), 119–28; Susan Magarey, 'Australia', in Spongberg, Curthoys and Caine (eds), 43–54; Patricia Grimshaw, 'Writing the History of Australian Women', in *Writing Women's History: International Perspectives*, eds Karen Offen, Ruth Pierson and Jane Rendall (London: Macmillan, 1991), 133–56.

Both asserted the ubiquity of women's inequality in most areas of life experience.[5] Women's work was the focus of much early research. Authors described the complexity of women's paid and unpaid work, in the public workforce and in the home, defining also as women's labour their social and cultural work in the wider family and community. Notable were Beverley Kingston's examination of the colonial period, *My Wife, My Daughter, and Poor Mary Ann*;[6] Edna Ryan and Anne Conlon's *Gentle Invaders* on the equal pay struggle;[7] and the collection of innovative papers that appeared in Ann Curthoys, Susan Eade (Magarey) and Peter Spearritt's co-edited special issue of *Labour History, Women at Work*.[8]

The first of what would become a series of Women and Labour conferences took place at Macquarie University in 1978; it was followed by the publication of selected papers, *Women, Class and History*.[9] Marilyn and I met at this conference, which took place amidst an atmosphere of excitement about history as a key pathway to gender equality, and we forged a lasting collegial friendship there. Having published in 1972 a study of women's suffrage in New Zealand (my country of origin), I had been recently appointed to a temporary lectureship in women's history at the University of Melbourne.[10] On leave from her PhD enrolment at Monash University, Marilyn had brought her eight-month-old daughter, Katherine, with her to Sydney where they stayed with Ann Curthoys, also a young mother. In the 1970s, while an MA student at the University of Tasmania, Marilyn had been a founding member of the local women's liberation movement and the Women's Electoral Lobby. She was, she recalls, particularly inspired by the theoretical orientation of the Hobart Women's Action Group, which produced the radical newsletter *Liberaction*.[11] She became part of a national team of research assistants (which also included Ann

---

5   Anne Summers, *Damned Whores and God's Police: The Colonisation of Women in Australia* (Melbourne: Penguin, 1975); Miriam Dixson, *The Real Matilda: Women and Identity in Australia 1788 to the Present* (Melbourne: Penguin, 1976).

6   Beverley Kingston, *My Wife, My Daughter, and Poor Mary Ann: Women and Work in Australia* (Melbourne: Thomas Nelson, 1975).

7   Edna Ryan and Anne Conlon, *Gentle Invaders: Australian Women at Work, 1788–1974* (Melbourne: Thomas Nelson, 1975).

8   Ann Curthoys, Susan Eade (Magarey) and Peter Spearritt (eds), *Women at Work, Labour History*, no. 29 (1975).

9   Elizabeth Windschuttle (ed.), *Women, Class and History: Feminist Perspectives on Australia, 1788–1978* (Sydney: HarperCollins, 1982).

10 Patricia Grimshaw, *Women's Suffrage in New Zealand* (Auckland: Auckland University Press, 1972).

11 Personal communication from Marilyn Lake.

Curthoys) working on a large International Women's Year archival project led by Kay Daniels, a senior lecturer in history at the university. The resulting two-volume publication, *Women in Australia: An Annotated Guide to Records* (1977), which Daniels co-edited with Mary Murnane and Anne Picot, was a ground-breaking work that facilitated the rapid expansion of original research in women's history across Australia.[12] Marilyn had moved to Melbourne in 1976 to commence work on her doctorate.

This early enthusiasm about the potential of a new women's history had a major impact on the ways women's historians became integrated into tertiary institutions. Marilyn became a central member of the group of activist researchers keen to establish women's history as a transformative academic pursuit. The entry point to the academy for many feminist scholars was through new positions in the emerging interdisciplinary field of Women's Studies, within which historians played a leading part.[13] Feminist historians, who usually met at national conferences but also at smaller workshops, established intellectual, cultural and methodological frameworks—including journals—within which innovative work took shape. They were talented scholars, who taught with commitment, supervised theses, organised seminars and undertook related administration with a drive that was truly impressive.

As was typical for new directions in the discipline, much of this scholarship appeared first as journal articles and chapters in edited collections, followed by numerous full-length studies. From their foundational work, Beverley Kingston, Ann Curthoys, Susan Magarey and Kay Daniels continued to influence the discipline through the 1980s and beyond. Beverley Kingston taught at the University of New South Wales for thirty years, also influencing a new generation of women historians through her writing.[14] Ann Curthoys inaugurated Women's Studies programs at the Australian National University and University of Technology, Sydney, becoming an influential theorist, exemplified in her book *For and Against Feminism*.[15] Susan Magarey also taught in ANU's newly established Women's Studies course before returning to Adelaide in 1983 as founding director of the

---

12 Kay Daniels, Mary Murnane and Anne Picot (eds), *Women in Australia: An Annotated Guide to Records* (Canberra: Australian Government Publishing Service, 1977).
13 See Lyndall Ryan, 'Women's Studies', in Caine (ed.), 365–9.
14 See 'Kingston, Beverley', in Smart and Swain (eds).
15 Ann Curthoys, *For and Against Feminism: A Personal Journey into Feminist Theory and History* (Sydney: Allen and Unwin, 1988). See 'Curthoys, Ann', in Smart and Swain (eds).

Research Centre for Women's Studies at the University of Adelaide and founding editor of *Australian Feminist Studies*. Her biography of Catherine Spence, based on initial work for an Honours thesis, was core to suffrage studies.[16] Kay Daniels's influence extended from the University of Tasmania through publications including the collection *So Much Hard Work: Women and Prostitution in Australian History*, which theorised a neglected area of women's labour.[17]

Others quickly became notable in this burgeoning academic initiative of the late 1970s and 1980s.[18] Lyndall Ryan, historian of the first Tasmanians, established Women's Studies programs in Queensland at Griffith University and at Flinders University in South Australia, after an earlier career as one of the first so-called 'femocrats' in the Commonwealth Public Service.[19] The founder and first convenor of the Australian Women's Studies Association, she worked in South Australia alongside Margaret Allen,[20] whose interest in Women's Studies also arose out of her involvement in the South Australian women's liberation movement. Another key figure in this group was the education historian Alison Mackinnon, eventually of the University of South Australia.[21] Jill Julius Matthews taught Women's Studies at the Australian National University, establishing a research specialisation in women's social and cultural history and published the path-breaking *Good and Mad Women*.[22] Also in Canberra was Desley Deacon, who wrote *Managing Gender* on the entry of women to the public service. Desley subsequently took up a teaching position in the United States before her return to the ANU.[23] Judith Allen, a key influence

---

16 Susan Magarey, *Unbridling the Tongues of Women: A Biography of Catherine Helen Spence* (Sydney: Hale & Iremonger, 1985). See 'Magarey, Susan', in Smart and Swain (eds).

17 Kay Daniels (ed.), *So Much Hard Work: Women and Prostitution in Australian History* (Sydney: Fontana/Collins, 1984). See 'Daniels, Kay', in Smart and Swain (eds).

18 Entries on historians noted in this chapter and numerous other Australian women historians can be found in Smart and Swain (eds).

19 Lyndall Ryan, *The Aboriginal Australians* (Brisbane: University of Queensland Press, 1981). See 'Ryan, Lyndall', in Smart and Swain (eds).

20 See 'Allen, Margaret', in Smart and Swain (eds).

21 Alison Mackinnon, *One Foot on the Ladder: Origins and Outcomes of Girls' Secondary Schooling in South Australia* (Brisbane: University of Queensland Press, 1984). See 'Mackinnon, Alison', in Smart and Swain (eds).

22 Jill Julius Matthews, *Good and Mad Women: The Historical Construction of Femininity in Twentieth Century Australia* (Sydney: Allen & Unwin, 1984). See 'Matthews, Jill Julius', in Smart and Swain (eds).

23 Desley Deacon, *Managing Gender: The State, the New Middle Class and Women Workers 1830–1930* (Melbourne: Oxford University Press, 1989). See 'Deacon, Desley', in Smart and Swain (eds).

on feminist scholarship in Sydney, became a noted historian of women and crime and biographer of the Sydney feminist Rose Scott, before leaving to take up a position in the United States.[24]

The Sydney historian, Jill Roe, biographer of Stella Miles Franklin, promoted women historians and women's history from her position at Macquarie University, serving a generous period as president of the board of the *Australian Dictionary of Biography* and eventually as the second woman president of the Australian Historical Association.[25] At the same time feminist scholars interested in Aboriginal history began to interrogate historical documents heavily skewed towards settler perspectives, focusing particularly on the very different work experiences of Aborigines and their relationships to the state. In Queensland, Kay Saunders, in collaboration with Raymond Evans, made early contributions to knowledge and debates on Australia's race relations.[26] In *Born in the Cattle*, based on her PhD thesis, Ann McGrath focused on Aborigines in the Northern Territory cattle industry;[27] Heather Goodall in *Invasion to Embassy* wrote about Aborigines and land in New South Wales;[28] Peggy Brock in *Outback Ghettos* examined Aboriginal missions in South Australia;[29] and in *For Their Own Good* Anna Haebich examined state control of Aborigines in the south-west of Western Australia.[30]

Marilyn established her particular place in the field of women's history during the 1980s when she completed her doctoral thesis, juggling—like

---

24 Judith Allen, *Sex and Secrets: Crimes Involving Australian Women since 1880* (Melbourne: Oxford University Press, 1990), and *Rose Scott: Vision and Revision* (Melbourne: Oxford University Press, 1994).

25 See 'Roe, Jill', in Smart and Swain (eds); Jill Roe, *Stella Miles Franklin: A Biography* (Sydney: Harper Collins, 2008).

26 See 'Saunders, Kay', in Smart and Swain (eds); Raymond Evans, Kay Saunders and Kathryn Cronin, *Exclusion, Exploitation and Extermination: Race Relations in Colonial Queensland* (Sydney: Australia and New Zealand Book Company, 1975); Kay Saunders, *Workers in Bondage: The Origins and Bases of Unfree Labour in Queensland, 1824–1916* (Brisbane: University of Queensland Press, 1982); Kay Saunders and Raymond Evans (eds), *Gender Relations in Australian History: Domination and Negotiation* (Sydney: Harcourt Brace Jovanovich, 1992).

27 Ann McGrath, *'Born in the Cattle': Aborigines in Cattle Country* (Sydney: Allen & Unwin, 1987). See 'McGrath, Ann', in Smart and Swain (eds).

28 Heather Goodall, *Invasion to Embassy: Land in Aboriginal Politics in New South Wales, 1770–1972* (Sydney: Allen & Unwin, 1996).

29 Peggy Brock, *Outback Ghettos: Aborigines, Institutionalisation and Survival* (Melbourne: Cambridge University Press, 1993).

30 Anna Haebich, *For Their Own Good: Aborigines and Government in the Southwest of Western Australia, 1900–1940* (Perth: University of Western Australia Press, 1988).

many young women—short-term teaching and the care of young children. Her daughters were born in 1977 and 1981. The 1978 Women and Labour conference that had so usefully brought together many feminist scholars had a productive outcome for women's history in Victoria when three Melburnians, based at La Trobe University, Margaret James, Margaret Bevege and Carmel Shute, undertook responsibility for convening the second Women and Labour conference in 1980. The labour feminist activist Zelda D'Aprano was a key figure there.[31] Melbourne networks were strengthened as a number of participants found employment within tertiary institutions. They included Diane Kirkby, biographer of Alice Henry, and the historical sociologist of the family, Kerreen Reiger, both also at La Trobe University; RMIT's Judith Smart, scholar of women's activism in early twentieth-century Victoria, who became the first woman to edit *Australian Historical Studies*; Monash scholars Marian Aveling (later Quartly), Marjorie Theobald, Farley Kelly and Ailsa Zainu'ddin; Renate Howe, of Deakin University, with her interests in transnational suffragist collaborations, and the welfare historian, Shurlee Swain, first at Deakin University, then at the Australian Catholic University. One outcome of this collective effort was Marilyn Lake and Farley Kelly's edited collection *Double Time*, a compendium of individual and group biographical essays on women in Victorian history commissioned by Penguin to mark Victoria's sesquicentenary in 1985.[32] Its publication was a conscious gesture towards earlier generations of women historians, who had similarly marked major commemorations with dedicated publications.

One year earlier, Marilyn had completed her PhD thesis, which was published in 1987 by Oxford University Press as *The Limits of Hope* (a title she then thought reflected her own condition vis-a-vis the (non)likelihood of finding permanent employment).[33] At that stage she held the contract position of Ashworth lectureship in Social Theory at the University of Melbourne (having previously held a four-year tutorship at Monash University and a short-term lectureship at RMIT). Soon after, however, she was appointed founding director of Women's Studies (a tenure-track position), located in the History Department at La Trobe University where

---

31 See Patricia Grimshaw, 'Zelda D'Aprano, Leadership and the Politics of Gender in the Australian Labour Movement 1945–1975', *Labour History*, no. 104 (May 2013): 101–18.

32 Farley Kelly and Marilyn Lake (eds), *Double Time: Women in Victoria: 150 Years* (Melbourne: Penguin, 1985).

33 Marilyn Lake, *The Limits of Hope: Soldier Settlement in Victoria, 1915-1938* (Melbourne: Oxford University Press, 1987).

she established a major in Women's Studies and then—with the appointment of a number of bright young feminist scholars in History, Philosophy, English and Legal Studies—an Honours degree, a Masters by coursework degree and a PhD program. Liz Conor, Esther Faye, Fiona Paisley, Ruth Ford, Catriona Elder and Natasha Campo were some of the program's distinguished graduates. Marilyn also taught six of the subjects on offer in Women's Studies herself.

Until then little children had kept her close to home, but in 1988 she accepted her first invitation to present a keynote paper at an overseas conference—the 5th Annual Conference of the Stout Research Centre for the Study of New Zealand Society, History and Culture, held at Victoria University in Wellington. Invited to speak on the theme of 'women and war', Marilyn presented an early version of 'Female Desires', about women's sexual agency in World War II, prompting a senior New Zealand historian to ask through pursed lips: 'Did those women realise there was a war on?' In Wellington one of her hosts was Charlotte Macdonald, who became a life-long friend and colleague. More than twenty years later they travelled to Johannesburg together to participate in a workshop organised by Isobel Hofmeyr and Antoinette Burton on 'Ten Books that Shaped the British Empire'.[34] By that time women's history had been established as an international project for some twenty-five years.

In 1987, the newly formed Australian Women's History Network (AWHN) became an inaugural component of the new International Federation for Research in Women's History (IFRWH).[35] In turn the IFRWH affiliated with the International Committee of Historical Sciences/ Comité international des sciences historiques (CISH) at its quinquennial conference in Madrid in 1990. Under the inaugural presidency of Norway's Ida Blom, women's history organisations from some forty-five countries became involved with the federation; the diversification increased each year. At subsequent CISH conferences, IFRWH ran special women's history streams that complemented the proliferation of feminist historical panels throughout the conference program more generally. In 1995, Marilyn was invited to the 18th CISH conference in Montreal to act as discussant for a

---

34   See Marilyn Lake, 'Charles Pearson's *National Life and Character*: Imperial Co-production', in *Ten Books that Shaped the British Empire: Creating an Imperial Commons*, eds Antoinette Burton and Isobel Hofmeyr (Durham NC: Duke University Press, 2014), 90–111.

35   See Patricia Grimshaw, 'Looking Backwards: The Origins of the Australian Women's History Network', in *Lilith*, forthcoming 2018.

plenary panel of papers from six different countries on the theme of 'Family, Sex and Power', an intimidating task, she recalls, that took her at least six months to prepare. The source of the invitation was Claire Moses, founding editor of the US journal *Feminist Studies* and a good friend of Martha Vicinus, with whom Marilyn had stayed at Ann Arbor when on her first sabbatical leave in 1991. Pursuing women's history at an international level was facilitated and made so much more enjoyable through the personal friendships that enlivened our academic endeavours. In Britain, Marilyn enjoyed the warm hospitality of Catherine Hall and Sally Alexander; in the Unites States, Sonya Michel, Linda Kerber, Laura Frader, Antoinette Burton and Alice Kessler-Harris kindly took her in; while in Sweden Barbara Hobson's Stockholm apartment provided a welcoming home away from home.

It was during the 1990s that Australian women's history became fully enmeshed with the work of women's historians in many other countries as international collaborations, comparative approaches and new disciplinary frameworks (such as those provided by the 'new imperial history' and postcolonial theory) took flight. The transnational dimension of women's history had been highlighted in Australia by the many scholars working in Australian universities in non-Australian areas, who contributed notable work in women's history in British, European, American and Asian history. Among those at the forefront of the new international scholarship were the modern British historian Barbara Caine and the early modernist Patricia Crawford, both of whom also contributed generously to Australian women's history and brought breadth and fresh insight to it thereby.[36] Marilyn would contribute an essay on 'A History of Feminism in Australia' to Caine's *Companion to Feminist History* published by Oxford University Press in 1998.[37]

A book-length version was published the next year as *Getting Equal: The History of Feminism in Australia*—the use of the definite article annoyed many but was insisted on by her publisher at Allen & Unwin. By the turn of the century, the new women's history was transforming understandings of Australian history at both academic and popular levels. Marilyn played a leading part in the planning of *Creating a Nation*, the short feminist history of Australia that she and I co-authored with Ann McGrath and Marian

---

36 For extended discussion, see Grimshaw, 'Transnationalism and the Writing of Australian Women's History'.
37 Lake, 'A History of Feminism in Australia'.

Quartly in 1994. The book was distinctive in two ways; it situated women as integral to key landmarks in Australia's past, and it sustained a narrative of racial divisions—between colonised and colonising—along with those of gender and class, including dedicated chapters focused on Aboriginal women's experiences of colonialism written by Ann.[38] The book's new narrative of the shaping of Australia was widely appreciated as a brave attempt at inclusiveness, though it also had its sceptical/hostile critics. Reprinted several times, it sold thousands of copies and attracted moving correspondence from women pleased to see that at last they had a history of Australia in which women played central roles. The following year Marilyn joined Joy Damousi in co-editing an anthology that brought together an influential set of essays—some classics even then and some new—reflecting on *Gender and War*. It has also been reprinted many times since.[39]

A distinctive aspect of Marilyn's historical analysis has been her deployment of gender as a theoretical category, apparent in her first revisionist and frequently cited and reprinted article in the *Australian Historical Studies*' 'Historical Reconsiderations' series called: 'The Politics of Respectability: Identifying the Masculinist Context'.[40] *The Limits of Hope*, published one year later, also demonstrated how taking gender into consideration through a focus on women, families and masculinity illuminated the supposedly male domains of politics and power (Foucault was another influence) and the work of farming and housework. It foreshadowed the major contribution Marilyn's gendered perspective would bring to studies of the impact of war, masculinity and Australian identity more generally, which others explore in this volume.

The American historian of early modern Europe, Natalie Zemon Davis, anticipated the use of gender as an analytical category in the mid-1970s, and the concept became influential with Joan Scott's 1986 article in the *American Historical Review* (published in the same year in which Marilyn's 'Politics of Respectability' examined the gendered nature of nationalist discourse in Australia).[41] Globally there were historians who feared the shift might imply a lessening of the political dimension of feminist scholarship;

---

38   Patricia Grimshaw, Marilyn Lake, Ann McGrath and Marian Quartly, *Creating a Nation* (Melbourne: McPhee Gribble, 1994).

39   Joy Damousi and Marilyn Lake (eds), *Gender and War: Australians at War in the Twentieth Century* (Cambridge: Cambridge University Press, 1996).

40   *Australian Historical Studies* 22 (86) (April 1986): 116–31.

41   Joan Scott, 'Gender: A Useful Category of Historical Analysis', *American Historical Review* 91 (5) (December 1986): 1053–75.

Australian practitioners were also divided. Most became convinced, nevertheless, that gender provided a key to understanding power relationships more generally. Gender shaped power just as power shaped gender. Marilyn's fruitful analytical adoption of gender—in studies of citizenship, feminism, nationalism and history itself—was a component in the attention her work attracted on a world stage. British historian Leonore Davidoff became convinced of the title of *Gender and History* for the new journal she would establish in 1989 after she had earlier visited us in Melbourne.[42]

While numerous other Australians brought their work on to an international stage, even a cursory look at Marilyn's overseas conference presentations in the 1990s indicate the energy she brought to the challenge as well as the interest her work elicited. In 1990 she spoke at the 8th Berkshire Conference on the History of Women at Rutgers University. In 1992, she was invited by Catherine Hall, on the basis of 'The Politics of Respectability'—*Australian Historical Studies* attracted a wider audience than some might think—to speak at an international workshop at the Rockefeller Center in Bellagio, Italy, on gender and nationalism, also attended by Australian colleagues Ann Curthoys and (sometime Australian) Dipesh Chakrabarty. Later in 1992, she presented a paper to the Social Sciences History Association Conference in Chicago. In 1993, she and I both spoke at a workshop at the University of Bielefeld, Germany, and at the international conference on suffrage in Wellington. In 1996, we again presented papers at the Berkshire conference, this time at Chapel Hill. All up, Marilyn thinks she has presented papers at six Berkshire History conferences.

Some exciting gendered history was also happening in Scandinavia. Marilyn first went to Stockholm when Barbara Hobson, a historical sociologist and friend of Sonya Michel, invited her to join a symposium on citizenship and gender (held in a Swedish castle!) in 1994. This led to the establishment of the international journal *Social Politics* (of which Marilyn became a contributing editor). The next year she edited and wrote the introduction to the special issue *Citizenship: Intersections of Gender, Race and Ethnicity* (intersectionality has a long history) with a range of contributors from India, South Africa, the United States and Britain.[43] Barbara Hobson was then successful in raising millions of dollars in funding—primarily

---

42   Personal communication Leonore Davidoff to author.
43   Special issue *Citizenship: Intersections of Gender, Race and Ethnicity, Social Politics* 2 (2) (Summer 1995).

from the Bank of Sweden—to support a series of related conferences at the Advanced Research School in Comparative Gender Studies at Stockholm University from 1997 until 1999, which Marilyn was pleased to attend. The focus was the gendered nature of 'recognition struggles', drawing on the theoretical work of Charles Taylor and Nancy Fraser, who participated. She and Nancy Fraser also taught postgraduate subjects in an international Masters degree program at Stockholm University—Marilyn's was on the gender of national narratives—that attracted students from as far away as Peru and Japan. The series of conferences led to the publication of the Cambridge volume, *Recognition Struggles and Social Movements: Contested Identities, Power and Agency*, edited by Barbara and including Marilyn's essay 'Woman, Black, Indigenous: Recognition Struggles in Dialogue' examining the conversations between white feminists and Aboriginal women, especially around history, in Australia.[44]

In the 1990s, questions of citizenship and nationalism were popular topics for historians working comparatively. At the end of the decade, Marilyn was invited to Oslo, Norway, where she presented two papers at the 19th CISH conference held in 2000, one a talk for the roundtable on 'Gender, Race, Xenophobia and Nationalism' curated by Ida Blom and including Geoff Eley and Catherine Hall,[45] and the other a paper on the special theme of 'Masculinity as Practice and Representation', organised by Karen Hagemann, Stefan Dudink and John Tosh, scholars with whom Marilyn would work on a number of later research projects.[46] During the past four years she has joined the team working on the *Oxford Handbook on Gender, War and the Western World Since 1600*, led by Karen Hagemann and Stefan Dudink, joining conferences in Chapel Hill and at the Berkshire History Conference at Hofstra University to discuss her contribution called 'The "White Man", Race and Imperial War during the Long Nineteenth Century'.

Through these conferences and joint projects, Marilyn became part of stimulating international networks and was active in bringing overseas

---

44   Barbara Hobson (ed.), *Recognition Struggles and Social Movements: Contested Identities, Power and Agency* (Cambridge: Cambridge University Press, 2003).

45   This was the basis of the book edited by Ida Blom, Catherine Hall and Karen Hagemann, *Gendered Nations/Nationalisms in the Long 19th Century: Europe and Beyond* (Oxford/New York: Berg, 2000).

46   Marilyn Lake, 'Translating Needs into Rights: The Discursive Imperative of the Australian White Man', in *Masculinities in Politics and War: Gendering Modern History*, eds Stefan Dudink, Karen Hagemann and John Tosh (Manchester: Manchester University Press, 2004), 199–219.

feminist historians—Sonya Michel, Antoinette Burton, Catherine Hall, Sally Alexander, Judy Walkowitz, Karen Hagemann—to visit Australia. She was an active member of the committee that planned the very well attended IFRWH conference I convened in Melbourne in 1998. It attracted more than a hundred delegates from outside Australia and generated enormous goodwill, much joyous singing and intellectual insight. In 2001 Marilyn joined Katie Holmes and myself in editing the volume based on a wide-ranging selection of the papers as *Women's Rights and Human Rights: International Perspectives*.[47] Increasingly feminist historians began to research the history of earlier feminists' international engagements and their work with organisations such as the International Woman Suffrage Alliance, the International Council of Women, the Women's International League for Peace and Freedom, the League of Nations, the Pan-Pacific Women's Congress, the YWCA and the United Nations.

One aspect of this engagement that became increasingly well known was the international campaign by women activists for Aboriginal rights through the British Commonwealth League and the League of Nations—rights for mothers, for children and land rights. Marilyn published her first article on that champion of Aboriginal rights, Mary Bennett, in the journal *Women's History Review* in 1993.[48] Much more work on Bennett by a number of scholars would follow, leading eventually to the establishment of a women's history prize in Bennett's name and two major biographies that have come out in the last five years. Marilyn's work on Aboriginal history in the 1990s extended to the biography of Faith Bandler, detailing the commitment of an activist of Pacific Islander and Indian descent, who became a leading advocate of Aboriginal rights during the long referendum campaign from 1957 through to 1967. Working closely with Faith, her family and friends on this project, Marilyn was thrilled when Governor General Sir William Deane agreed to launch the book at the State Library of New South Wales in 2002 and also when it won the HREOC award for non-fiction. For Marilyn, Faith's beaming face on these occasions was the best reward of all.[49]

---

47 Patricia Grimshaw, Katie Holmes and Marilyn Lake (eds), *Women's Rights and Human Rights: International Historical Perspectives* (London: Palgrave, 2001).

48 Marilyn Lake, 'Colonized and Colonizing: The White Australian Feminist Subject', *Women's History Review* 2 (3) (1993): 377–86.

49 Marilyn Lake, *Faith: Faith Bandler, Gentle Activist* (Sydney: Allen & Unwin, 2002). Personal communication with the author. HREOC stands for Human Rights and Equal Opportunity Commission, since 2008 Australian Human Rights Commission.

Adopting new theoretical perspectives and employing fresh evidence, the new women's and gender history has effected a major transformation in Australian history and had a significant impact at the international level. Feminist work in the fields of education and the professions, health policy and social work, religion, philanthropy and missions, sexual desire and identity, family history and demography, migration and ethnicity, British imperialism and settler colonialism often connected to both grass-roots publics at home and academic scholars abroad. Scholars working in the fields of settler colonialism and Aboriginal history, such as Ann Curthoys, Vicky Haskins, Ann McGrath, Penny Edmonds, Fiona Paisley and the late Tracey Banivanua Mar, have made a major mark. In 2007 Marilyn was invited to join scholars from Africa and Asia on a Presidential Panel, 'Feminist History in a Postcolonial World', at the American Historical Association annual conference in Atlanta, Georgia, in honour of President Linda Kerber.

Like other Australian historians, Marilyn has published in a range of international journals including *Gender and History*, the *Journal of the History of Sexuality*, *Women's History Review*, the *Journal of Women's History* and *History Workshop Journal*. Her Australian articles have also been selected for reprinting in international anthologies. Her article on 'frontier feminism' has been reprinted in a volume edited by Clare Midgley[50] and again by Nupur Chaudhuri and Ruth Pierson.[51] Oxford's 'Reading in Feminism' series has twice reprinted articles Marilyn first published in Australia. Thus Australia-based work—historical work about Australia—came to circulate widely. Joan Scott selected 'Female Desires: The Meaning of World War II' for the collection *Feminism and History*,[52] while Joan Landes selected 'The Inviolable Woman: Feminist Conceptions of Citizenship, 1900–1940' for her collection *Feminism: The Public and the Private*.[53] Gordon Martel from Canada also included 'Female Desires' in the Routledge publication, *The World War Two Reader*.[54]

---

50 Clare Midgley (ed.), *Gender and Imperialism* (Manchester: Manchester University Press, 1998), 123–36.
51 Nupur Chaudhuri and Ruth Pierson (eds), *Empire, Nation, Colony: Historicizing Gender and Race* (Bloomington, Ind: Indiana University Press, 1998), chapter 5.
52 Joan Scott (ed.), *Feminism and History: Oxford Readings in Feminism* (Oxford: Oxford University Press, 1996).
53 Joan Landes (ed.), *Feminism: The Public and the Private: Oxford Readings in Feminism* (Oxford: Oxford University Press, 1998), 223–40.
54 Gordon Martel (ed.), *The World War Two Reader* (London: Routledge, 2004), 359–76.

Marilyn's time at Harvard University, when she joined the History Department as Chair in Australian Studies between 2001 and 2002, was clearly formative in her transnational turn, as she reflected on the historiographical implications of placing Australian history in a larger international framework. (She also happened to be there as the horror of 9/11 unfolded and the world changed forever.) Having completed work on the biography of Faith Bandler—and researched the African American dimensions of Faith's family's identifications with Black civil rights campaigns and bought Langston Hughes' poetry at the Harvard bookstore—she embarked on the project that would become the multi-prize-winning book *Drawing the Global Colour Line: White Men's Countries and the International Challenge of Racial Equality*—written with Henry Reynolds.[55] Gender remained a major theme of analysis; at a Harvard seminar when Marilyn explained the 'white man' as a gendered and racialised figure one member of the department looked perplexed when he commented that he could see the racialised aspect but not the figure's gendered dimension. There were several seminar series, attracting visitors such as Linda Gordon and the late Adam McKeown, with whom she would subsequently work. Marilyn taught with and learnt much from Harvard scholars Evelyn Brooks-Higginbotham and Laurel Thatcher Ulrich. She enjoyed the company of other history faculty including Nancy Cott and Susan Pedersen, and spent time with feminist friends then living in Cambridge: Laura Frader (affiliated with the Centre for European Studies), Alice Kessler-Harris (a visitor that year at Radcliffe College while writing her biography of Lilian Hellman), and the Australian biographer, the late Hazel Rowley, whose biography of African American writer Richard Wright was launched at Harvard soon after Marilyn arrived.

Through the first two decades of this century, Marilyn extended her researches into imperial and settler colonial history and wrote a short memoir in this context for Antoinette Burton and Dane Kennedy's collection *How Empire Shaped Us*.[56] She has also continued to write for newspapers—some fifty articles over her career—and speak to a range of community audiences. She has maintained her significant contribution to women's and gender history through her scholarship and public activism, in attending and organising meetings and conferences, in mentoring postgraduate students and early career scholars. Not least in importance for the

---

55   Marilyn Lake and Henry Reynolds, *Drawing the Global Colour Line: White Men's Countries and the International Challenge of Racial Equality* (Cambridge: Cambridge University Press, 2008).
56   Lake, 'In and Out of Empire'.

position of women in the profession has been her willingness in recent years to exercise leadership as president of the Australian Historical Association and as an active Fellow of the Australian Academy of the Humanities (and its council) and the Academy of the Social Sciences in Australia. Her participation in history at many levels is set to continue into her retirement. Her next book, encompassing many years of research and reflection, *Progressive New World: How Settler Colonialism and TransPacific Exchange Shaped American Reform*, is due out with Harvard University Press early in 2019.

In February this year, 2018, just forty years since our first meeting at the Macquarie Women and Labour conference, Marilyn and I gave papers at the conference 'Australian Mothering in Historical and Contemporary Perspective', convened by early career researchers Carla Pascoe and Petra Bueskens at the University of Melbourne. Marilyn grounded her paper, 'Mothers' Rights and Children's Needs: Maternal Citizenship in a Comparative and TransPacific Frame', in American comparative perspectives drawing on research for her forthcoming book. It seemed an appropriate moment to reflect on her extensive engagement with the experiences of Australian women past and present. Of the field of women's history, it is perhaps not an exaggerated claim to make that the recovery of the significance of women's past lives has shaped in constructive ways the chances and choices of a generation of Australian women. Marilyn Lake was and continues to be one of the notable feminist historians who furthered this endeavour. She has promoted a focus on women and gender as a means of situating women's history within an illuminating social, political and transnational frame, work that has attracted both a national and an international audience. Her intellectual breadth enabled her to take Australian history directly into local and global forums, helping to establish the field's legitimacy.

Chapter 4

RADICAL FEMINISTS AND RESPECTABLE RADICALS

Progressive Feminism and the Mainstream Women's Movement in Australia

Judith Smart

All histories and historians have a genealogy that is both professional and personal, the former largely discoverable via the conventions of footnotes/endnotes and bibliographies. The latter is often less evident but just as important. As late twentieth and early twenty-first-century feminists, we proclaimed the link between the personal and the political. As feminist historians we also acknowledge the link between the interpersonal and the interpretative, for we pride ourselves on working through sharing in informal as well as formal ways—via friendship, food and fun, and sometimes sympathy and tears, as well as through professional exchanges at conferences and seminars—and a festschrift is an ideal context for breathing some personal memory and feeling into a celebration of achievement.

I first met Marilyn in 1976 when she came to Melbourne to start her doctorate on soldier settlement in Victoria after World War I. I had begun a doctorate too—on Melbourne during World War I—though it took me a lot longer than Marilyn to complete it. Marilyn's reputation preceded her—she had just published *A Divided Society*,[1] the product of her MA research on Tasmania during the Great War and the first of the revisionist state

---

1   Marilyn Lake, *A Divided Society: Tasmania During World War I* (Melbourne: Melbourne University Press, 1975).

histories to appear—histories that stressed the complexity of feeling, including opposition and division, on the home front during the war years rather than the 'birth of a nation' mythology of Gallipoli and uniform patriotic enthusiasm.[2] But the feminist perspective on war was only just emerging at this point and was not a dominant theme in Marilyn's book. Carmel Shute's pioneering article 'Heroes and Heroines: Sexual Mythology in Australia 1914–1918' had been published in *Hecate*, the journal she helped found in 1975, and was succeeded by '"Blood Votes" and the "Bestial Boche"' a year later.[3] These two articles marked the beginnings of a gendered perspective on Australian war history, and Carmel herself arrived in Melbourne from Queensland around this time in order to do a doctorate on women on the home front during World War II—sadly never completed. We three formed ourselves into a cohort we called 'The War Girls' to talk initially about the part played by women during the wars but later about the role of gender more generally. We have been meeting regularly ever since to catch up, share a meal and discuss the work we are doing.

This period also saw the flowering of what came to be called—somewhat problematically as Marilyn and others later showed—'second-wave feminism'. Among other things it stressed the importance of linking the personal with the political and saw the emergence of 'consciousness-raising groups'. Marilyn was the source of much wisdom on this, having been involved in early activism in Hobart with pioneering feminist historian Kay Daniels. Five or six of us in inner suburban Melbourne decided to form one. We made no claims to be great pace-setters; we were a very middle-class CR group and would meet regularly for dinner at a local restaurant in Prahran—aptly called La Cuisine Bourgeois. I cannot remember when we disbanded though I don't think we persevered beyond two or three years. But we have remained friends, and we all took our feminism into

---

2   Dan Coward started the revisionism with his doctoral thesis on NSW during the war but it remains unpublished ('The Impact of War on New South Wales: Some Aspects of Social and Political History 1914–1917' (PhD thesis, Australian National University, 1974). Subsequent published revisionist histories include Raymond Evans, *Loyalty and Disloyalty on the Queensland Homefront, 1914–18* (Sydney: Allen & Unwin, 1987); Bobbie Oliver, *War and Peace in Western Australia: The Social and Political Impact of the Great War, 1914–1926* (Perth: UWA Press, 1995); Judith Smart, 'A Divided National Capital: Melbourne in the Great War', *La Trobe Journal*, no. 96 (September 2015): 28–58.

3   Carmel Shute, 'Heroes and Heroines: Sexual Mythology in Australia 1914–1918', *Hecate* 1 (1) (January 1975): 7–22, and '"Blood Votes" and the "Bestial Boche": A Case Study in Propaganda', *Hecate* 2 (2) (July 1976): 6–22.

our varied spheres of work. An overlapping group undertook a program of reading, and we worked our way through early feminist histories by Miriam Dixson, Anne Summers, Anne Conlon and Edna Ryan, and Bev Kingston, as well as discussing new directions being explored in labour history, and speculating on how a feminist understanding might change frameworks of understanding for national story telling. In mid-1988, Marilyn, along with Patricia Grimshaw and Marian Quartly, founded the Melbourne Feminist History Group, which eventually morphed into the Australian Women's History Network, our section of the International Federation for Research in Women's History in which Pat played a key formative role.

With the completion of her doctoral thesis and its publication as *The Limits of Hope: Soldier Settlement in Victoria, 1915–1938* (1987), Marilyn's career and leading role as a feminist historian took off. Along with Susan Magarey, Pat Grimshaw, Ann Curthoys, Judith Allen and a few others, she began exploring the history of Australian feminism (as distinct from the history of women), alongside a re-reading and re-conceptualisation of Australian history from a feminist then a gendered perspective. *The Limits of Hope* had already begun to do that in relation to the legacy of World War I. It was followed in 1994 by the ground-breaking new gendered history of Australia, *Creating a Nation*, the product of an inspired collaboration between Marilyn, Pat Grimshaw, Marian Quartly and Ann McGrath.[4]

My specific focus here, however, is the contribution of Marilyn's scholarship to the writing of *Respectable Radicals: A History of the National Council of Women of Australia 1896–2006*.[5] In 2008 Marian Quartly and I commenced work on a history of the NCWA after being approached by the organisation's president, Leonie Christopherson, two years earlier. Over the next three years, with support from the Australian Research Council Linkage program and the NCWA as our partner organisation, we visited every state Council and the archival collections where their records were held, spent some weeks in the National Library where we helped organise the addition of another cache of NCWA records to their files, and interviewed over thirty key figures, including seven former presidents. We argued our case for funding on the grounds that:

---

4   Published by McPhee Gribble/Penguin. A second revised edition was published by API Network in 2006.

5   Marian Quartly and Judith Smart, *Respectable Radicals: A History of the National Council of Women of Australia 1896–2006* (Melbourne: Monash University Publishing, 2015).

> Until the 1970s the National Council of Women of Australia was the major representative national women's coalition, taking the voices of Australian women to national government and, through the International Council of Women, to the League of Nations and the United Nations. The NCWA was thus the principal force behind the exercise of Australian women's political citizenship across most of the twentieth century. The absence of a comprehensive history of this important peak body is a gap in current understandings of women's activism and feminism in twentieth-century Australia.

It was, in other words a major project, but, as we also made clear, it was one that necessarily rested on the shoulders of other historians of Australian feminism, both those who had gone before and those still researching and writing. They are many, and we drew heavily on their work and insights, but most important among them for our understanding was undoubtedly Marilyn Lake.

In *Getting Equal: The History of Australian Feminism* (1999),[6] Marilyn explored the activities and ideas of self-consciously progressive Australian post-suffrage feminists throughout the twentieth century, ranging over political representation, welfare and social reform, education, nationality, Aboriginal rights, war, peace and international co-operation. Quite simply, our project would not have been do-able without Marilyn's pioneering work on the path-setters of Australian feminism and her major contribution to theorising, conceptualising and periodising the movement as well as debunking many of the myths associated with its history. Among these were: 'that there have been but two wave of feminism with a long lull in between'; 'that ... they didn't do anything with the vote'; 'that [they] failed politically because they largely failed to win election to parliament'; and 'that [they] were only concerned to advance the interests of white, middle-class career women'.[7] In building on Marilyn's work, we have been able to debunk another myth—that they failed to mobilise a large cross-section of mainstream women's organisations on feminist and other issues.

Marilyn demonstrated more clearly than anyone before her that there was no hiatus between the two so-called 'waves' of feminism. The architecture for a history was laid out a year earlier in her contribution to Oxford University Press's *Australian Feminism: A Companion* (1998), in which she

---

6   Marilyn Lake, *Getting Equal: The History of Australian Feminism* (Sydney: Allen & Unwin, 1999).

7   Lake, *Getting Equal*, 9.

described five phases: the protectionist focus of the nineteenth-century 'woman movement'; the stress on independence alongside maternalist protectionism during what she termed the 'era of the woman citizen' in the first three decades of the twentieth century; an increasing emphasis on equality of opportunity and downplaying of difference from the 1940s to the 1960s, alongside declining interest among younger women; rejuvenation and radicalisaton with a new focus on sexual freedom as a right during the 'women's liberation' period in the 1970s and 80s; and, finally, from the 1990s, a 'post-colonial'-influenced questioning of 'woman' as a universal category and the reformulation of feminism as coalition-building rather than a given 'natural' identity of interests.[8]

Getting Equal was organised around issues rather than phases but the pattern of changing focus Marilyn had already traced underpinned the interpretative trajectory of the book. *Getting Equal* took as its main focus Australia's leading twentieth-century liberal feminists, those who were political activists and key figures in the explicitly rights-focused organisations affiliated to the International Woman Suffrage Alliance and its successors. They were proudly radical, taking up unpopular issues and running with them—from Catherine Spence, Rose Scott and Vida Goldstein, through Linda Littlejohn, Bessie Rischbieth, Mary Montgomerie Bennett, Constance Ternent Cooke and Jessie Street, on to Germaine Greer, Elizabeth Reid, Anne Summers and many many others. Our national heroines were paraded before us in Marilyn's book. Only a few of them had been the subjects of previous major biographical studies.[9]

These were not the women Marian and I researched and wrote about in our history of the National Council of Women of Australia. Our women largely followed where Marilyn's women led, though they did not always follow very enthusiastically and sometimes they did not follow at all and instead retreated—or at least some of them did. But because NCWA leaders were largely supportive of the independence, equality and rights agendas, and managed to bring their hundreds of affiliates along with them (however reluctantly or passively) in support of equal pay, marriage law reform,

---

8   Marilyn Lake, 'A History of Feminism in Australia', in *Australian Feminism: A Companion*, ed. Barbara Caine (Melbourne: Oxford University Press, 1998): 132–42.
9   Notably Susan Magarey, *Unbridling the Tongues of Women: A Biography of Catherine Helen Spence* (Sydney: Hale & Iremonger, 1985); Judith Allen, *Rose Scott: Vision and Revision in Feminism* (Melbourne: Oxford University Press, 1994); and Janet Bomford, *That Dangerous and Persuasive Woman: Vida Goldstein* (Melbourne: Melbourne University Press, 1993).

equality of opportunity and equality before the law etc., we characterised them as 'mainstream feminists' and called the book *Respectable Radicals*.

We added twenty-six leaders of these women to supplement the pantheon of feminist heroines Marilyn (and others) had been building. They can be found in an online exhibition called 'Stirrers with Style' on the Australian Women's Register website and, in abbreviated version, in the book.[10] The AWR itself, an initiative of Pat Grimshaw through the National Foundation for Australian Women, followed a year after the publication of *Getting Equal* and has grown to nearly 6500 entries, boosted by the addition of *The Encyclopedia of Women and Leadership in Twentieth-Century Australia* to the AWR website in 2014.[11] Marilyn's book was a significant milestone in this renewal of interest in women's biography, long seen as conservative and privileging the ruling classes.

Respectable Radicals rests firmly on Marilyn's prior scholarship and builds on her work. Without the foundations she had established in her book, ours could not have assumed the extent, continuous history and conceptual sophistication of feminist organisation and activism against which to measure and compare the National Councils and would necessarily have been a very different book. The chronological phases, the categories and concepts, and the themes and issues stressed in *Getting Equal*, while varying somewhat from those we developed in *Respectable Radicals*, were nevertheless our indispensable primary point of reference.

The organisation of *Respectable Radicals* is both chronological (we divided it into four periods) and thematic (each period includes chapters focused on issues relating to home and family, to equality, and to international engagement, as well as to organisational change). Our periodisation for the first two sections (1896–1950) broadly followed Marilyn's first two phases emphasising protection, maternal citizenship and independence, though we also put some emphasis on equality battles from the 1920s onwards. There were during this period some areas of difference between most Council leaders and the feminist pace-setters. Marilyn's work alerted us to some of these, and they helped structure our discussion. One was the greater impact

---

10   Jan Hipgrave, Marian Quartly and Judith Smart, *Stirrers with Style! Presidents of the National Council of Women of Australia and Its Predecessors* (Melbourne: eScholarship Research Centre, University of Melbourne, 2014), at http://www.womenaustralia.info/exhib/ncwa/.

11   Judith Smart and Shurlee Swain (eds), *The e-Encyclopedia of Women's Leadership in Twentieth-Century Australia* (Melbourne: Australian Women's Archive Project, eScholarship Research Centre, University of Melbourne, 2014), at http://www.womenaustralia.info/leaders.

of professional women on Council activism and policy. Lawyers and doctors were influential on policy, the former in the interests of legal equality and the latter for more ambiguous purposes relating to maternal responsibility for family health and wellbeing. Here I focus on some examples of medical doctors' generally conservative pressure on NCW thinking about maternal feminism, beginning with the 'baby bonus'. Though not always decisive, the doctors' assertion of expertise had the effect of restraining the Councils from taking more progressive positions on some key issues.

Marilyn had researched the role of Labor Party women such as Muriel Heagney in Prime Minister Andrew Fisher's introduction of the Maternity Allowance in 1912—a one-off payment to a white woman, single or married, on the birth of a child. She then traced the subsequent defence of the scheme by advanced feminists in the non-party political organisations as well as Labor women, both groups framing it first as a step towards a mother's pension, then, more politically, as recognition of the citizen-mother's right to payment for her services to the state.[12] The highlighting of this issue triggered our attention to it in NCW records, where greater ambivalence was evident, some of the Council leaders and delegates initially seeing the payment as not only endorsing immorality and undermining individual responsibility but also as inefficient and giving insufficient emphasis to the problems of ignorance among young mothers.[13] Dr Edith Barrett was the force behind a deputation from the Victorian Council to present the view that provision for 'proper care and treatment during confinement' would be more effective than an unconditional one-off payment to individuals.[14]

While the impact of the Great War on families and the growing concern for independent economic security for married as well as single women kept the idea of ongoing payment of mothers alive in Council circles as well as more progressive ones, the parallel concern that the 'baby bonus' was an inefficient means of supporting new mothers and their babies was emerging in all states and becoming dominant in the Victorian and South Australian Councils by the early 1920s. As the national government also began to question the efficacy of the payment to new mothers, the Victorian NCW organised a nation-wide conference of women in Melbourne, the national

---

12 Marilyn Lake, 'State Socialism for Australian Mothers: Andrew Fisher's Radical Maternalism in its International and Local Contexts', *Labour History*, no. 63 (November 1992): 1–24, and *Getting Equal*, chapter 3.
13 *Argus*, 15 November 1912, 14.
14 Recollection of Dr Edith Barrett, then secretary of NCWV. See *Argus*, 21 March 1923, 19.

capital, in March 1923. With 120 organisations involved, it was the largest and most representative conference of women yet held in Australia.[15]

Noting the role of women doctors in the rising criticism of the baby bonus, Marilyn pointed out that 'at the behest of government' the National Council of Women in Victoria had in 1921 sponsored a report by 'three female medical experts' who had concluded that the bonus was ineffective as well as expensive.[16] The growing role of medical doctors in the Council movement was already evident to Marian and me in the emergence of baby health centres for the medical supervision and training of new mothers (NSW 1914 and Victoria 1917) and in infant welfare reforms, but it also explained the regulationist position most Councils adopted on Venereal Diseases control during the war years, contrary to the long-term opposition of nearly all women's organisations to the victimisation of women under Contagious Diseases legislation.[17] Marilyn's work reinforced our awareness of the growing emphasis on medical control and expertise in Council circles during the post-war years and later.

At the maternity bonus conference, the Victorian and South Australian Councils followed the advice of the Australian Branch of the British Medical Association and women medicos like Dr Edith Barrett who argued that the bonus had done nothing to increase the birth rate or decrease infantile or maternal mortality. Barrett was not advocating the employment of more medical men, for their increased involvement under the baby bonus regime had achieved no improvements. Her solution was medical supervision in hospitals; government money should thus be diverted from individual grants to new mothers to 'subsidising of existing State maternity hospitals' and 'bush nursing, district nursing, baby health centres, and other child welfare work'. She was supported by the South Australian NCW delegate, who favoured a 'more helpful and scientific method for the mother and child', and cited the British Medical Association's advocacy of 'the extension of maternity hospitals and antenatal clinics'.[18]

In 1923, the medical women were unable to carry all the NCW delegates with them, let alone persuade those from labour and radical feminist groups. NSW's Council delegate, for example, argued that: 'No mother should be driven into a hospital against her will'. Both the Western

---

15   Quartly and Smart, 69.
16   Lake, *Getting Equal*, 76–7.
17   Quartly and Smart, 74–5, 82–5.
18   *Argus*, 21 March 1923, 19.

Australian and Queensland Councils had conducted surveys and discovered that, while most doctors favoured diverting the funds, the vast majority of ordinary women they consulted found the bonus extremely helpful and wanted it continued.[19] The conference, as Marilyn also notes, passed two resolutions, the first supporting retention of the bonus and the second, in recognition of the medical arguments, arguing for government supplementation of the allowance by funding 'projects for mother and child welfare'.[20]

In the following years, state and federal Councils agitated with some success for dedicated programs in obstetrics in university medical courses. This, as well as legislation for greater medical control over midwifery and the introduction of new specialisations like mothercraft nursing—also urged by the National Councils—saw increasing medical hegemony over maternity.[21] Medical women's engagement in these debates demonstrated the growing influence of the disciplinary and efficiency-driven side of modern progressivist reform thinking encouraged by the demands of war, as opposed to the more liberal and democratic wing dominant before the war years.[22] Pre-war progressivism is a subject to which Marilyn has been devoting considerable and insightful attention in more recent years with her work on the turn-of-the-century exchanges between Australian and American social reformers and liberal thinkers, and her expression of regret that so much of the idealism of that period was lost in the post-war celebration of militarism and masculinism represented by Anzac.[23]

In the Great Depression emergency of the 1930s, the Councils, this time with no dissent from medical women, joined with all women's groups in agitating for restoration of full payment of the baby bonus after it had been reduced as an austerity measure.[24] Nevertheless medical women in these years continued to exert a conservative maternalist influence, notably on Council debates about birth control. The 1935 conference of the National

---

19 *Argus*, 21 March 1923, 19.
20 *Argus*, 22 March 1923, 9.
21 Quartly and Smart, 78–9.
22 Judith Smart, 'Was the Great War Australia's War? A Domestic Perspective with Particular Reference to Victoria', in Craig Wilcox (assisted by Janice Aldridge) (ed.), *The Great War: Gains and Losses—Anzac and Empire* (Canberra: AWM/ANU, 1995).
23 Marilyn Lake, '1914: Death of a Nation: Presidential Address Australian Historical Association Annual Conference, Brisbane, 2014', *History Australia* 12 (1) (2015): 7–24; and *Progressive New World: How Settler Colonialism and Trans-Pacific Exchange Shaped American Reform* (Cambridge, MA: Harvard University Press, forthcoming).
24 Quartly and Smart, 160–1.

Council of Women of Australia saw a lengthy discussion on abortion and contraception, which, according to president May Moss, was 'almost the most interesting debate we have yet had'.[25] Victoria had submitted resolutions seeking the prevention of abortion and a ban on the advertisement of contraceptives, and Queensland introduced an 'emergency resolution' asking the Councils to gather information about law and practice in the various states with a view to deciding the best means to prevent abortion. Delegates agreed that abortion was an 'evil' that should be prevented, but disagreed about how best to do this—and especially about the place of contraception in this process.

Lillie Goodisson, a New South Wales delegate and a leading light in the NSW Racial Hygiene Association, supported access to birth-control measures to minimise abortions. But Queensland's Dr Ellice Dart, arguing against this, proposed the teaching of sex hygiene in schools by 'proper people', narrowly defined as religious professionals and medical experts in mothercraft. Information about birth control should be strictly limited to married women and come only from the family doctor; the poor who had no doctor could get sympathetic advice at public hospitals. Dart believed that the stricter enforcement of laws against advertisement and sale of contraceptives would be the best remedy against abortion.[26] The implication was that fear was the best deterrent, and it was an argument that attracted the support of many religious and moral conservatives in the Councils. The conference resolved 'that all State Councils undertake to endeavour to get legislation enacted which will make the distribution of advertising matter for contraceptives etc. a punishable offence'. At the ensuing conference in Adelaide in 1936, the delegates went further, recommending 'that each State council urge its government to press for legislation concerning the sale, advertisement, exhibition and distribution of contraceptives similar to the Victorian Act of 1935'.[27]

In structuring our account of NCWA's history in *Respectable Radicals*, Marian and I opted to define our third period (1950–1970) as beginning and ending some ten years later than Marilyn's third phase (equality of opportunity). In doing so we both complicated her argument and helped explain falling support for her feminist frontrunners in the 1950s and the declining interest among the young by the 1960s. We called this period

---

25 NCWV, *Report for 1935*, 9–10.
26 NCWA Conference Minutes, August 1935, NCWA Papers, MS7583, Box 11, National Library of Australia.
27 *Advertiser*, 19 September 1936.

'The Golden Years' marked by the NCWA's favourite-daughter status during the Menzies years and beyond. Throughout this period delegates to the UN's Commission on the Status of Women came from NCWA ranks, and the Council was first port of call for government ministers wanting advice on anything to do with women. NCWA's very success from 1950 was at the expense of the radical pace-setting feminists such as Jessie Street, a founder of CSW, who was now, in the Cold War context, stigmatised as a communist or fellow traveller. Other early progressives, notably Bessie Rischbieth, responded to the polarising politics of the period by establishing a kind of rapprochement with our respectable radicals against Street and new left-leaning groups such as the Australian Union of Women.

While, as Marilyn notes, the 'adherents of feminism aged and dwindled in number' during the 1950s and 60s, our 'mainstream feminists', represented by the National Councils, were not sidelined as Street and others were. Rather, their numbers ballooned in terms of affiliated organisations from some 490 in the early 1950s to more than 600 in the early 1970s.[28] While they did pay attention to the main equality questions Marilyn identified among 1940s Charter feminists, especially equal pay, access to work, social welfare, nationality rights and marriage law reform, their commitment to maternalist citizenship became stronger rather than weaker in the 1950s and 60s. During these decades, the 'home and family as the secure centre of the moral universe, the well-spring of moral action' seemed to 'be under threat' not only from communism but from 'declining moral values, divorce, materialism, increasing rates of illegitimacy, single parenthood, desertion, juvenile delinquency and, perhaps worst of all, working mothers'.[29] This emphasis on family, rather than its commitment to equality, boosted membership and gave the National Councils the ear of government, effectively excluding the remaining radical feminists and turning away the generation of young women growing up in the 50s and 60s.

Thus when Women's Liberation, Marilyn's fourth phase in the history of Australian feminism, came to life in the early 70s, our 'respectable radicals' were ill equipped to respond to demands for sexual freedom and revolution, and soon found that their political influence could no longer be assumed, as alternative and politically savvy organisations emerged—specifically the Women's Electoral Lobby. Like Women's Liberation and its off-shoots, WEL members felt they owed nothing to the Councils or earlier radical

---

28 Quartly and Smart, 254.
29 Quartly and Smart, 267–8.

feminists, conveniently forgetting what these women had achieved and, in many cases, reinventing methods and arguments they had used long before. Finally, then, like the Charter feminists before them, our respectable radicals in the Council movement declined in influence and began to dwindle in numbers, and NCWA could no longer credibly claim to represent the voices of Australian women as they had previously done, although they did participate in new representative bodies inaugurated by the Whitlam government and its successors.

With only a few exceptions, NCW leaders were either unsympathetic or unresponsive on issues relating to the demand for sexual liberation. And they failed to neutralise some of the more outspoken critics in their ranks. Even if they did not condone their views, they did not explicitly reject them. Medical women played a role in this backlash and, once again, were mostly a force for conservatism. A prominent example was Dr Claire Isbister, a consultant paediatrician at the Royal North Shore Hospital in Sydney and convenor of the Child and Family Committee for NCWNSW, who campaigned against maternity leave and pensions for unmarried mothers, as well as the ready availability of the contraceptive pill.[30]

Isbister told guests at a NSW Child Care Week luncheon early in 1973 that the Australian family was threatened by great social problems, 'and some of these problems are being permitted and even created by academic experts, governments and fanatical selfish minorities'. Unmarried mothers were paid to keep their babies, de facto couples lived off government support, married couples struggled to find childcare when preference was given to working women, and teenagers contemplated 'trial marriage'. 'So who is getting the best deal at present, the responsible committed parents or the irresponsible?'[31]

Dr Isbister's views found a sympathetic hearing in several state Councils, especially among the delegates of affiliated organisations based in the churches. Their influence was probably strongest in the South Australian Council, where president Margaret Davey was a prominent member of the Young Women's Christian Association. Davey was subsequently NCWA president from 1976 to 1978. In late 1973 the British campaigner for family values, Mary Whitehouse, made her first Australian tour, and Davey's state board publicly supported her position, rallying and marching with

---

30   Quartly and Smart, 370.
31   Claire Isbister, 'The Rights of the Child', *NCWA Quarterly Bulletin* 2 (9), March/April 1973.

her Festival of Light. After a visit from Isbister, NCWSA put forward as a discussion topic at the NCWA executive meeting in August 1974 the proposal that the federal government should set up a 'Ministry of the Family' in order to defend 'the integrity of the family unit as the basis of a sound society. We feel that present processes undermine the importance of the family unit'.[32]

In May 1975, Isbister visited Brisbane at the invitation of the Presbyterian Women's Association and the National Council of Women.[33] Her address to the Council was nothing short of a call to arms. She 'emphasised the role NCW must play in fighting for the maintenance of the family unit, and fighting against all those things which are corrosive forces in today's world'. The force singled out for special attention was 'the Women's Liberation Movement insofar as its credo would lead people, and young men and women especially, to abandon certain moral principles which are vital not only for the social but the physical well-being of the community'. The outcomes of unrestrained sexuality were venereal diseases, abortions, and mental illness for women on the pill, whom she described as 'hormonally castrated'. 'If we believe that the "advanced" women's groups are undermining what we stand for, NCW ought to state where it stands on the rights, the needs and the responsibilities of a woman.'[34]

The Queensland executive was moved by this 'stimulating talk' to call a special meeting to consider how 'to make the voice of NCW more clearly and widely heard in the land'.[35] The meeting agreed that NCW should take on the role of 'spokesman for women who do not subscribe to the theories and principles of Women's Lib', with the central belief that 'family life is the keystone, with both parents having equality in their roles, but carrying out their functions as wife and mother, husband and father, as a women and a man'.[36] A 'Declaration' was prepared and circulated to affiliates, but the enthusiasm generated by Isbister's visit seems to have faded fast; the Methodist Church of Australia was the only affiliate to respond.[37]

---

32   NCWSA Annual Report 1973–74, published as *NCWSA Newsletter* 5 (9): 9.
33   NCWQ Executive Minutes, 11 November 1974, Box 16045, 7266 Minute Books, NCWQ Papers, State Library of Queensland (SLQ).
34   NCWQ Council Minutes, 15 May 1975, Box 16045, 7266 Minute Books, NCWQ Papers, SLQ.
35   NCWQ Executive Minutes, 19 May 1975.
36   NCWQ Executive Minutes, 9 June 1975.
37   NCWQ Executive Minutes, 20 October 1975.

As the NCWA convenor for Health Child and Family in 1978, Isbister prompted Margaret Davey's national board to protest against proposed federal family support funding that took no account of 'blood relationship, legal adoption or any legal commitment' such as 'the responsibility of marriage'. While the board did not go so far as to nominate Isbister as the NCWA representative on the International Year of the Child National Committee, as requested by NSW Council, it did not reject her views, and thus continued to position itself as socially conservative during this crucial decade.

Conclusion

The story we have told in our fourth and last section, 'Remaking the National Councils 1970–2006', is overall one of fragmentation and the fight to survive, adding both complexity and substance to Marilyn's characterisation of the fifth phase of Australia's feminist history as one of coalition building and acknowledgement of difference. Forced now to acknowledge that the Councils could no longer claim to represent Australian women as a whole, NCWA turned from the late 1980s to devising different ways of relating to other women's organisations and to the federal government.[38]

Marilyn's work on the leading radical feminists of the twentieth century made possible Marian's and my history of the mainstream feminist movement in Australia during the same period, establishing patterns and concepts from which we sometimes diverged and which we sometimes contested. But it is the mark of Marilyn's scholarly achievement that *Getting Equal* served us—and will continue to serve others—as the indispensable foundational work on the history of Australian feminism. We thank you for that gift Marilyn.

---

38   Quartly and Smart, chapter 14.

Chapter 5

PEACE POLITICS AND WOMEN'S LIBERATION

Kate Laing

The twentieth century saw the increasing employment of internationalism within the women's movement as a mode of engaging with the wider world of politics and social justice. During World War I new women's groups emerged with internationalism at their core. They devised organisational structures that drew diverse cultures and nationalisms together to lobby new post-war international assemblies such as the League of Nations and the International Labour Organization (ILO). These women's groups also utilised international political pressure and example to progress campaigns for domestic and national rights. The international sphere became a place to share ideas and gendered experiences beyond the arbitrary confines of national borders, and the contacts they made enabled women to broaden their networks of support, validation and respect. Marilyn Lake, in her vast writings on feminist history in Australia, made the observation that 'one can't study the history of Australian feminism without realising how internationally engaged feminists were—despite the distances and costs involved'.[1] As international political engagement defined many feminists in Australian history, feminists defined a gendered experience of internationalism. The men who dominated the delegations to those first international gatherings at the League of Nations, the ILO, and later the United Nations, were primarily interested in advancing national priorities and saw their positions as extensions of their national roles. In contrast, 'women's

---

1   Marilyn Lake, 'Histories Across Borders', in *Australian History Now*, eds Anna Clark and Paul Ashton (Sydney: NewSouth, 2013), 281.

experience of international activism produced convinced internationalists' whose practical and philosophical commitment to the idea of internationalism coloured their entire political agenda.[2]

Understanding the history of internationalism—a focus of Lake's work in *Drawing the Global Colour Line* and other contributions to journals and edited collections—is integral to our wider understanding of Australia's past.[3] Putting Australian history in an international context allows for deeper consideration of 'the ways in which Australian national identity and the white imperial ambition were forged—and contested'.[4] Lake, among others, has demonstrated that a narrow focus on national stories 'cuts us off from the world and reduces our history to a small number of favoured and mostly masculinist narratives', often revolving around Australia at war.[5] Her work has complicated and extended our understanding of Australia's past by drawing attention to international perspectives in feminist history and by directly confronting the dominance of the Anzac myth, which has trumped all other narratives in Australia's popular history.[6] Buoyed by massive funding from government and the private sector, Anzac commemoration has militarised Australia's popular history by encouraging school children and communities more generally to honour the 'Landing' at Gallipoli in 1915 as the birthplace of the nation. Lake has paved the way for more histories that challenge the dominance of Anzac. My own research into the Women's International League for Peace and Freedom (WILPF), established in 1915, builds on this foundation and contributes

---

2   Marilyn Lake, 'Women's International Leadership', in *Diversity in Leadership: Australian Women, Past and Present*, eds Joy Damousi and Kim Rubenstein (Canberra: ANU epress, 2014), 74.

3   Marilyn Lake and Henry Reynolds, *Drawing the Global Colour Line: White Men's Countries and the Question of Racial Equality* (Melbourne: Melbourne University Press, 2008); Marilyn Lake, Katie Holmes and Patricia Grimshaw (eds), *Women's Rights and Human Rights: International Historical Perspectives* (New York: Palgrave, 2001); Marilyn Lake, 'Women's International Leadership', 71–90; Marilyn Lake, 'The ILO, Australia and the Asia-Pacific Region: New Solidarities or Internationalism in the National Interest?', in *The ILO from Geneva to the Pacific Rim: West Meets East*, eds Nelson Lichtenstein and Jill M. Jensen (London: Palgrave Macmillan, 2015), 33–54. On internationalism as a political movement, see Glenda Sluga, *Internationalism in the Age of Nationalism* (Philadelphia: University of Pennsylvania Press, 2013).

4   Lake, 'Histories Across Borders', 270.

5   Lake, 'Histories Across Borders', 271.

6   Marilyn Lake and Henry Reynolds, with Joy Damousi and Mark McKenna, *What's Wrong With Anzac?: The Militarisation of Australian History* (Sydney: UNSW Press, 2010).

to a more balanced understanding of Australia at war by focusing on the vision of women peace activists for an Australian identity based on peace and social justice rather than the valorisation of war.[7]

During the 1960s and 70s peace activism and theories of internationalism were complicated by new rhetoric from the local Women's Liberation Movement (WLM), which in its own way grew out of international networks and embraced internationalism through the UN International Women's Year (IWY) 1975 and the subsequent UN Decade for Women. Balancing national interests with international ideals and finding a place within the new feminist rhetoric created tensions for the activists of WILPF who were conscious of their own history and traditions. Margaret Holmes recalled their efforts to appear 'middle class', 'respectable' and distinct from the new generation of radicals, 'so that people wouldn't be able to say that the war was only opposed by a ratbag lot of youngsters'.[8] Yet, in labelling themselves so, they reinforced the distinction that many conservative status quo groups used to destabilise and dismiss the movement and its more radical elements. After prioritising involvement with the UN Decade for Women 1975–1985, which forced collaboration with other NGOs, international civil servants, national governments, and a range of feminist groups, WILPF's ideology too began to change. This chapter will detail WILPF Australia's involvement in anti–Vietnam War protests and its subsequent transformation after the explosion of WLM feminist activism challenged it to adapt and renew its radical critique of gender relations and war.

WILPF and the Vietnam War protests

WILPF established an active group in Sydney in 1960.[9] Using information from their international networks, Sydney branch members began monitoring and agitating on the issue of conflict in Vietnam in 1963—much earlier than other Australian peace groups. They placed advertisements in local and national papers that urged readers to send letters to members of parliament,[10] and, at the 1964 Congress for International Cooperation

---

[7] This article is based on a chapter from my PhD thesis: Kate Laing, 'Fighting for a New World Order: The Women's International League for Peace and Freedom in Australia 1915–1975' (PhD thesis, La Trobe University, 2017).

[8] Margaret Holmes, 'Proud to be a Proper Peacenik', *Australian*, 18 July 1990, 3.

[9] Michelle Cavanagh, *Margaret Holmes: The Life and Times of an Australian Peace Campaigner* (Sydney: New Holland, 2006).

[10] Annual report WILPF NSW 1963–64, WILPF NSW Branch Records 1960–1990, MLMSS 5395, Box 1, State Library of NSW.

and Disarmament (CICD) conference in Sydney, WILPF member Betty Gale, who had recently travelled to Vietnam, was one of the only speakers to mention the Vietnam conflict. It was not until Menzies introduced conscription later that year that the peace movement really gathered momentum to respond to Australia's involvement.[11] In 1965 WILPF was joined by others women's groups protesting against the war, including Save Our Sons, which focused on conscription, and Women For Peace, a WILPF-affiliated action group.[12]

These women's groups were defined by their method of protest, which was explicitly and strategically maternal. SOS members drew on their identities as mothers to articulate their opposition to conscription, and WILPF also participated in vigils and 'mothers in mourning' activities.[13] In concurrent campaigns against nuclear testing, these women's groups used emotive maternalist imagery emphasising child protection and defined themselves as 'feminine but not feminist'. Like earlier women's rights activists, they built on traditional understandings of feminine identity, emphasising the importance of women as mothers and thereby reinforcing gender roles in the broader society that radical gender theory aimed to deconstruct.

By 1970, new energy had been injected into the organised women's movement fuelled by the radicalising experiences of women activists against the Vietnam War. Life was changing for women in Australia. In the 1950s and 60s, scientific developments offered the promise of revolutionary emancipation in sexual relationships, with effective and rapid treatment available for the three principal sexually transmitted diseases then prevalent, syphilis, chlamydia, and gonorrhoea, and, most importantly, reliable contraception in the form of the Pill.[14] While many of the ideas about sex and sexuality had been championed by radicals long before the 1960s, the wider

---

11 B. Gale, 'Summary of paper presented by Mrs. B. Gale at Seminar on 26 October on Australia's Relations with Asia', Australian Congress for International Cooperation and Disarmament Conference 1964, CICD Collection, Box 49, Series 3/51, University of Melbourne Archives. See also Ann-Mari Jordens, 'Conscription and Dissent', in *Vietnam: Remembered*, ed. Gregory Pemberton (Sydney: Weldon Publishing, 1990), 62.

12 Ann Curthoys, '"Shut up you bourgeois bitch": Sexual Identity and Political Action in the Anti/ Vietnam War Movement', in *Gender and War: Australians at War in the Twentieth Century*, eds Joy Damousi and Marilyn Lake (Melbourne: Cambridge University Press, 1995), 311–41.

13 Curthoys, '"Shut up"'. See also 'Women in Black Hoods Fail to Shake Menzies at Poll Rally', *Sydney Morning Herald* (*SMH*), 24 November 1964.

14 Marilyn Lake, *Getting Equal: The History of Australian Feminism*, (Sydney: Allen & Unwin, 1999), 220.

acceptance of associated social changes, along with the radicalising protests of the Vietnam War, turned the decade into an era 'encrusted with legend'.[15] Many women experienced greater sexual freedom as a consequence.

In the middle decades of the twentieth century several path-breaking feminist books gave a new language to the women's movement.[16] They were followed in the 1970s by analyses of women in Australian history that challenged conventional understandings of the role of gender in our past.[17] They encouraged women to think differently about their place in society and often explicitly rejected the priorities of earlier maternalist feminism. Anne Summers wrote that upholding the 'structural inequalities of the family', as the early anti-war women's groups did, contradicted the aim of feminist independence. When discussing Vida Goldstein's Women's Peace Army, Summers noted 'they did not appear to recognize the irony and the ultimate anti-feminism of their basic assumptions', and 'Goldstein and the other members of the Women's Peace Army were endorsing a conservative, if not outright reactionary, view of women and their social functions'.[18] Summers defined the stereotypes of Australian women as either 'damned whores' or 'God's police', products of a society that assigned social functions on the basis of sex. Despite their radicalism in their context, Peace Army members were, to unsympathetic Summers, God's police.

The new wave of women's organising, inspired by new theories of gender and equipped with a new language of 'sex roles' and 'sexism' to discuss it, began on university campuses and within peace movements in the late 1960s and early 1970s. 'Sexism' offered a framework in which to discuss structural inequalities, but the analysis focused more on the individual than women's role in the family. Sexuality and bodily autonomy were primary concerns. This differed from women's rights campaigns of the past in acknowledging

---

15 Frank Bongiorno, *The Sex Lives of Australians: A History* (Melbourne: Black Inc., 2012), 222.

16 Notably, Simone de Beauvoir, *The Second Sex* (New York: Knopf, 1952); Betty Friedan, *The Feminine Mystique* (Melbourne: Penguin, 1963); Kate Millett, *Sexual Politics* (London: Rupert Hart-Davis, 1970); and Germaine Greer, *The Female Eunuch* (London: Paladin, 1971).

17 Anne Summers, *Damned Whores and God's Police: The Colonization of Women in Australia* (Melbourne: Penguin, 1975); Beverley Kingston, *My Wife, My Daughter, and Poor Mary Ann: Women and Work in Australia* (Melbourne: Thomas Nelson Australia, 1975); Miriam Dixson, *The Real Matilda: Woman and Identity in Australia 1788 to the Present* (Melbourne: Penguin, 1976); Edna Ryan and Anne Conlon, *Gentle Invaders: Australian Women at Work 1788–1974* (Melbourne: Thomas Nelson Australia, 1975).

18 Summers, 428 (revised 2002 ed.).

women's desire for sex and aiming to make women sexually free through access to contraception and abortion, rather than through repression of their sexuality.[19] Women had new economic aspirations in Australian society that motivated their call for change too. The WLM, however, was also a 'generational rebellion', rejecting mothers and maternity.[20]

Women engaged in the Vietnam War protests were spurred to think about oppression in the light of the national struggle of the Vietnamese. Through direct experience in the anti-war movement, they began to think more deeply about the need for their own liberation. The name Women's Liberation Movement (WLM) was a conscious reflection of the language of liberation associated with the Vietnamese resistance movement. Many young women had become frustrated with the condescension of male comrades in the peace movement. In 1970 activist Kate Jennings gave a speech at a Vietnam War moratorium march at Sydney University that controversially pointed out the inconsistencies of men in the New Left:

> our brothers of the left and in the peace movement will think that what I am about to say is not justified, this is a moratorium ... Women are conscripted every day into their personalised slave kitchens. Can you with your mind filled with the moratorium, spare a thought for their freedom, identity, minds, and emotions?[21]

Significantly it was the same impulse that had caused the Sisterhood of International Peace and WILPF to organise autonomously in 1915—they wanted to have a louder and distinctive voice in the male-dominated anti-war campaigns and not be consigned to menial tasks within the movement.

WILPF and its interaction with the WLM

For WILPF, whose membership in the 1970s consisted primarily of older married women, some of the new language and theory of the WLM was confronting. The focus on abortion, contraception and sexuality challenged some church-going members. In Australia and internationally, WILPF was not at the forefront of women's liberation. But many members experienced

---

19   Marilyn Lake, 'Sexuality and Feminism: Some Notes in their Australian History', *Lilith: A Feminist History Journal*, no. 7 (1991): 29. See also Lake, *Getting Equal*, 223.
20   Patricia Grimshaw, Marilyn Lake, Ann McGrath and Marian Quartly, *Creating a Nation* (Melbourne: McPhee Gribble/Penguin, 1994), 301.
21   Kate Jennings, *Trouble: Evolution of a Radical: Selected Writings 1970–2010* (Melbourne: Black Inc., 2010), 8.

insults as a result of their efforts in the Vietnam peace movement similar to those suffered by WLM women. For example Margaret Holmes and other members bristled at being asked 'why aren't you back at home looking after your husbands and kids?'[22] Many had grown up in an era of rigid gender segregation and had not politicised the experience, seeking instead to instrumentalise roles for women embedded in that structure to advance their politics. WILPF saw itself primarily as a peace organisation. Members' early feminist identity and commitment had lessened once they realised that women's suffrage 'had not put an end to or even diminished wars'.[23] This difference of opinion divided the older parts of the women's movement from the new; older women activists were willing to employ patriarchal language to achieve their ultimate goal of peace. Peace was more important than feminism.

The rise of the transnational WLM at first provoked WILPF to reassert its identity as a peace organisation rather than a feminist one. Serious discussions took place about whether it should remain a women's group at all. In 1968, British WILPF member Margaret Tims wrote a circular letter to the international membership advocating that WILPF should eschew identity as a women's organisation, because 'the two causes—of peace and freedom in the general sense and of women's freedom in the particular sense—are no longer synonymous and should be treated separately'.[24] As enfranchised citizens women were part of the system, no longer 'outside' politics, and must therefore share responsibility for its failures and achievements. As more women gained positions of power, especially in Australia, with the growth of 'state feminism' and 'femocrats' working within the political system and in light of the rising critique of white feminists by Aboriginal activists, it became harder for WILPF to assert that women were not complicit in decisions about war and violence.[25]

While Tims's suggestion that WILPF women no longer organise in a gender-specific way was not acted upon, the Danish section did remove 'Women's' from its title in 1969 and was congratulated by the international chair, Elise Boulding, for doing so. She wrote, 'perhaps our sisters are right

---

22   Holmes, quoted in Siobhan McHugh, *Minefields and Miniskirts: Australian Women and the Vietnam War* (Sydney: Doubleday, 1993), 239.
23   Catherine Foster, *Women For All Seasons: The Story of the Women's International League for Peace and Freedom* (Athens, Ga: University of Georgia Press, 1989), 40.
24   Margaret Tims, April 1968 circular letter to WILPF, quoted in Foster, 55.
25   Lake, *Getting Equal*, 253; Patricia O'Shane, *Aboriginal Political Movements: Some Observations* (Armidale: University of New England, 1998).

and it's time for women to become people'.²⁶ By 1974, when Kay Camp was international president of WILPF, her husband William Camp became a member of WILPF and more men joined, including Australian pacifist Dr Keith Suter.²⁷ Some WILPF leaders such as Gertrud Baer tried to maintain the link between women and peace, but the League gradually 'evolved into being a peace organisation whose members happened to be women' and, with the acceptance of male members, even this changed.²⁸ However, some WILPF members, while sceptical and somewhat hesitant about associating with the WLM, still promoted women's issues and equality more generally. WILPF concern about the new feminist ideologues stemmed from their insistence on an equality that did not account for women's 'difference'. The US section of WILPF, in writing about the relationship with the WLM in 1970, stated: 'WILPF was born of the suffrage movement ... Our criticism is that some feminists equate equality and similarity—the idealization of masculine attributes'.²⁹

While Australian WILPF leaders ensured that the organisation kept its distance from the WLM, the new movement energised individual members. Irene Greenwood, in her 70s at the time, enjoyed the new 'awakened consciousness' and felt it was 'no new phenomenon'.³⁰ However, other members of WILPF, when asked if they were feminists, were quick to draw the distinction between the organised WLM, with which they were not involved, and general support for women's equality. Betty McIntosh, president of the Western Australian WILPF branch in the 1970s, answered:

> I don't feel I want to drop other things I'm doing for the sake of pursuing feminism, and yet I have always been strongly in favour of women's rights and personally involved in a number of areas where recognition of women is very important ... I think there's a difference between organised feminism and feeling the strength of feminism. I

---

26 Foster, 56.
27 Cavanagh, 302; Erika Rathgeber to Edith Ballantyne, 5 July 1978, and Ballantyne reply, 10 July 1978, WILPF Collection, Box 53/4, Swarthmore College Peace Collection (SCPC), University of Colorado at Boulder (UC) Archives.
28 Foster, 32.
29 Foster, 56.
30 Irene Greenwood, 'Chronicle of Change', in *As a Woman: Writing Women's Lives*, ed. Jocelynne A. Scutt (Melbourne: Artemis Publishing, 1992), 113.

think when we use the term loosely, we do refer to organised feminism. And I've just never had the time to devote to that.[31]

WILPF's members' reluctance to become involved with this new wave of organised women's groups points to difficulties women had organising across generations with different motivations, perspectives and experiences. Indeed Stella Cornelius, Australian vice president of WILPF in 1987, believed that WILPF members tended 'to be matriarchs', and, while they would 'very happily [work] with other women's groups that attract younger women', they were more 'like a motherly organisation in the women's activities for peace'.[32] WILPF, insistent on producing 'well considered and thoroughly investigated' work, wanted to present as the 'sensible' group and 'not revolutionary'.[33] Other groups that worked alongside them viewed WILPF as old and overly bureaucratic.[34]

Historian Suellen Murray has noted that, in the women's peace movement of the 1980s, 'while many involved … would not have claimed to be radical feminists, the politics of radical feminism was influential'.[35] WILPF was not intimately involved in the new direction of the movement, but members were starting to reconceptualise the links between violence and gender. Influenced by feminist theory, WILPF began articulating the link between international violence and domestic forms of violence such as rape and battery. For example, the US section held a conference in 1967 called 'Women's Response to the Rising Tide of Violence'.[36] In 1971, the Western Australian WILPF branch held a symposium called 'The Understanding of Human Aggressiveness' at which a sociologist, psychologist, psychiatrist, and biologist discussed the issue of gendered violence. While male violence and aggressiveness were not specifically targeted, the report used gendered language throughout, referring to 'mankind', 'man', and 'his very nature'.[37] This language was much more binary than that previously used.

---

31 Betty McIntosh, interviewed in 1985, in Scutt (ed.), 176.
32 Stella Cornelius, 'Peace Worker and Businesswoman', in *The Matriarchs: Twelve Women Talk about their Lives to Susan Mitchell* (Melbourne: Penguin, 1987), 130.
33 Agnes Stapledon, 'Head of British Peace League; Left Sydney 40 Years Ago', *SMH*, 24 November 1966.
34 Amy Swerdlow, *Women Strike for Peace* (Chicago: University of Chicago Press, 1993), 9.
35 Suellen Murray, '"Make Pies Not War": Protests by the Women's Peace Movement of the Mid 1980s', *Australian Historical Studies* 37 (127) (April 2006): 81.
36 Foster, 41.
37 Roma Brown and Betty King, 'The Understanding of Human Aggressiveness Seminar Report', 24 June 1971, WA Branch of WILPF.

By the 1970s, the membership of WILPF was ageing, and many sections had difficulty recruiting younger members. In the Australian branch, new member Jennifer Fischhof joined after the Vietnam War protests. Her youth and vitality were much feted by the older membership: 'She is just the sort of woman we need, young, active and tremendously motivated'.[38] Fischhof became active in WILPF and tried to engage older members with the campaigns run by the WLM. She was also a member of the newly formed Women's Electoral Lobby (WEL), established in 1972. Writing to Edith Ballantyne at the Geneva office, Fischchof described the difficulty she had in interesting older members in the WLM:

> WILPF in Australia is unknown!!! I have tried hard this year to put WILPF on the map in Australia, but there seems to be a fear that by working with other groups that WILPF will lose its identity. I feel discrimination against women is a WILPF issue, but cannot get anyone in WILPF to work with Women's Lib and a new big group here, the Women's Electoral Lobby.[39]

Just as many WILPF women, more concerned with peace activism than feminism, rejected engagement with the WLM, many WLM members were concerned that 'peace activism could be tied too closely to particular discourses about femininity, ones that feminists were working hard to challenge'.[40] Maternity and nurturance were often invoked in discussions of peace. This did not serve the interests of feminists 're-imagining gender well beyond the confines of motherhood and wifedom'.[41] In the 1970s and 80s, when SOS and the Pine Gap Peace Camp both explicitly employed the rhetoric of maternalism, the equality/difference debate again divided feminists and pacifists. Some Women's Liberationists feared 'that any form of women's pacifism may be positively subversive of feminist purpose'.[42] However, unlike more conservative women's groups such as the National Council of Women and the Country Women's Association, WILPF did

---

38   Fischchof to Ballantyne, 11 May 1974, Reel 55, WILPF Papers 1915–78 [microform], Series III, National Sections and Other Countries, 1914–1979, Australia Section (Reels 54–55), Sanford, NC: Microfilming Corp. of America, *c.* 1983.
39   Fischchof to Ballantyne, 15 February 1974, Reel 55, WILPF Papers.
40   Suellen Murray, 'Taking the Toys From the Boys', *Australian Feminist Studies* 25 (63) (March 2010): 5.
41   Murray, 'Taking the Toys', 5.
42   Jo Vellacott, 'A Place for Pacifism and Transnationalism in Feminist Theory: The Early Work of the Women's International League for Peace and Freedom', *Women's History Review* (*WHR*) 2 (1) (1993): 24.

not expressly criticise WLM aims, despite finding it hard to locate themselves within them.[43] Fischhof remained involved in both peace activism and feminism, attended international meetings in the UN Decade of Women, and continued to participate in both WILPF and the WLM, gradually helping to combine the rhetoric of one with the other.

When 1975 was declared International Women's Year by the UN,[44] three themes were chosen to structure the year: equality, development, and peace. Australia's Whitlam government, having appointed Elizabeth Reid as its women's adviser, allocated over $2 million towards grants for events and projects.[45] WILPF's Irene Greenwood was appointed to the IWY national advisory committee. Reid had a difficult job bringing together the various sections of the women's movement during 1975, and the committee was criticised by the mainstream media and by sections of the movement itself. The media represented IWY as 'feminism as excess, equated with the extravagance attributed to the Whitlam government in general'.[46] WLM activists such as Mavis Robertson criticised the allocation of funding for prioritising non-feminist proposals over WLM projects that were committed to change.[47] WILPF too was disappointed, noting that peace was constantly dropped from the agenda. While being pleased that IWD events were well attended and 'spectacular', its leaders lamented that 'nothing is ever said by anyone except us about the third objective, namely peace. So that is what we are concentrating on'.[48]

WILPF decided to devote its energy to the conference planned by the UN for IWY and held in Mexico City. Because the number of observers at the main UN event was limited, WILPF's main arena of engagement was through the Tribune satellite conference organised for NGO representatives excluded from the official gathering. Both conferences were lively and controversial, and represented as the 'NGO-ization of activism, particularly transnational women's activism'.[49] Feminists Betty Friedan and Germaine

---

43   Marian Quartly and Judith Smart, *Respectable Radicals: A History of the National Council of Women of Australia 1896–2006* (Melbourne: Monash University Publishing, 2015), 390, 396.

44   Jocelyn Olcott, 'Globalizing Sisterhood', in *The Shock of the Global: The 1970s in Perspective*, ed. Niall Ferguson (Cambridge, MA: Belknap Press, 2010), 281–93.

45   Lake, *Getting Equal*, 258.

46   Lake, *Getting Equal*, 259.

47   Lake, *Getting Equal*, 259.

48   Rothfield to Ballantyne, 14 March 1975, Box 53/4, WILPF, SCPC, CU Archives.

49   Olcott, 287. The Tribune conference was characterised in the media as divisive and disruptive.

Greer, among others, wrote about their experiences of both the UN conference and the Tribune, criticising the national delegations for promoting their national interests rather than engaging in genuine discussion of sexism.[50] Reid's speech was among the few to confront this focus on women as 'instruments' for national goals.[51] WILPF's main impression of the conference and the Tribune was their disappointing failure to focus on the 'peace' pillar.[52] International general secretary Edith Ballantyne worked alongside Australian WILPF member Evelyn Rothfield to organise a 'peace caucus' that pressed for a UN world disarmament conference, but they were told that 'such matters would unnecessarily "politicize" the decade'.[53]

Pushing the peace angle also posed difficulties throughout the Decade for Women. What limited discussion of peace there was centred on a resolution that equated Zionism with racism, causing countries supportive of Israel to abstain from voting for the Plan of Action.[54] At the 1980 women's conference in Copenhagen, Australia voted against the whole Plan of Action because it criticised Zionism. This focus on the Arab–Israeli conflict, and the discussion of economic development and decolonisation, forced WILPF to engage with groups like the Women's International Democratic Federation (WIDF) that were supportive of violence in liberation struggles.[55] While WILPF simultaneously reaffirmed its commitment to non-violence, the issue highlighted the difficulty of engaging with the violent insurgencies that so often characterised the later phases of anti-colonialist movements. Nonetheless, its members energetically participated

---

50 Betty Friedan, *It Changed My Life: Writings on the Women's Movement* (New York: Dell Publishing Company, 1977), 343; Germaine Greer, *The Madwoman's Underclothes: Essays and Occasional Writings* (New York: Atlantic Monthly Press, 1987), 200.

51 'Australia Wants Changes in Plan', and 'Ms Reid Hits Back', *Xilonen*, Mexico City, 24 June 1975. See also Elizabeth Reid, 'Between the Official Lines', *Ms. Magazine*, November 1975.

52 Rothfield to Ballantyne, 18 July 1975, Box 53/4, WILPF, SCPC, CU Archives.

53 Foster, 76.

54 Kristen Ghodsee, 'Revisiting the United Nations Decade for Women: Brief Reflections on Feminism, Capitalism and Cold War Politics in the Early Years of the International Women's Movement', *Women's Studies International Forum* 33 (1) (January 2010): 6.

55 WIDF was a rival international organisation often accused of communist affiliation. See Francisca de Haan, 'Continuing Cold War Paradigms in Western Historiography of Transnational Women's Organisations: The Case of the Women's International Democratic Federation (WIDF)', *WHR* 19 (4) (September 2010): 547–73; Katharine McGregor, 'Opposing Colonialism: The Women's International Democratic Federation and Decolonisation Struggles in Vietnam and Algeria 1945–1965', *WHR* 25 (6) (November 2016): 925–44.

in the UN Decade for Women as a central arena for expressing internationalist principles. WILPF played a pivotal role in the associated NGO forums, signalling a further shift of focus towards concentrating its resources on lobbying through the UN.

While WILPF may not have been at the forefront of feminist second-wave movements, the rapid changes in society nevertheless substantially transformed the organisation. Increased scholarship on gender and peace coming from university departments newly populated with women, including Lake, gave WILPF a new lens through which to examine its core purpose. Similarly, participation in the UN Decade for Women modified WILPF's ideology through connections with the wider feminist movement, other NGOs, international civil servants and national delegations. In 1983 scholar Cynthia Enloe, now a member of WILPF, published her work *Does Khaki Become You? The Militarisation of Women's Lives*, which demonstrated militarism's reliance upon individuals performing gender roles at their most conventional, influencing WILPF to rethink its mode of organising.[56] In 1989 philosopher Sara Ruddick published *Maternal Thinking*, which revived the maternalist perspective after second-wave feminist thought rejected it, helping shift the transnational WLM closer to WILPF's viewpoint.[57] In her description of motherhood and the politics of caring, Ruddick maintained that men could fulfil the roles traditionally left to women.

At the 1986 WILPF triennial congress held in the Netherlands, keynote speaker Dr Catharina Halkes unpacked the word 'patriarchy', made popular in the 1970s by feminist scholars, and linked it to the idea of peace.[58] In thus highlighting the theoretical underpinning of patriarchal societies as a major cause of war she recast and reaffirmed WILPF's justification for autonomous organisation. Halkes condemned the 'rigid role distribution' that made women 'accustomed to think that they have to keep peace only in the house, in the family and in personal relations' and thereby 'influence their husbands and children ... to help avoid war'.[59] Women were not inherently more peaceful than men; rather, 'differences between the sexes

---

56   Cynthia H. Enloe, *Does Khaki Become You?: The Militarisation of Women's Lives* (Boston: South End Press, 1983).

57   Sara Ruddick, *Maternal Thinking: Towards a Politics of Peace* (London: Women's Press, 1990).

58   Catharina J.M. Halkes, 'Women's Work for Peace in a Patriarchal Society', in *Women Unite for Justice and Peace*, 23rd International Congress of WILPF, The Netherlands, 1986, subsequently published as 'Peace and Patriarchy', *Pax et Libertas* 51 (4) (December 1986).

59   Halkes.

stem from social conditioning—learned behaviour by which women and men come to see the world, and act in it, in substantially different ways'.[60] It was not men who were the problem, but 'the patriarchal system which dehumanizes many men', encouraging them to 'kill the enemy of tenderness, love and care within themselves. The linking of male sexuality to aggression is the root of both patriarchy and war'.[61] Furthermore Halkes suggested that 'peace is not possible in a patriarchal society', and that opposing male aggression with 'feminine motherliness' only reinforces patriarchal ideas about differently gendered moral codes. The way forward for peace was to 'throw off shackles of fear and lack of self-confidence'.[62] From 1989 onwards all congresses of WILPF referred to 'patriarchy' as a root cause of war, and recognised the need to dismantle oppression of women as part of the program for a peaceful society. Though it did not happen all at once, and WILPF was not immediately on board with second-wave feminist activism, a radical interpretation of feminist theory became part of its core organising principles, enabling the organisation to recast long-present strands of thought into the new vocabulary.

Conclusion

Lake's research has charted the radical changes in definitions of feminism over time, noting 'the feminist of one era can look like an oppressor in another'.[63] WILPF was founded in 1915 when prevailing feminist thought was maternalist in orientation. The organisation has maintained continuous activity for over one hundred years, and has therefore had to reassess and reshape its political thinking as political fashions changed. Analysing the catalytic moments of that change helps us understand WILPF's longevity and adaptability.

The Vietnam War changed Australian society. Newly politicised university students expanded their activism, while young women spoke out about the marginalisation they experienced in the new protest organisations. This posed one of the biggest challenges to WILPF, which was compelled to engage with new ideas about gender equality and feminism.[64] WILPF had

---

60   Halkes.
61   Halkes.
62   Halkes.
63   Marilyn Lake, 'On History and Politics', in *The Historian's Conscience*, ed. Stuart Macintyre (Melbourne: Melbourne University Press, 2004), 98.
64   Lake, *Getting Equal*, 221.

to define its understanding of peace activism anew while reorganising the national section. Nevertheless, WILPF was one of the first organisations to protest about Australia's escalating role in the war, stimulated to do so by information received through international channels. Keeping up to date with overseas newspapers, circulars, WILPF and UN reports gave members the knowledge that propelled their activism. However, once again, they had to debate whether they should agitate and protest against the war or remain focused on studying the causes of war. Parallel with the anti-war movement, the WLM began to discuss ideas about femininity, women in the workforce and family responsibilities. Engaging with this new and subversive discussion in the 1970s required a change in WILPF's approach.

Historian Ann Curthoys recollected as a participant in the 1970s WLM that movement women 'anxiously distinguished' themselves from activists in established groups such as the Union of Australian Women and WILPF.[65] She termed the ignorance and arrogance shown by the WLM 'matricidal feminism'—women were 'shaking hands with our sisters yet rejecting our mothers'.[66] WILPF was certainly confronted by this 'matricidal feminism', which excluded their ideas and devalued their history. Despite this, WILPF eventually absorbed ideas generated by the new women's movement and radicals within the universities. In particular, the concept of 'patriarchy' gave WILPF the language to understand the gendered focus of their organisation and to interpret their activities within a framework seeking to dismantle gendered oppression.

---

65 Ann Curthoys, preface to Barbara Curthoys and Audrey McDonald, *More Than a Hat and Glove Brigade: The Story of the Union of Australian Women* (Sydney: Bookpress, 1996), ii.

66 Curthoys, preface, ii.

Chapter 6

SCHOLARLY ACTIVISM IN WOMEN'S STUDIES

Liz Conor

Thirty years ago I fronted up to the La Trobe University open day to enquire after a BA. I had spent my school-leaving years schlepping in Melbourne's cafes, saving to backpack around Europe for two years. On my return I was hell bent on acquiring languages, mortified at my European friends' linguistic virtuosity. I was also intrigued by feminist continental philosophy. That open day was my first meeting with Marilyn Lake. She affably informed me that to do Women's Studies I would have to undertake two core Australian history subjects. I inwardly curled my lip at what would indeed become core learning and remains so to this day. I had returned home laden with brattish misplaced contempt for Australian parochialism. After thrill-seeking in Europe, I found my homeland boring. The whole joint seemed like a small country town. I was enthralled by the Scottish Highland Clearances, the IRA, Weimar Berlin, the French Resistance, Marx, Sartre and de Beauvoir—all things European.

My shameful deficit in languages sparked an interest in linguistics. Women's Studies at La Trobe was part of a suite of first-year subjects focused on acquiring and understanding language. In some irretrievable depository of my brain lies a store of Pure Grammar. It was linguistics that placed in my hands Dale Spender's *Man Made Language*, and I was hooked by the intervention, the praxis of feminist scholarship from that moment. I lopped a few letters—ill-defined as patrilineal—off my then name, Lizzie O'Connor, and, thus newly minted, began my career in Women's Studies—which is what Marilyn mostly taught me.

The year I commenced, 1987, was also the year John Dawkins, then Minister for Education, brought down his green paper, sparking a series of reforms in the tertiary sector. These 'reforms' aimed to improve the 'international competitiveness' of Australian universities, which we now know was shorthand for a slavish adherence to the precepts of neoliberalism. It entailed the slashing of federal funding, the commercialisation of knowledge and the subjection of universities to corporate managerialism, where market values ride roughshod over curiosity, contemplation and the unpredictable adventure of crafting, all the while critiquing, explanation. Humanities schools were demoralised through endless, disheartening restructures within the hollow metrics of ranking and output, while the salaries of VCs (who were mostly men) bulged like Barnaby Joyce's Beetroot. These same reforms would ultimately see the demise of Women's Studies since it was said to have 'triumphed' by being absorbed into the mainstream (rather than 'grazing by' it as Jill Matthews so wryly put it). Women's Studies departments have since closed in the US and the UK as well as here.

Dawkins had proposed HECS in his green paper, and it was introduced in 1989. I joined the protests and my double life as an activist and student/scholar commenced. My point in this chapter is that feminist activism and Women's Studies were inextricably linked, and at our present juncture we need to draw on those traditions today. Dawkins argued that while, in theory, no tuition fees should provide greater equality of educational opportunity, in reality free-fee students were drawn overwhelmingly from higher income families. Unsurprisingly redress was not found in making education less accessible, and who could put up scholarships for disadvantaged students after rounds of gutting cuts? The squeeze is felt in the classroom (those not attended online). Yet while student numbers increased as a proportion of the population, federal funding was slashed over the ensuing decades—in 2016 by $1.4 billion and another $1.2 billion in 2017—flinging the Group of Eight's craven support for fee deregulation back in their teeth.

For a generation of baby boomers who rode their gratis law degrees all the way to the front bench to then saddle onerous HECS–HELP debts on the shoulders of young adults is somewhat ungracious, if not intergenerational fleecing. Nevertheless, this initial economy of scale of HECS debts less than $10,000 allowed me to combine a PhD with mothering, and, when one of my daughters became mysteriously gravely ill, I had the support of interrupted-career and bridging fellowships and flexible-time fractions from three munificent workplaces. Each helped me muddle through the precarity of contract and sessional work, expended grants and ultimately a resigned post. Being a Women's Studies graduate ironically did not insure me from depending on my then partner for 7.7 of the 13 years between my PhD being conferred and finally sniffing the promise of tenure aged fifty. He was my principal funding body. Ironically, in order to complete a PhD in feminist thought, I depended on a male breadwinner and assumed the domestic and care loads, plonking me in a 'feminine mystique' no less mystifying for my increasingly arch and implacable feminist analysis. Still, a proportional HECS debt was not daunting for me. But for younger women the triangulated pincer of extended study/training, combined with declining fertility while partnering a mortgage makes a humongous HECS debt unviable and crushing.

Looking back, Marilyn was a mainstay, a mentor and an indispensable champion. From the time she commented on an essay with 'You must go on', thus sealing my fate, I have been ever in Lake's wake, and not just in terms of depending on her formative and foundational scholarship. During her time at La Trobe I invented a binder full of excuses to knock on her door knowing she would always generously give hours of her highly pressured time in often hilarious reveries on everything from mothering to politics, feminism and, dare I say, Australian history. Marilyn converted me and I sit at my desk rather sheepishly, one of only two history beneficiaries in 2015's ARC Future Fellowship round. Since Marilyn let me pursue a directed reading on Foucault in my honours year, I never looked back. I submitted two essays that bristled with spelling and grammar mistakes, with incomprehensible titles about 'omni-elided males' and the discursive field of pornography. In her comments Marilyn noted that the display of the female body was in fact superseded in pornography by worship of the penis—clearly I needed to pay closer attention. She also asked whether discourse analysis is entirely compatible with psychoanalytic readings and thought I needed to pay far more attention to the codes of meaning entailed in different media forms.

Marilyn impressed on me the importance of foregrounding the materiality of imagery (or any text) by historicising it. For example, she connected Miss Australia back to Britannia, a nationalist fantasy of inviolate femininity: 'the female figure worked as an abstract symbol in the public domain precisely because real women were excluded from politics and other formal power structures'.[1] As a print historian examining the Modern

---

1   Marilyn Lake and Penny Russell, 'Miss Australia', in *Symbols of Australia*, eds Melissa Harper and Richard White (Sydney: UNSW Press and National Museum of Australia Press, 2010), 94.

Girl,[2] I remembered this instruction. We find a wealth of meaning in any particular visual library (and because of Marilyn they were for me gendered and then colonial) when we historically contextualise, or collocate imagery with cultural production/producers of the time, and situate them within contingent mediascapes. Considering Surveyor-General Thomas Mitchell's prints, for example, we start to see the relation of imagery to colonial governance in his topographical charting of sovereign lands (see illustration).

'Dance at the Report of a Pistol', Plate 14, Major T.L. Mitchell, *Three Expeditions into the Interior of Eastern Australia*, vol. 1 (London: T&W Boone, 1839), 248
(Courtesy Newcastle Regional Library)

Not only do they reference Mitchell's earlier engagement with lithography as the new printing technique he used for his topographical intelligence in the Peninsular wars, but they also cast light on his illustrations of conciliation, engagement and, here, warning of the 'natives'. Firing a pistol shot into a tree, in part out of curiosity, Mitchell had hoped to appease this group who instead 'repeated their gesticulations of defiance with tenfold fury ... demonic looks, hideous shouts and a war cry' after which, unsurprisingly, 'any further attempt to appease them was out of the

---

2   Liz Conor, *The Spectacular Modern Woman: Feminine Visibility in the 1920s* (Bloomington: Indiana University Press, 2004).

question'.³ In an attempt to deflect concerns in the Colonial Office regarding his party's massacre of at least seven Aboriginal people on the Murray River near Robinvale in May 1836, which delayed his much-sought-after knighthood, Mitchell was careful here to detail the friendly exchanges he had had with tribes elsewhere. The cause of the 'evil disposition' of this group was 'unimaginable' to his party, and their 'inveterate hostility' would probably 'ere long force upon us the painful necessity of making them acquainted with the superiority of our arms'.⁴ He was thankful for the dread his pistol shot had incited. Mitchell thus preempts criticism of his ambush and firing on this same, still-hostile, group four years later. He could no longer count on the patronage of Sir George Murray, Secretary of State for the Colonies, in the Colonial Office, and, in his disputes with Governors Darling, Bourke, Gipps, FitzRoy and Denison, his illustrated published expedition journals served to generate a wider popularity that enabled him to bypass them and retain the confidence of the Colonial Office. Along with the critical roles of his maps in parceling the sovereign lands he had 'opened', and in some cases violently seized, these lithographs were key to the creation and regulation of distinct but connected colonial publics. Interpreted in this context, this image provides a portal into the complexities of colonial surveying, patronage and governance, part of the information revolution Zoe Laidlaw has described,⁵ and it also reflects contemporary changes to print culture, not the least the steam-powered rotary lithograph press in 1843.

'It is the supreme art of the teacher to awaken joy in creative expression and knowledge', said Albert Einstein. Women's Studies undoubtedly achieved this. As the program's foundational director at La Trobe, Marilyn was the hub from which Women's Studies' interdisciplinary offerings were explored. Talk about breadth. I was treated to an array of inspirational, unforgettable teachers in Barbara Creed's Feminist Film Theory, in Lucy Frost's Feminist Literary Criticism, in Adrian Howe's Feminist Legal Studies, as well benefiting from the influences of Freya Matthews and Phillipa Rothfield in

---

3   Thomas Mitchell, *Three Expeditions into the Interior of Eastern Australia*, vol. 1 (London: T&W Boone, 1839).

4   Extracts from Proceedings ... Relating to Major Mitchell's Attack on Aborigines, 1836, *SRNSWCSO* 4/118; *Australian*, 8 November 1836; Mitchell, *Three Expeditions*, vol. II, 101–02; *HRA*, I, xviii, 590–1; Roger Milliss, *Waterloo Creek Massacre: The Australia Day Massacre of 1838, George Gipps and the British Conquest of New South Wales* (Melbourne: McPhee Gribble, 1992), 128–36.

5   Zoe Laidlaw, *Colonial Connections 1815–45: Patronage, the Information Revolution and Colonial Government* (Manchester: Manchester University Press, 2005).

philosophy, and exposure to Alison Ravenscroft's postcolonialism and Katie Holme's environmental history. I look back on these utopian years wistfully, when burying oneself in piles of reading could not take a backseat to deadlines. These experiences provided precisely the core articulation of Women's Studies, empowerment through knowledge.

The year of my entry into this scholarly cornucopia, 1987, was also four years after Australia became a party to the international bill of rights for women, the Convention on the Elimination of All Forms of Discrimination against Women, in 1983.[6] And it was three years after the Commonwealth *Sex Discrimination Act 1984*. The Office of the Status of Women had been formed in 1983—although the shoulder-padded 'Femocrat' had already been typecast in the Fraser years as the 'Minister Assisting the Prime Minister in Women's Affairs'. Incendiary activism did not entirely give way to pragmatism, as we interlaced into the structures we had combatted. As they ran in parallel, some of us were equivocal about making compromises with equality-based and liberal feminism. These were tremendously exciting times for women, but the gains, the admissions into extant structures were dominated, it has to be owned in retrospect, by settler-heritage middle-class women. They were full of hope and determination to correct the manifold expressions of entrenched gender asymmetry. For all our 'western-centrism', we feminists were acutely aware of the critical role of education in effecting change in workplace participation and economic autonomy, in decision-making and policy, and most urgently in violence against women and girls. But there were whole worlds of oppression some of us had barely glimpsed. The intergenerational traumas of colonialism, slavery, flight from war and persecution—these were rude awakenings for still largely unmarked white feminists.

This was also the year women students began to outnumber men students, though this failed to overturn gender segregation in the higher echelons of most of the professions we entered. Having born witness to so many glass ceilings shattering like toffee, when I thudded into the brick wall of maternity it felt I had run headlong into the bulwark of liberal feminism as it blocked out the demands of socialist feminism. Labour force participation still depended on either having a wife, or not needing one—that is, remaining childless. While barriers had tumbled for childless women, when it came to accommodating carers into the workplace no amount of community-based childcare and maternity leave could counter the exhaustion women experienced doing the double (and, with study, triple) shift discussed by Marilyn

---

6   At http://www.un.org/womenwatch/daw/cedaw/cedaw.htm.

and others in *Double Time*.[7] These basic needs remain unchanged; if a child has not slept, neither has at least one of its parents. Thus, when the 'daughters of feminism' angrily accused us of indifference to the trials of maternity, we were able to produce rejoinders drawing on the historical record. We still have a way to go in the battle for domestic equity, and accommodating carers into the workforce, but it is not for want of trying.

Higher education as a social mobility mechanism has let women down; the female pay gap increases, we continue to be subjected to violence, we are disproportionately impacted by cuts to state welfare in elder care and childcare provisions, and a new wave of unapologetic misogyny emanates from the pussy-grabbing clawback of 'victimised' white men within Trumpism. That said, no graduate of Marilyn's could witness or participate in #MeToo without thinking through the vicissitudes of fame, race and class as they fomented and framed women's varied responses within this critical mass of 'silence breakers'. Marilyn was critical to a great many of us in identifying gender as a primary field in the organisation of power and within the institutions that field underpins, from parliament to the public sector to the media, where men still dominate.

In her lively, vivid teaching Marilyn shifted norms, challenging the entrenched gender bias of knowledge systems produced by and for men for centuries. It was at times mind-blowing; I remember in my first tute being riveted as a student applied and amplified these teachings to her sense of injustice at not being able to pallbear her father's coffin despite having turned, washed and lifted him through his last months. The personal, we discovered in those tutes over and again, was manifestly political. And I simply would not date a boy who had not read Kaja Silverman.

Women's Studies was not about dismantling patriarchal epistemologies, but engaging with, challenging, expanding and, in so many cases, reinvigorating and endowing those ideas with new impetus and relevance. Feminist psychoanalysis was a case in point. It did not instil dogma but scepticism, the first attribute of critical thinking. It did not entrench some feminist orthodoxy but instead questioned unexamined political dogma. Marilyn's teachings gave momentum to feminism, and many of us sprang with firebrands from the classroom to the rally, working together in a variety of direct action collectives.

---

[7] Marilyn Lake and Farley Kelly (eds), *Double Time: Women in Victoria—150 Years* (Melbourne: Penguin, 1985).

In Women's Studies we scrutinised women's contribution to culture and history alongside the meanings assigned to the category 'woman' in philosophical, literary, socio-cultural, and historical thought. It was incendiary. But any category or identity-based discipline was also unsustainable once the exclusions it was founded upon became apparent.

It was also Marilyn who introduced me to Judith Butler's writing about the performativity of gendered identity. We were constantly appraising and criticising feminism in its myriad manifestations, and this drive to evaluate is what powered its momentum, what made it a movement, as much as the collective rallies roiling down Swanston Street. Postcolonial feminism is more than a case in point here; it completely remapped feminist thought into the many strands now animating settler–colonial studies. The intersectionality (or what in the '90s we called, 'multiple points of identification' or 'overlapping fields of power') of race, sexuality and class attended our every inquiry. Marilyn expansively and respectfully invited into our purview the central question posed to students and practitioners of Women's Studies: 'which women?' The ethnocentrism of feminist thought identified by women of colour brought us into the standpoint theory of situated knowledges. Through postcolonial feminist thought and the critique of heteronormativity, we learnt that gender norms are largely enforced by violence and it is the dispossessed and uprooted who bear the brunt of that violence.

We learnt conflicting theories of gender, including the contest over Women's Studies as a subject-based or category-based enquiry, soon after accused by deconstructivists of 'ontological chastity'. We also learnt a lot of big words. Since Women's Studies aimed to make higher education more inclusive for women, a logical extension of this field was to become more inclusive of men through critiques of hegemonic masculinity and heteronormativity. But the transferral of Women's Studies into Gender Studies has never overcome the entrenched conviction that women are not only the second sex but the marked sex. And, over the last decade, a number of Australian universities have dismantled their Gender Studies programs— albeit in the face of widespread student protest.

From Australia we have looked over at the rupturing tumult in heteronormavity in the US and seen the waves begin to break on our shores with the naming of Don Burke, Craig McLachlan and Robert Doyle. Gender equality has been startlingly dismantled in the USA, and 'down under' we like to prostrate ourselves before all American caprices. How long before the Bannonites in the Liberal–National Party Coalition push for women who abort to be 'punished', as President Trump promised? How long before Australian cabinet makers reskill in Texan joinery to make the world's tiniest caskets? Therein, ludicrously, foetal remains at any stage will be laid to rest. It is to states such as Texas that Trump wants to devolve abortion law. The Tea Party must be roiling in the rank sweat of the enseamèd bed they have made with their Trumposter, leaving the entire GOP to stew in its own corruption.

Trump's bravado about accusations of sexual assault cannot have been incidental to his opposing the First Woman Presidential Candidate (FWPC—this deserves its own acronym, and surely should take precedence over the Family Worship and Prayer Centre or the Forest and Wood Products Council). Trump's four most powerful cabinet positions are occupied by white men. His cabinet is a caligari of billionaire somnambulists. His sexism has been so persistent and flagrant it can be charted over decades: there is even a ranking for 'Trump-grade sexism'.[8] He also seems hellbent on squandering anything achieved towards the collective good since the Enlightenment. But he reserves his most repugnant smearing for women. When we are not deemed attractive enough to be up for grabs, we are fat, pigs, slobs and disgusting animals. Esteemed senators—notably Elizabeth Warren—are 'Pocahontas' and willing to 'do anything' for campaign funds. Trump also promised to appoint a Supreme Court justice who will overturn the landmark 1973 *Roe v Wade* ruling on women's reproductive rights. And, at the time of writing, he has succeeded, with the swearing in of Brett Kavanaugh—their bromance blossoming through a shared history in sexual misdemeanours. Trump's opportunistic stance on abortion will likely embolden the Australian anti-abortion movement. Indeed, in May 2018 they popped up like perennials, startling Queensland MP Rob Pyne when he introduced his Woman's Right to Choose Bill aimed at decriminalising abortion in his state (abortion also remains in the NSW criminal code).

Within our fatal shores (two women murdered every week) an anti-feminist backlash is underway everywhere you look. Kicking off the latest wave of femexecration was Victorian football identity Eddie McGuire's gaffe in June 2017 about 'holding under' *Age* journalist Caroline Wilson. Feminist columnists are inundated with a tsunami of threats—trolling—and derided as 'hysterical'. This discursive violence is far from immaterial

---

8   See https://www.telegraph.co.uk/women/politics/donald-trump-sexism-tracker-every-offensive-comment-in-one-place/, accessed 25 June 2018.

given these columnists attract such vitriol because they write about the gender pay gap (still around 16 per cent), occupational segregation, gender asymmetry on company boards (fifteen of the two hundred boards comprising the Australian Institute of Company Directors have no women), one in three elderly women living in poverty (often having failed to accrue sufficient superannuation savings owing to caring responsibilities), and rising rates of domestic violence.

These are some of the inequities still material to women that Women's Studies once made a central object of analysis within an unapologetically tendentious feminist critical tradition. The threats of violence mean we continue to occupy space differently, often with a sense of trepidation, our knuckles wolverining keys, buying alarm grenades for our daughters. Inequality continues to shape our world view, our expectations of career 'merit', and income security. It also stimulates that thirst to understand the nature of the discrimination we face, its historical derivations and daily operations, the work that it does within governance, economy, citizenship, culture, and the practices of knowledge that sustain it. On that last point, like all peoples ascribed identity categories by which their every move is defined, women are acutely aware that knowledge is power.

And that is why, thirty years ago, I fronted up to the Women's Studies table that open day to inquire about majoring in the broad array of courses on offer. Therein I found a passel of femo-comrades and ratbags. We fagged for hours over each others' kitchen tables, pot-valiant on castration theory. We sometimes literally burst from the tutorial to the rally. Our praxis was frequently chemically enhanced and very often vainglorious. And, like all Bright Young Things, we may have been a teensy bit attracted to certainty and occasionally sneering of ambiguity (despite being schooled to hold them 'in tension').

Does the historical record of feminist struggle, the epistemic interventions and the revival of these localised attacks on the feminine body warrant its own disciplinary identification—a return to Women's Studies? Can the particularity of this renewed *malleus maleficarum*, centred on the category woman, be accommodated within Gender Studies? Or did we lose a strategic analysis of a shared corporeality by querying the exclusions embedded in that category until it Balkanised into pronouns and acronyms. If Women's Studies served in the past to produce activists who were informed by but moved beyond epistemological interventions, is it the place of the academy to challenge the entrenched gender bias of knowledge systems produced by and for men for centuries? Was Women's Studies a genuine intrusion into the 'dominant paradigm', or merely a meditation? How do we defend its subsequent incarnation, Gender Studies?

Since Women's Studies had first and foremost aimed to make higher education more inclusive for women, the impetus for this field had to be more inclusive of those who also spurned patriarchy through critiques of hegemonic masculinity and heteronormativity. As Jacqueline Rose has recently argued, feminism should be 'natural bedfellows' with queer men, especially trans who 'shed maleness'. Transgender women should find an ear and an intellectual home within Women's Studies precisely 'because so many of them have suffered such personal pain in prizing open the question "Who is a real woman?"'[9] And this raises the further question, how can a scholarly discipline base itself on an identity category whose very ontology is, like any category demarcated by group membership and social kind, inherently exclusionary?

This was the unassailable reasoning through which Women's Studies was rebadged as Gender Studies. Yet, as we have seen through these programs' recent closures, mainstreaming gave hardly any security to the investigation and interrogation of gender in universities. Rather the study of gender was co-opted and diluted. It is no coincidence that both the unbridled 'alt-right' in the US and the hard right here (with its recent fixation on Section 18C of the Racial Discrimination Act), deeply resist their identification as White Men. It is discriminatory, they have snivelled.[10]

Arguments to preserve Women's Studies against the nomenclature of Gender Studies were incompatible with the destabilisation of the sovereign subject underway within poststructuralism. Women's Studies was a subject-based enquiry, leaving it open to the accusations by deconstructivists of 'ontological chastity' already referred to here. In hindsight, Women's Studies' amendment to Gender Studies did not honour the activist women who established Women's Studies departments in Australia, most of them historians. Nor should Gender Studies be taken as a signal that women

---

9   Jacqueline Rose, 'Who Do You Think You Are: Jacqueline Rose on Trans', *London Review of Books*, 5 May 2016, 14, http://eprints.bbk.ac.uk/18467/1/18467.pdf, accessed 25 June 2018.

10   SBS News, 'White Men File Complaint Claiming Indigenous MP Linda Burney Has Been Racist to them', at https://www.sbs.com.au/news/white-men-file-complaint-claiming-indigenous-mp-linda-burney-has-been-racist-to-them, accessed 25 June 2018. See my 'Raging Bullfrogs, Goadboys, 18C and other Masculinist Misadventures', *Meanjin Quarterly* 77 (2) (June 2018): 88–103, https://meanjin.com.au/essays/raging-bullfrogs-section-18c-and-other-masculinist-misadventures/, accessed 25 June 2018.

have overcome being allotted positions not only as the second sex but the marked sex.

It is now left for us to ask whether the discontinuing of both Women's and Gender Studies programs is yet one more of neoliberalism's intellectual deprivations, or whether this mainstreaming overcame the purported ghettoisation of an indispensable critical tradition. Was it part of the backlash to which Susan Faludi alerted us, and under which liberal feminism co-opted the feminist ethic of economic independence and twisted it into 'the consumer ethic of buying power'? Do the latest permutations of this backlash—barefaced and predatory misogyny from the leader of the free world—warrant the reinstating of Women's Studies? I think not—not once the category woman was intercepted by woman-identifying people committed to shedding the coercive binary of gender identification. It is Gender Studies we must now defend and reinstate.

If education level, more than income, is the biggest factor in explaining both the Trump and the Brexit turn, it is assuredly not élitism to argue that higher education is critical to an informed citizenship. It is more critical than ever to clamour for proven critical traditions that resist the 'coercive violence of gendering', as Jacqueline Rose puts it.[11] Scholarly enquiry cannot be sustained on the basis of any form of closure, of which exclusion inherently partakes. It is gender that became the category for analysis, not women, or the feminine, or feminists, or mothers.

Meanwhile, as we quibble over strategic essentialism, Trump and his ilk subscribe zealously to an imagined essence of women and seek to contain its disruptions within definitional parameters. While we resist the category they will go all out to enforce its ontological bounds, thereby laying out the agenda for our resistance. In the west, under Trump in the US and in Australia among the hard right, the feminist coalface has been superimposed yet again over women's bodies and localised to those sites that, by coming under attack, serve to confirm an essence that becomes biological and unassailable. We need allies, comrades of every identification. Trumpism incites a call to arms to women, whoever they may be, with all of us attending to the particular temporalities of reproductive rights, from those denied abortions to those denied artificial insemination and IVF.

Thus a 'Statement by Feminist Scholars on the Election of Donald Trump' did the rounds. Its hundreds of signatories pledge to 'act now', to:

---

11   Rose, 'Who Do You Think You Are', 6.

protect reproductive justice, fight for Black lives, defend the rights of LGBTQIA people, disrupt the displacement of indigenous people and the stealing of their resources, advocate and provide safe havens for the undocumented, stridently reject Islamophobia, and oppose the acceleration of neoliberal policies that divert resources to the top 1% and abandon those at the bottom of the economic hierarchy.[12]

I signed it (the Trump Dump must be, by token of his borderless menace, a transnational movement). I sign a handful of online petitions everyday, out of sheer helplessness and with a growing sense of frustration. This one commits me to 'resist', to 'challenge', to 'stand and fight'. 'What are we waiting for?', it asks. How about a more concrete plan than to 'push ourselves into new, and more precise and radical analytical frameworks'.

We have known since the years of Victoria's Kennett government that petitions, even the largest rallies in history, no longer have purchase beyond building consensus and expressing community—invaluable, foundational, but only in the activating stage. Even #MeToo, for all its unprecedented galvanising, does not chart an activist strategy to counter sexual violence beyond the outing of notable men by multiple accusers, thereby inducting rape into the Hollywood Hall of Fame. Unless the streets are taken, occupied and blockaded within a raft of solidarity measures, from general strikes to targeted sites of non-violent direct actions such as intercepting and obstructing boardrooms, we find ourselves now paddling in the activist toddler pool. Indeed, though it received scant media attention, in eighteen US cities women not only rallied but went on strike after Trump's election. It was a canny intervention, even just to remind Americans they have recourse to strike. Each one of the salutary commitments outlined by feminist scholars above needs to hyperlink to proven campaigns already on the ground, with instructions on how to donate, how to contribute, and how to *physically* stand with protesters at their sites of resistance. Bodies in the way. That is where we are at. The Women's March on Washington needed to hunker down in tents for as long as it takes. Rally planners should be organising encampments rather than permits.

Radical analytical frameworks have abounded since Rousseau's *Social Contract*, and they have been known to incite revolution, so the Trumping of these traditions warrants diligent analysis. But more urgently we need to

---

12 'Statement by Feminist Scholars on the Election of Donald Trump', https://fembot.adanewmedia.org/blog/2017/02/13/statement-feminist-scholars-election-donald-trump-president-united-states/, accessed 25 June 2018.

be collaborating on manifestos, treatises and stratagems designed to foment and sustain resistance. The dispersed frontlines need to be polynodal, rhizomes robustly linking the academy to the blockade, a committed praxis—each informing the other. Gender Studies, the last bastion of Women's Studies, has come under attack in the US and the ripples have spread here. If it can still find the time to eschew the identity-based politics of competitive suffering, while maintaining a bulwark for women whose wombs and 'pussies' are up for grabs, it might also turn its attention to how working-class white men gauge their economic exclusion through scroterial ballot tantrums—not that we would ever reduce manhood to body bits.

I will always aspire to carry some of Marilyn's responsive, incisive, unstinting, vibrant engagement into my own teaching and scholarship. I am not quite sure how she did it, but she managed to make these extremely complex and challenging questions a hoot while never losing sight of their gravity or consequence. When I arrived at La Trobe the place I had been assigned in this world was that of a 'Bit of Fluff'. I do not exaggerate when I say that it was Marilyn who gave me a place and purpose. Maria Montessori may be correct in saying, the greatest sign of success for a teacher is to be able to say, 'The children are now working as if I did not exist'. Marilyn's teaching and what she taught me were so profoundly enabling and stirring she has been and will be present in every word I set down. I can only hope they do her justice.

Chapter 7

'MY WORK DOES NOT WAIT FOR REVOLUTIONS'

Elizabeth Reid and the Possibilities of State Feminism in Iran[*]

Roland Burke

My first sustained academic engagement with Marilyn took place in Sydney in July 2008. Marilyn was discussant for a paper I had prepared on the transnational aspect of critiques of the Universal Declaration of Human Rights. She immediately spotted the empirical chasm that underlay my argument but subsequently generously assisted my successful application for an Australian Research Council Discovery grant on the intellectual history of arguments against universal human rights. The research for this chapter comes from a satellite project that emerged from the ARC research and also owes its shape to Marilyn. It explores the interaction of state feminism and international human rights in Iran during the last years of the Shah's regime through the figure of leading Australian feminist Elizabeth Reid, by then heading up a joint Iran–United Nations enterprise on women and development centred in Tehran.

---

[*] This research was supported by the Australian Research Council, Discovery Project DP110100952. The article draws on an interview conducted by and curated at the Oral History Collection of the Foundation for Iranian Studies, edited by Gholam Reza Afkhami and Seyyed Vali Reza Nasr. The author expresses his gratitude to the Foundation.

At the end of September 1978, Elizabeth Reid, former adviser to Prime Minister Gough Whitlam, prepared a short letter from Tehran on her recent work as director of the Asia Pacific Centre for Women and Development (AWPCD). Amidst the bloody conflagration of the pre-revolutionary protests, Reid observed, with impressive equanimity, 'there is no more Ministry for Women', and the central women's organisation offices were being physically attacked by the mob. Princess Ashraf Pahlavi, twin sister to the Shah and patron of the official Women's Organization of Iran (WOI), was facing a show trial 'at best'. The forecast was bleak—and prescient—'religious hypocrites' would, she wrote, 'trample down the women'.[1] Reid's principal partner, the first—and last—official Iranian Minister for Women, Mahnaz Afkhami, would be unable to return to her homeland following the execution of numerous Iranian feminists in the early years of the Islamic Republic, a fate Afkhami would have shared. Despite well-warranted pessimism, a composed Reid still furnished her correspondence with a cheery closing salutation—'do write again'.[2] By November 1978, she would await telegrams, hopeful after a handful of messages 'breached the strikes, tear gas and flames which ring the Centre at present'.[3] Even amidst the spectre, and often the spectacle, of mass violence, she returned to the enterprise. 'My work', she asserted, 'does not wait for revolutions'.[4]

This chapter assesses the uneasy equilibrium between the Shah's political project and the energetic international organisation for women's advancement that emerged from Iran across the 1960s, reaching its zenith in the final years of the regime. Through the figure of Reid, leading feminist, veteran of national and international political institutions, and adept navigator of real and bureaucratic politics, it identifies the tensions, both productive and pernicious, that shaped the Iranian project and its interactions with languages of Western second-wave feminism and universal human rights. The inherent disposition to progressive reform amongst many women's rights advocates, and the intrinsic limits of the political architecture that enabled the rapid

---

1   Reid, Correspondence, 9 September 1978, Papers of Elizabeth Reid, MS 9262, Series 1, Correspondence, Committee of International Women's Year, Folder 23–24 Correspondence, May 1977 – December 1978, National Library of Australia (NLA); also 19 August 1978 to a friend at the Department of Foreign Affairs, mapping the essence of the contest—between two powerful élites—with an acuity often missing from Western commentators.
2   Reid, Correspondence, 9 September 1978. See also Elizabeth Reid, 'Iran: An Inside View', *National Times*, 20 January 1979.
3   Reid, Correspondence, 2 November 1978.
4   Reid, Correspondence, 19 August 1978.

successes of Iranian women activists, never reached durable equilibrium. Nevertheless, the two-decade entente between state and women's advocacy furnished substantial agency to those who could seize its opportunities.[5]

For Afkhami, in an assessment composed long after her short period as minister, the Shah's was 'an authoritarian system that was committed to economic and social development'. While operating 'within that framework', the Shah's state 'encouraged gender equality and rights'.[6] The WOI's successes were unfeasible 'without the support of the modernizing state and its political organs, which were controlled by men'. Canalising the state where possible, WOI stressed 'the modernizing impulses of the political leadership in favour of women's projects' as its principal strategy, and it was functional despite 'the ruling elite's essentially unsympathetic attitude to women's rights'.[7]

Amidst the efflorescence of independent social movements and a rising generation of human rights NGOs that embraced the politics of purity as the singular index of virtue, the apparent compromise and state co-option of Iranian feminism was viewed with no little distaste. By the later 1970s, the liberal internationalist milieu had lost its tolerance for pragmatist accommodation. But liberal adamantine prescriptions of maximal purity offered little practical wisdom to those who had, however partially and problematically, leveraged state power for wider emancipatory goals. For almost two years, Reid, amongst the most effective advocates for equality within the Whitlam government, sought to assist Iranian women in their own reform effort.[8] Her tenure coincided with the terminal era of Iranian reform and the dissolution of a two-decade constellation of circumstances

---

5   Analogous examples of this constrained agency in a statist frame operated in Soviet bloc women's organisations, see for example, Kristen Ghodsee, 'Rethinking State Socialist Mass Women's Organizations: The Committee of the Bulgarian Women's Movement and the United Nations Decade for Women, 1975–1985', *Journal of Women's History* 24 (4) (Winter 2012): 49–73; and Francisca de Haan, 'Continuing Cold War Paradigms in Western Historiography of Transnational Women's Organisations: The Case of the Women's International Democratic Federation (WIDF)', *Women's History Review* 19 (4) (2010): 547–73.

6   Mahnaz Afkhami, '"Sunlight, Open Windows, and Fresh Air": The Struggle for Women's Rights in Iran', in *Shirin Neshat: Facing History*, eds Melissa Chiu and Melissa Ho (Washington, DC: Smithsonian Books, 2015), 45.

7   Mahnaz Afkhami, 'The Women's Organization of Iran', in *Women in Iran from 1800 to the Islamic Republic*, eds Lois Beck and Guity Nashat (Urbana: University of Illinois, 2004), 133.

8   On Reid's national work, see summary biographies, Papers of Elizabeth Reid, at http://www.nla.gov.au/ms/findaids/9262.html#bioghist1, accessed 1 March 2018.

that had allowed the state-monopoly feminist group, the WOI, to win substantial success.[9]

Literature on the connections between women's rights and human rights is both imposing and impressive, and so too the growing literature on internationalism and women's advocacy.[10] Consecrated in the NGO alliances and resurgent activism of the Second World Conference on Human Rights in Vienna in June 1993, reaffirmed at the World Conference at Beijing in 1995 and its successors, the mutuality of both constellations of rights discourse is sufficiently well established to be a commonplace in UN terminology, if not in the life of most states and many of their citizenries. The logic of the chiastic formulation of women's and human rights is unimpeachable, and both concepts are mortally compromised without such connection. However, it is a limited heuristic for those cases where the ability to secure both was radically decoupled. From Seneca Falls to the fate of the United States Federal Equal Rights Amendment, the political contradictions between the practice of human rights and women's rights have been apparent. Iran under the Shah is perhaps the signature case of paradoxes that are not easily navigated even in retrospect, much less by those historical actors embedded within them.

Iran's unusual position in the twentieth-century history of women's rights is precarious.[11] Its place in human rights history is predominantly represented as an example of the subversion and abuse of rights.[12] This study of Reid and the ill-starred Iranian project seeks to parse the tensions and paradoxes of women's rights activism in the context of authoritarian

---

9 On the Women's Organization of Iran, see, Afkhami, 'The Women's Organization of Iran', 107–35; Eliz Sanasarian, 'Women's Movement as a Social Movement in Iran' (PhD thesis, SUNY (Buffalo), 1980); Parvin Paydar, *Women and the Political Process in Twentieth-Century Iran* (Cambridge: Cambridge University Press, 1995); and Hamideh Sedghi, *Women and Politics in Iran* (Cambridge: Cambridge University Press, 2007), 61–192.

10 For example, see Rawwida Baksh and Wendy Harcourt, *The Oxford Handbook of Transnational Feminist Movements* (Oxford: Oxford University Press, 2015); Glenda Sluga, *Internationalism in the Age of Nationalism* (Philadelphia: University of Pennsylvania Press, 2013); Sluga, '"Add Women and Stir": Gender and the History of International Politics', *Humanities Australia* 5 (2014): 65–72; and the pioneering work by Leila J. Rupp, *Worlds of Women: The Making of an International Women's Movement* (Princeton: Princeton University Press, 1997); also Donna Sullivan, 'Women's Human Rights and the 1993 World Conference on Human Rights', *American Journal of International Law* 88 (1) (1994): 152–67; and Ursula O'Hare, 'Realizing Human Rights for Women', *Human Rights Quarterly* 21 (2) (May 1999): 364–402.

11 For example, see 'Iran: An Anthropologist Engaging the Human Rights Discourse and Practice', *Human Rights Quarterly* 34 (2) (May 2012): 507–45; and Sedghi.

12 Reza Afshari, *Human Rights in Iran: The Abuse of Cultural Relativism* (Philadelphia: University of Pennsylvania Press, 2001).

government. Under the Shah's regime, between 1953 and 1979, a grand modernisation and development enterprise allowed appreciable expansion of freedoms and welfare for women—yet a wider liberalisation was almost entirely foreclosed. A modest but insightful collection of analyses of the Iranian case led by Afkhami has revealed precisely how this *modus vivendi* between feminist and autocrat enabled a measure of freedom.[13] My research connects this domestically focused narrative to a larger international context and, in particular, the ways Western feminists engaged with a situation that was quite unlike that prevailing in their home countries.

Pankhurst and Persepolis? The Pavhlavi's project of feminist self-fashioning

Under Shah Mohammed Reza Pahlavi, women's advancement, in some form, was embraced in the new regime's program of international self-fashioning. Less than a decade after the Shah's 1953 seizure of power, an ascent facilitated by the United States and Great Britain, a professed commitment to equality, welfare, and education had become an ideological lodestar of the Shah's governance—his so-called 'White Revolution—in a paternalistic modernising state.[14] Across the early 1960s, the Pahlavi government advertised its claim to powerful feminist credentials—and provided some meaningful evidence of their substance. A raft of legislative reforms in women's suffrage, education and legal status was rapidly adopted. While often cast in contemporary reporting as beneficent dispensation from the monarch, the reform program revealed real agency from women.[15]

Internationally, women's advancement was studiously cultivated as perhaps the foremost moral claim in the Shah's diplomatic repertoire and was particularly evident during the successful visit of the United Nation's Commission on the Status of Women in March 1965. Fusing a narrative

---

13 Mahnaz Afkhami, 'A Future in the Past: The "Prerevolutionary" Women's Movement', in *Sisterhood Is Global: The International Women's Movement Anthology*, 2nd edition, ed. Robin Morgan (New York: CUNY Press, 1996), 330–38.

14 Mohammed Reza Pahlavi, *The White Revolution* (Tehran: Kayhan Press, 1961). Women's advancement was integral to the White Revolution's rhetoric, and one of its legislative pillars. See Manouchehr Ganji, *Defying the Iranian Revolution: From a Minister to the Shah to a Leader of Resistance* (Westport, Conn.: Praeger, 2002), xix–xx.

15 Evident, for instance, in suffrage reforms and national mobilisations for literacy promotion. See 'Suffragettes Clash With Clerics in Iran', *Christian Science Monitor*, 26 March 1963; and 'Iran Women Demand Part in Campaign for Literacy', *Globe and Mail*, 28 March 1963, 17.

of national progress, of which the improved social and legal position of women was the mainstay, with ceremonial visits by Commission members to key sites in the Pahlavi mythopoeia, it was something of a public relations triumph. Nor was it devoid of meaningful content; alongside generous opportunity for exalting the Shah's progress, the visit included a productive session of the Commission and an occasion to raise its profile worldwide.[16] For the UN, and for a human rights program that was struggling for both resources and prestige, the imposing shadow of Persepolis—and a comfortable level of funding by the Shah—enabled a markedly higher profile than a more prosaic annual session in New York or Geneva.[17] It was a mutually beneficial exchange in two currencies of prestige, although one that required some glossing over of deficiencies in the Shah's broader political orientation. The illiberal character of the Iranian system in a wider sense was readily set aside for the thematically focused deliberations of the CSW, which could find plausible promise and progress in its principal domain of interest. Iran further refined its reformist and progressive credentials in September 1965 with the successful hosting of the UNESCO Congress on the Eradication of Illiteracy, a project that coincided with its own domestic campaign for women's literacy.[18]

By the late 1960s and into the 1970s, the Iranian strategy for leveraging domestic reforms for diplomatic purposes was highly evolved. It produced self-congratulatory statements for the Western press.[19] In the figure of Princess Ashraf Pahlavi, cosmopolitan, adept with the media, and comfortable on the Upper East Side of New York, it possessed close to what the UN human rights system considered a celebrity icon.[20] While Western

---

16   See summary by US feminist and diplomat, Gladys Tillett, 'Expanding the Participation of Women in National Life', *Department of State Journal* LIII (1358) (5 July 1965): 40. For speeches, including Princess Ashraf Pahlavi, see Summary Records of the Commission on the Status of Women, 18th session, 1–2 March 1965, 412th to 414th meetings, E/CN.6/SR.412–414.

17   John Humphrey, A.J. Hobbins and Louisa Piatti, *On the Edge of Greatness: The Diaries of John Humphrey*, Vol. 4 (Montreal: McGill University Libraries, 1994), 69.

18   UNESCO, *Inaugural Speeches, Messages, Closing Speeches, World Congress of Ministers of Education on the Eradication of Illiteracy, Tehran 8–19 September 1965* (Paris, 1965). On participation of women in the literacy program, see Farian Sabahi, 'Gender and the Army of Knowledge in Pahlavi Iran, 1968–1979', in *Women, Religion and Culture in Iran*, eds Sarah Ansari and Vanessa Martin (Richmond: Curzon, 2002), 99–126.

19   Notably, Statement by the Imperial Organization for Social Services, 'Welfare, Medicare Network Extends across Iran,' and 'Dawning of a New Era for Iranian Women,' *The Times* (Supplement), 21 May 1974, vi–vii.

20   Linda Blandford, 'People: Shah's Twin Off to Work, Her Liberated Highness', *Observer* 16 March 1975, 34; and William Fulton, 'Rights Fighter Charming Iran

democracies had been represented by highly capable women delegates almost from the outset and had able representation across the decades from prominent figures such as socialite and social activist Marietta Tree and the strong-minded Baroness Dora Gaitskell, Ashraf remained distinctive. With a career that spanned negotiation with Stalin, in which she was not bested, when she was barely an adult, and the almost unparalleled authority that came as twin sister to an absolute monarch, Ashraf ensured that Iran was a major force in General Assembly politics. The Shah's nascent campaign to lead the Group of 77, the coalition that broadly corresponded to the Third World, also provided her with an agenda to press forward energetically.

Rather than despatching sortie emissaries outward to press Iran's case, the Shah sought to bring the world to his glittering reform and development project. In April 1968, having beaten European contenders for the honour, the Shah welcomed a vast and distinguished audience to the First World Conference on Human Rights. Delegates from the Prague Spring, NAACP leader Roy Wilkins, and future Nobel Laureate Rene Cassin assembled in the Shah's New Majlis building to consider the state of human rights. The building was the venue for a parliament that normally held decidedly consensual and timorous debates.[21] In May 1974, a more modest event, a speaking tour by some of the leading international feminists organised by the WOI, brought two of the luminaries of the second wave to Iran, with Betty Friedan and Germaine Greer sharing the stage—though scarcely anything else.[22]

Including a full itinerary of travel and audiences with both Iranian women and, for Friedan, a meeting with the Shah and Empress themselves, it was a major public event, widely reported in the Iranian press.[23]

Princess', *Chicago Tribune*, 1 December 1971, A6. For the generous self-reported assessment of her contribution, see Ashraf Pahlavi, *Faces in a Mirror* (Englewood Cliffs, NJ: Prentice Hall, 1980), ix, 153–8, 193, 173–5.

21   Roland Burke, 'From Individual Rights to National Development: The First UN International Conference on Human Rights, Tehran 1968', *Journal of World History* 19 (3) (September 2008): 275–96.

22   'Programme of Ms. [Helvi] Sipilä, Ms. Friedan, and Ms. Greer Visit to Iran, 21 May – 26 May'; items from *Tehran Journal* and *Kayhan*, May 1974, in Betty Friedan Papers, 1933–1985, 1974, MC 575, folder 976, Iran trip, 1974: press clippings, printed material, Schlesinger Library, Radcliffe Institute, Harvard University, Cambridge, MA. Cf Leslie Goodman-Malamuth, 'Kate Millet Takes on the Shah', *Daily Californian*, 24 May 1974.

23   Approximate transcript, interview with Mohammed Reza Pahlavi and Empress Farah, May 1974, in Friedan Papers, MC 575, folder 972, Iran trip 1974: notes; speech by Princess of Iran; Women's Org. of Iran.

Perceptions of the tour also began to reveal an incipient rupture in attitudes toward the WOI, however, and the beginnings of a sharper scepticism about the Shah's state feminist enterprise. Greer was scathing in her review and remained so in 1988.[24] Friedan was initially much more optimistic, though she did appear to retreat from this position in the later 1970s. Writing for *Ladies' Home Journal* in June 1975, Friedan concluded that, although the regime's deployments of women's rights were instrumentalist, the efforts of Iranian women activists to secure them, and to make them at least vaguely meaningful, were serious. Venturing dangerously close to orientalist cliché, she asked rhetorically whether there was any real emancipation in an 'ancient land ruled by an iron-handed autocrat'? Nevertheless, the Shah 'felt he could not lead his nation into the modern world, as he intends, without liberating Persian women', and appeared to be delivering on that vision.[25]

The tour itself was well timed, aligning with trends within the General Assembly and the wider purchase of women's liberation struggles worldwide. Women's rights rose in prominence, if not in resourcing, at the UN across 1974 and 1975, with International Women's Year (IWY) and its attendant Conference (WCIWY) held in Mexico City. Iran was amongst the most conspicuous sponsors of the WCIWY, a beneficence that would become a provocation for the reactionary clerical élite and a rallying point in the protests of the late 1970s.[26] As chair of the consultative committee that mapped out IWY, Ashraf served as symbolic leader of the initial conference planning.[27] Reid joined an impressive Australian delegation to the WCIWY.[28]

---

24 Germaine Greer, 'Women's Glib', *Vanity Fair* 51 (6) (June 1988): 32, 37–8; see also the intriguing work from Rachel Buchanan, 'The Iran Album (1974): Some Sleeve Notes', *Archivaria* 86 (Fall 2018), forthcoming.

25 Betty Friedan, 'Coming Out of the Veil,' *Ladies' Home Journal* XCII (6) (June 1975): 71, 98–104. Friedan's several re-drafts of this piece reflected considerable deliberation—see Friedan Papers, folder 970, Iran trip, 1974: First Draft, Coming Out of the Veil.

26 'Message of Her Imperial Majesty, Farah Pahlavi, Shahbanou of Iran, on the Occasion of the International Women's Year, 1975', *Iran Newsletter* (Information Section, Imperial Embassy of Iran, 10 January 1975); Sedghi, 172.

27 Frances Johnson, 'How Iran Princess Views Conference', *Xilonen*, 1 July 1975, 5; Ashraf Pahlavi, 'And Thus Passeth International Women's Year', *New York Times*, 5 January 1976, 29.

28 Jon Piccini, '"Women are the oldest colonial group in the world": Elizabeth Reid on Human Rights and Women's Rights in Mexico City, 1975', *Australian Women's History Network*, March 2017, at http://www.auswhn.org.au/blog/elizabeth-reid-mexico-city-1975/, accessed 11 March 2018.

Mexico City itself was not quite the celebration of international women's solidarity that its official press materials and communiques suggested.[29] Between crushing altitude, apocalyptic traffic congestion, and a security service justly maligned for its brutality after its massacre of protestors prior to the 1968 Olympics, the experience of Mexico was, for many—especially those countless legations stricken with food poisoning—onerous.[30] Vicious debates between Third World delegates, instructed to demand global wealth redistribution as a precondition for any progress on women's rights and aversive to any mention of 'sexism', rendered easy platitudes about sisterhood farcical.[31] Nevertheless, despite the official acrimony, and the chaos of the NGO forum (Tribune), simple proximity and interpersonal exchange did at least provide sinews for future global organising.[32]

Elizabeth Reid's principal engagement with Iran emerged from the frameworks that circulated in the WCIWY and its immediate aftermath. With the regime in Iran already approaching its moment of terminal crisis, her work there would commence just as the Shah's power and ambition crested and the regime's women's advancement project reached its zenith. Reid had been sought out by Ashraf shortly after her resignation from the Whitlam government, and was offered the directorship role for the new

---

29   For official perspective, see *Meeting in Mexico: The Story of the World Conference of the International Women's Year, Mexico City, 19 June – 2 July 1975* (United Nations, 1976); and *Report of the World Conference of the International Women's Year*, 1975, 19 June – 2 July, E/Conf.66/34, 1976. Cf the informal record of the Conference newspaper, *Xilonen*, published daily (copies held by author); Virginia Allan, Margaret Galey, and Mildred Persinger, 'World Conference of International Women's Year', in *Women, Politics, and the United Nations*, ed. Anne Winslow (Westport: Greenwood Press, 1995), 29–42.

30   Further elaborated by Roland Burke, 'Competing for the Last Utopia? The NIEO, Human Rights, and the World Conference for the International Women's Year, Mexico City, June 1975', *Humanity* 6 (1) (Spring 2015): 47–61.

31   See Betty Friedan, 'Scary Doings in Mexico City', in *It Changed My Life* (Cambridge, MA: Harvard University Press, 1998), 442; Germaine Greer, 'World Conference, United Nations International Women's Year', *Chatelaine* (September 1975), republished in Greer, *Madwoman's Underclothes*. Cf Elizabeth Reid, 'Mexico City: Was It a Fiasco? Between the Official Lines', *Ms.* (November 1975): 88–91, 100–01.

32   For recent scholarly treatment of the 1975 WCIWY, and its sequelae, see Jean Quataert, and Benita Roth, 'Guest Editorial Note: Human Rights, Global Conferences, and the Making of Postwar Transnational Feminisms', *Journal of Women's History (JWH)* 24 (4) (2012): 11–23; Jocelyn Olcott, 'Empires of Information: Media Strategies for the 1975 International Women's Year', *JWH* 24 (4) (2012): 24–48; Avonne S. Fraser, 'Making History Word by Word', *JWH* 24 (4) (2012): 193–200; Agnès Desmazières, 'Negotiating Religious and Women's Identities: Catholic Women at the UN World Conferences, 1975-1995', *JWH* 24 (4) (2012): 74–98; Charlotte Bunch, 'Opening Doors for Feminism: UN World Conferences on Women', *JWH* 24 (4) (2012): 213–221.

Asia Pacific Centre for Women and Development. It was no gentle entreaty: 'Wherever she is in the world, find her', Ashraf reportedly instructed her subordinates, and 'Bring her here'.[33] It appears Reid was merely on the other side of Central Park in New York, a rather anticlimactic conclusion to the invitation process—and she soon departed for Iran to assist the creation of the new international assistance centre, to be headquartered in Tehran.

While operating under UN auspices, as part of the Economic and Social Commission for Asia and the Pacific (ESCAP), the APCWD was enabled by Iranian resources and opened on 27 February 1977, timed to coincide with the annual celebration of women's suffrage in Iran. Its charter reflected the kind of emancipation that was feasibly advanced under the Shah, improved status for women being interlaced with a wider modernisation effort. In working to set up the centre and manage useful operations, Reid saw how partial and fragile the gains were and soon discovered how quickly a generation of reform could be dismembered. Ventures out of the centre encountered the desperate material poverty of urban Iranian women and an atmosphere that often shifted into menace without warning.[34] Security of the entire edifice of the Iranian state was steadily in decline throughout the Centre's life.[35] By September 1978, Reid was instructing staff to work at home, owing to the mounting risks of physical travel around the city.[36]

Given her recent experience under the Whitlam government seeking to maximise the possibilities for women that the state could afford, Reid was acutely aware of the power of institutionally sponsored reform but just as conscious of its limits.[37] Reflecting on her endeavours in 1988, Reid observed

---

33 Elizabeth Reid and Mahnaz Afkhami, Interview with Elizabeth Reid, Vol. I, 14 April 1988, Oakland, New Zealand, Foundation for Iranian Studies, Program of Oral History, available at http://fis-iran.org/en/content/reid-elizabeth, accessed 29 December 2017, transcript pagination, 15.

34 Travel journalist Christine Osborne provides some sense of the atmospherics, though Reid's papers suggest very substantial problems. See 'Fighting for Basic Women's Right's in Iran's Male-dominated Society, *Women's Weekly*, 31 August 1977, 51–2. Cf Reid, Correspondence, 16 October 1977.

35 The downward course is well charted by local headlines, preserved amongst Reid's papers: 'Six Deaths, 300 Arrests Reported in Riots', *Kayhan*, 6 August 1978, 1; 'Majlismen Shown Martial Law Text', *Kayhan*, 20 August 1978, 1; 'Iran Fighting for Survival', *Kayhan*, 3 September 1978, 1; 'Martial Law to be Lifted "soon as is possible"', *Kayhan*, 1 October 1978, 3.

36 Reid, Correspondence, 3 September 1978.

37 Michelle Arrow, 'Working Inside the System: Elizabeth Reid, the Whitlam Government, and the Women's Movement', *Australian Women's History Network*, 5 March 2017, available at www.auswhn.org.au/blog/elizabeth-reid/, accessed 2 March 2018.

that she 'had to begin by working out what governments can and can't do', and then, triaging 'what needs to be done first and how you go about getting it'.[38] It encapsulated an approach characterised by the practical deployment of political power, a strategy that did not always endear Reid to those in the Australian women's movement who judged such methods philosophically unsound. In Iran, Reid approached the challenge in a similar manner and observed the 'the same problem, same analysis' on impediments to women's freedom from lack of child care and maternal assistance.[39] Those had a number of effective policy solutions in Australia, drawing together state funds and community initiatives. However, in Iran, 'there was just no way that that was the solution. Absolutely no way'. While the problems were common, similar strategies for their resolution were not possible.[40]

The configurations of power in Iran were obviously not comparable, but, if anything, Iran provided a more favourable context for building within and upon an existing architecture operating under the patronage of the state. Non-governmental organisation, activism, and civil–society-led efforts certainly faced both reaction and lassitude in her home country, but they were at least viable. In Iran, the alternative path to the WOI was not the equivalent of Australia's Women's Electoral Lobby (WEL) but, rather, no organisation whatsoever. Despite the impossibility of conventional social organising and dissent under the Shah's gravely problematic regime, there were modest channels of action possible, and these had to be seized given the rising threat of violent anti-feminist clerical attack.

'Once more, the women are losing': the end of the centre, and the fate of women's rights in Iran

Human rights and the Shah's project, never convincingly compatible and always requiring drastic ellipses for coherence, had begun to diverge. For the generation of human rights NGOs that arrived in Iran in the early 1970s, the melange of authoritarianism, development rhetoric, and state-led welfarist initiatives did not constitute a human rights policy, nor was it a context in which such a policy could flourish. In philosophical terms, this judgment was sound—the Shah was no friend of the vision of inherent, indivisible and universalistic freedom enunciated in the UDHR. In his

---

38   Afkhami, Interview with Reid, 5.
39   Afkhami, Interview with Reid, 20.
40   Afkhami, Interview with Reid, 21.

personal disposition, as famously demonstrated to Italian journalist Oriana Fallaci, he was no feminist.[41] The Pahlavi government, as part of its 'White Revolution', adopted policies that overlapped with certain portions of the human rights canon, with some beneficial consequences for women, but with an ideological provenance that was remote from the animating ideas of human rights.[42]

This almost certainly placed a ceiling on the extent to which any WOI-type state feminism might deliver liberation, but the effects seemed real enough to Reid. Women's advancement as a national project did have a discernible impact, and, impressionistically, she found a kind of 'pride' amongst a cohort of Iranian women through the 'work of Women's Organization, the role of the Shahbanou [Empress] and Princess Ashraf in pushing women forward in different spheres, in different ways, the focus on education, literacy, girls in school'. 'I just felt', Reid recalled, in reference to the emergent class of university students, 'there was this tremendous taking off ... you could feel it'. Considered at the level of the structural defects and severe human rights abuses of the Iranian state, there was surely nothing to salvage—yet there were spaces of hope created within that system. In places like the new women's education facilities, 'you really could feel a feeling of change that these young girls felt that the world was suddenly one which they could enter, and enter actively'.[43]

The new 'human rights' that became the substance of this new NGO-led human rights movement held its own evasions and silences, and lacked much of an appreciation for the sort of women's activism possible in Iran at this time.[44] Properly voluble on violations of those rights involving the integrity of the person, where the grotesque record of the Shah's security services, SAVAK, was notorious, it was less visibly active on other realms of structural abuse. It spoke rather less on economic and social rights, or of the often-indispensable role of the state in securing welfare—arenas where

---

41   Oriana Fallaci, 'The *Shah* of Iran', *New Republic*, 1 December 1973, 16–21.
42   For the Shah's distaste for democratic and individual freedoms, see Frances Fitzgerald, 'Giving the Shah Everything He Wants', *Harpers*, November 1974, 55–84.
43   Afkhami, Interview with Reid, 25.
44   The 1970s 'breakthrough' of human rights activism has been the focus of much scholarship. For example, Jan Eckel, 'The Rebirth of Politics from the Spirit of Morality: Explaining the Human Rights Revolution of the 1970s', in *The Breakthrough: Human Rights in the 1970s*, eds Jan Eckel and Sam Moyn (Philadelphia: University of Pennsylvania Press, 2014), 226–59; Sam Moyn, *The Last Utopia: Human Rights in History* (Cambridge, MA: Belknap Press of Harvard University Press, 2010); Barbara Keys, *Reclaiming American Virtue: The Human Rights Revolution of the 1970s* (Cambridge, MA: Harvard University Press, 2014).

the Shah's record was somewhat less indefensible. Impatient with decades of dissembling by Western governments, which had a long record of support for ideologically friendly autocrats and frequently installed them, the new human rights activists of this period were ill equipped to devise strategies to manage an appalling state and a worse insurgency. In this struggle between two competing authoritarianisms, Reid assessed, 'once more, the women are losing'.[45] As she commented archly in a May 1978 letter, writing in the context of President Jimmy Carter's seeming ill-ease with further support for the Shah, 'pursuing a "human rights" policy here or elsewhere has proven to be a little more complex than idealists conceive'.[46] Maximalist purity was transmuted into an impracticable virtue.

In contrast, Reid's orientation was exemplified by her persistence and willingness to do what was possible, seeking to continue the purpose of the AWPCD even when its operation became ever more constrained and compromised. In correspondence to a UN colleague, Director of the Social Development and Human Settlements Program in Beirut, an exchange 'from one delicate situation to another', Reid inquired, in the midst of the usual administrative rhetoric, 'Did that bomb explode in a building in your area?'[47] Resigned to the reality that the UN Secretariat would invariably avoid moving the Centre, even as its members faced credible risk to their lives, Reid managed as best she could.[48] There was little interest in abstraction, for the main objects of concern were the micro-terrain around her and the AWPCD, the gardens and residences that might allow fleeing an attack (none were proximate), and the symbolic liabilities of a women's organisation (many).[49] Although she lamented the growing reversals already apparent in her interactions with Iranian women, her prime focus of despair was the fate of the project itself. 'In some ways', Reid confessed, 'it is the work that is killing my spirit, and the life, rather than the possibility of bodily harm'.[50]

Human rights activism in this mode provided fine material for condemnatory mobilisation and ill-defined counsel when and where engagement and gradualist incrementalism were delivering some gains. Western feminists confronting the problems of working in such environments were left to

---

45 Reid, Correspondence, 6 August 1978.
46 Reid, Correspondence, 28 May 1978, 2.
47 Reid, Correspondence, 12 September 1978.
48 Afkhami, Interview with Reid, 33.
49 Reid, Correspondence, 3 September 1977.
50 Reid, Correspondence, 3 September 1977.

intuit what was possible and whether it was worthwhile. For a time, Friedan was highly optimistic about the Shah, a position stated with embarrassing effusiveness shortly after the May 1974 tour. Even when looking back, she was mostly satisfied with the decision to visit.[51] Greer was inimical nearly from the outset. Kate Millet, actually amidst those progressive women within the Iranian protest movement, hoped for something else entirely.[52] Reid, like Millet, remained until the final collapse of the Shah's regime. Never did she adopt the kind of over-enthusiastic position of Friedan, who seemed almost wishful about the potential for an autocratic ally, nor the resolute dismissal of promise that characterised Greer's appraisal. Instead, she was relentlessly focused on the immediate—heartened, for instance, by the 'amazing strength in women' and that 'pride and a strength', and the fledgling protections that were dimly visible in the new Family Courts.[53]

For Reid, there remained real promise to build upon and a cohort of Iranian feminist leaders who were seriously engaged in the pursuit of an improved position for women. In a world where repressive regimes of all political orientations were prevalent, and seemingly ascendant, organising and pursuing the vision of equality entailed pragmatism and agility, not over-hopeful pieties. If operation in a full-scale liberal or social democratic state was an essential prerequisite for grasping what few opportunities existed, then the possibilities for any meaningful global cooperation were minimal. There was no straightforward mechanism for advancing women's welfare in an illiberal state, only pragmatic navigation, and working with what resources and opportunities were available. Even if these were never stellar, and diminished steadily as the Shah's power ebbed, there was useful work that seemed possible in the proximate, present and specific, however distasteful it seemed in the distant and the abstract.

---

51   'It was', Friedan wrote in her memoir, 'true that the Shah was repressive—the SAVAK, the secret police in Iran, were '"disappearing" people left and right'. Nevertheless, 'part of the Shah's attempt to modernize Iran was his embrace of women's rights'. Betty Friedan, *My Life So Far* (New York: Simon & Schuster, 2000), 284.

52   Kate Millet, *Going to Iran* (New York: Coward, McCann & Geoghan, 1982).

53   Afkhami, Interview with Reid, 23.

Chapter 8

TRANSFORMING AUSTRALIAN HISTORY

Humanitarianism and Transnationalism

Joy Damousi

I would have to go back a very long way to recall a time when Marilyn was not in my life. Our working relationship stretches over thirty years. I first met Marilyn in 1985 during the second year of my PhD thesis. My supervisor, Ken Inglis, had been animated about an exemplary thesis he had just examined and was very keen to bring Marilyn to the Australian National University so she could tell the history postgraduates how it was done. And that's what she did. I recall an inspiring talk, taking us through her research on the soldier settlement scheme, and how she had developed her argument, structured her thesis and pulled it all together. Ken had set us the highest and most exacting standards, and Marilyn had met them. It could be done! I also read the book from the thesis when *Limits of Hope* was published in 1987. Marilyn's name had become fixed in my mind.

When I returned to Melbourne in 1988 to take up a tutorship in the history department at Monash University the Melbourne Feminist History Group had just got off the ground, driven by Marilyn, along with Pat Grimshaw and Marian Quartly. For me, newly arrived back in Melbourne, the group provided not only a lively, intellectual and supportive network of feminist historians but also encouragement, confidence and a collective sense of purpose. Marilyn was at the core of the Feminist History Group's activities, discussing and debating ideas, new theories, and shifts in historical frameworks. There is one further quality that also stood out then and remains a hallmark of her scholarship. Marilyn's intellectual courage in pushing new arguments—even when hotly challenged or unfashionable—was, and continues to be, an inspiring quality and one that is comparatively rare among academics. When we published the edited collection *Gender and War* in 1995, the backlash from some of our colleagues was vociferous; fast forward fifteen years to *What's Wrong With Anzac*, and the toxic and misogynistic response from some members of the public was just as strident. Marilyn held the line, bolstered by the courage of her convictions. The highest quality research she would say will always win the day—whatever the response from critics—academic or otherwise. And so it has come to pass. The arguments in both books—*Gender and War* and *What's Wrong With Anzac*—set the parameters of a new debate, and much of what was argued has now become accepted, embedded and even mainstreamed within the historiography of Australia's experience of war. Marilyn has been an intellectual trail-blazer and unfailingly inspiring, energising and transformative in all that she has done.

* * *

Recently our work has dovetailed in approaching international history from an Australian perspective. Both *Drawing the Global Colour Line* and *Connected Worlds: History in Transnational Perspective* have provided valuable insights and frameworks that have informed my own recent work.[1] In *Drawing the Global Colour Line*, Lake and Reynolds exhorted historians to move beyond the national frame and consider 'whiteness' as a transnational phenomeon. Their aim was to:

> trace the transnational circulation of emotions and ideas, people and publications, racial knowledge and technologies that animated white men's countries and their strategies of exclusion, deportation and segregation, in particular, the deployment of those state-based instruments of surveillance, the census, the passport and the literacy test.[2]

---

1   Marilyn Lake and Henry Reynolds, *Drawing the Global Colour Line: White Men's Countries and the International Challenge of Racial Equality* (Cambridge: Cambridge University Press, 2008); Ann Curthoys and Marilyn Lake (eds), *Connected Worlds: History in Transnational Perspective* (Canberra: ANU E Press, 2005).
2   Lake and Reynolds, 4.

As the authors pointed out, there was an inherent paradox in this historical phenomenon; it was, at once, transnational in its 'inspiration and identifications but nationalist in its methods and its goals'.[3] Historians of immigration, noted Lake and Reynolds, also tend to tell 'self-contained national stories' that consider reactions to various immigrants such as the Chinese, Jews, Southern Europeans, Indians and others, viewing the international context as parallel, rather than 'dynamically inter-connected and thus mutually formative'.[4] The circulation of ideas, people, and commodities is also central to *Connected Worlds*, which locates the historical project very distinctively within a transnational framework. The definition of this project is thus

> shaped by processes and relationships that have transcended the borders of nation states. Transnational history seeks to understand ideas, things, people, and practices which have crossed national boundaries. It is generally in a complex relation with national history; it may seek to interrogate, situate, supersede, displace, or avoid it altogether. In their reaction against what they see as rigid and confining national histories, many of those enthusiastic about transnational history reach for metaphors of fluidity, as in talk of circulation and flows (of people, discourses, and commodities), alongside metaphors of connection and relationship.[5]

It is summarised in the follow terms:

> Transnational history has, then, many departure points and follows many lines of enquiry. Whatever form it takes, transnational history suggests that historical understanding often requires us to move beyond a national framework of analysis, to explore connections between peoples, societies and events usually thought of as distinct and separate.[6]

My recent work on post-war Greek migration and the memory of war in the diaspora, and on the history of child refugees and Australian internationalism, takes up many themes evident in Marilyn's work, which connects internationalism with transnationalism, gender and feminism. In both of

---

3   Lake and Reynolds, 4.
4   Lake and Reynolds, 5.
5   Ann Curthoys and Marilyn Lake, 'Introduction', in Curthoys and Lake (eds), 5–6.
6   Curthoys and Lake, 'Introduction', 6–7.

my projects, Australia is positioned internationally, as well as transnationally, taking the circulation of ideas, peoples, memories and emotions as articulated in *Connected Worlds* as central to framing these studies. Pivotal, too, in both cases are questions of gender and women, neither of which has been given much attention in migration histories or in the historiography of refugees.

One of the key objectives in my book *Memory and Migration* was to uncouple the history of international migration from nation-building and the history of the nation. In taking as its frame of reference the need expressed by transnational scholars such as Marilyn to move beyond the nation, I aimed to shift the discussion of international migration away from migrants and nation-building within the receiving nation, and to focus instead on the ways that the international fallout from war can affect relationships between cultures and generations when people cross national borders.

As a part of this study, I employed the concept of transnational families when analysing the impact of international migration and the flow of culture and politics. In doing so I moved the discussion beyond the development of the nation state within the framework of assimilation to explore new ethnic identities that emerge from a transnational understanding of family interactions and experiences. The experience of war formed a significant aspect of ethnic and personal identity and was a fundamental part of family history for those who migrated. In the post-war period, there was a profound gap in understanding of the complex experiences migrants brought with them to Australia, and this gap has never really been closed. Historians and sociologists alike have usefully considered the ideological aspects of the assimilation policy, but my contention here that assimilation was premised on the denial of an immigrant's past has not been widely studied. The failure of assimilationist policies to recognise the need to record, examine or even acknowledge individual and collective memories of crucial wartime experiences is a major omission I redressed in this project.[7]

Within this paradigm, migrant memories can be explored through an examination of the *place of the past* in the ways their recollections are constructed. Within the context of the international Greek diaspora, the transnational nexus has typically been explored through return migration by the second generation, and through the negotiation of ethnic identities within

---

7   Joy Damousi, *Memory and Migration in the Shadow of War: Australia's Greek Immigrants after World War II and the Greek Civil War* (Cambridge: Cambridge University Press, 2015), 50.

Greek families. What I have tried to conceptualise in linking international migration and transnationalism is an understanding of the memory of war within Greek communities as a transnational, not exclusively a national phenomenon.

In focusing on the particular experiences of mothers, who in wartime were forced to make decisions about the fate of their children, the specific dilemmas faced by women and the traumas they suffered become central to this account. These women's memories, together with those of their children when they migrated to Australia, tell a compelling international story of the enduring legacy of traumatic war experiences that transcends place and nation, but also illuminates the international history of the post-war period and Australia's vital role within it.

Shifting the focus to how children negotiated new ethnic identities, I position the story of the *paidomazoma*—where between 1946 and 1949 over 20,000 children were removed out of Northern Greece into Yugoslavia—within the transnational intersection of war, migration and national identity beyond national boundaries. I follow Lake and Curthoys in their understanding of transnationalism as

> the study of the ways in which past lives and events have been shaped by processes and relationships that have transcended the borders of nation states. Transnational history seeks to understand ideas, things, people, and practices which have crossed national boundaries.[8]

By tracing the movement of children of the *paidomazoma*, we can locate and identify transnational processes through the life experience of individuals. In doing so, we can further illuminate the enduring impact of this episode and how it has engendered fragmented identities within shifting cultural worlds.

A study of the *paidomazoma* also provides an opportunity to explore a unique relationship between war, children and motherhood, highlighting the traumatic dilemmas that the peculiar circumstances of the Greek Civil War created for mothers. It also adds a further dimension to histories of post-war migration to Australia more generally by demonstrating the enduring legacy of war experiences that transcend place and nation.[9]

The history of child refugees I am currently undertaking thus positions Australia internationally and, in so doing, sheds light on both Australia and

---

8   Curthoys and Lake, 'Introduction', 5.
9   Damousi, 175.

internationalism. A humanitarian movement engaged with child refugees developed in Australia from the early twentieth century. It took Australians overseas where in some instances they became a core part of key organisations shaping international events. Many, but not all, returned to Australia and attempted to reshape politics here. Invariably, it was women who engaged with international campaigns and carved out a sphere of activism within them. I will briefly mention four women whose efforts influenced international organisations and who attempted not only to foster the spirit of internationalism in Australia but also to encourage a fluid exchange between nations and across continents.

The first is Cecila John, an active member of a British organisation, the Save the Children Fund, from its inception in 1919. In Melbourne, John had campaigned against conscription in 1916 and 1917 and was active as a pacifist and feminist during the first decade of the twentieth century. John established an Australian branch of Save the Children after she and Vida Goldstein attended the Women's International Peace Congress in Zürich in 1919, where they were exposed to horrific images of starving children in Europe. John's efforts in the early years of the organisation were strenuous and challenging. She called a public meeting in Melbourne, formed a committee and, through the daily newspapers, opened subscriptions to fund the SCF and its international activities. John was an internationalist who travelled extensively during the 1920s in areas devastated by war and where children, in particular, had been displaced. In 1923, she visited Austria, Hungary and Greece. The international SCF recognised the Australian branch as John's work. She exemplified the role women could play in international affairs even though the world of diplomacy, foreign affairs and government was largely closed to them. John was a driving force nationally and internationally, and the SCF gave her a platform for assisting child refugees.

The second internationalist is University of Melbourne lecturer in ancient history Jessie Webb, whose advocacy for the women and child victims of the Armenian genocide through the League of Nations provides a further example of how activist women worked to position Australia in international affairs. Webb's advocacy in Australia is notable because she staunchly defended the League of Nations and its work during the 1930s, fostering a wider global perspective within her own country. In particular, she was a strong supporter of the humanitarian work of the League. A member of the League of Nations Union, which was formed in Melbourne in 1921 and included the international lawyer William Harrison Moore and later Attorney General John Latham, Webb spoke of the need for the League to undertake properly organised humanitarian work.[10] It was said she had 'an international mind'. In 1923, Jessie Webb became the substitute delegate for Australia to the League of Nations. The submissions for her nomination described her suitability for the task. The Victorian branch of the National Council of Women, for example, listed several qualities that were clear evidence of her capacity to lead.

> Miss Webb has frequently lectured in public, and she is noted for her wit and readiness of apprehension, as well as for her learning, and the fresh and vivid manner in which she presents the most difficult subjects. Those who know Miss Webb best value her highest, not only for her personal charm, but for her clear and judicial brain.[11]

Webb's experience of international travel also positioned her perfectly to undertake this role.

> Miss Webb made an extensive tour of Europe some years ago, and on her present trip she travelled through Africa from Cape to Cairo, and experienced ... the greatest value to one so keenly interested in modern problems. She is now in Greece, where she intends to stay for some time. Miss Webb speaks French fluently and also modern Greek and Italian to a certain extent.[12]

Webb's internationalism, above all, recommended her for the League of Nations position. 'We feel that she understands European problems from the point of view of those who are most affected by the solution of them—she has an international mind.'[13] The announcement of her appointment 'was received in academic circles with pleasure and gratification'.[14] She was even a favourite among conservatives, the *Farmers' Advocate* noting that her qualities and capacities as well as her 'personal side' are 'bound to make her a success'.[15]

---

10 *Argus*, 29 March 1924, p. 36.
11 Edith Barrett (Hon. Home Secretary, National Council of Women of Victoria) to The Hon. Prime Minister, 29 May 1923, AA Series A981/1, Item: League of Nations 4th Assembly 1, National Archives of Australia (NAA).
12 Barrett.
13 Barrett.
14 *Argus*, 12 July 1923, 9.
15 *Farmers' Advocate*, 19 July 1921, 10.

During her time as alternate delegate Webb wrote and campaigned in support of Karen Jeppe, a member of the Commission on the Deportation of Armenian Women and Children, who had begun a colony for women and children survivors of the Armenian genocide.[16] Seeking financial donations for this cause, Webb argued that Jeppe was

> doing some of the noblest work with which I have ever come in contact … It is a sad state of bondage that is endured by these Armenian women. Torn from homes and families, and I do wish a few hundreds of pounds could be promptly raised by the Australian States.[17]

Webb was effective in raising £200 in Melbourne[18] to enable Jeppe to continue her home for women.[19] It was humanitarian work of this kind under League auspices that convinced Webb of the value of international co-operation. It could have an effect, she argued, and there were many causes to which Australia could make a significant contribution. She argued in these terms in defence of the League and against claims that it was 'futile':

> The League was doing excellent work in its humanitarian sphere, but unfortunately such work indirectly weakened the League for the fulfilment of its main object, namely the maintenance of peace with justice. Moreover the League could not carry out the recommendations of its Humanitarian Committee without having some money at its disposal. Australia held an honoured place in the League, and the first thing to strike an Australian delegate upon returning home was the question whether Australia could not do more for the League than she was doing in the one department in respect of which all the nations were very ready to co-operate, namely its humanitarian work.

The Communist Esme Odgers provides a third example of international activism at work. In NSW, during the 1930s, she was a member of the Young Communist League and editor of the pro-Communist, *Women of Today*.[20] Odgers became immersed in the Spanish Civil War and volunteered to join the Republican cause. In 1937 she travelled to Britain

---

16   *News* (Adelaide), 19 July 1924, 1; *Age*, 1 March 1924, 17; Bruno Cabanes, *The Great War and the Origins of Humanitarianism, 1918–1924* (Cambridge: Cambridge University Press, 2014), 250.
17   *Register* (Adelaide), 4 March 1924, 6.
18   *Argus*, 6 August 1924, 6.
19   *Evening News*, 3 June 1924, 11.
20   *Australian Worker*, 4 September 1937, 14.

and then to Spain with her lover and fellow communist Sam Aarons, one of the leading Communist Party activists. On arrival in England, she visited the National Joint Committee for Spanish Relief and was so impressed with their efforts that she immediately offered assistance.[21] An appeal was launched in 1937 by John Langdon-Davies and Eric Muggeridge known as the 'Foster Parents' Plan for Children in Spain' (later called PLAN), the 'foster parents' being financial supporters who committed themselves to contribute one shilling per day, an amount calculated to be enough to sustain one child. The organisation solicited support specifically for children orphaned by the Spanish Civil War.[22]

In 1937, Odgers ran what became known as children's 'colonies'. In January 1939, after the fall of Barcelona, these children were evacuated to Biarritz in France where Odgers and Muggeridge established a colony. By then, 902 foster children were being hosted under PLAN's auspices, supported by international donations. In 1938, Australia's Spanish Colony was set up in Torrentbo, fifty miles from Barcelona. Odgers agitated for support for the Australian Spanish Colony through donations, and she publicised the cause by providing graphic and emotive descriptions of the needs of children in the Australian colony to the Australian press.[23] Fostering children became popular, leading to support well beyond left-wing and pacifist groups. While there was a precedent for international humanitarian assistance in the history of Australian efforts to support Armenian victims in the first decades of the twentieth century,[24] the Spanish Civil War marked a significant shift by focusing exclusively on children. This was in large part because of the child sponsorship and 'foster parent' program that Odgers successfully promoted from Spain, which uniquely drew together supporters in Australia from across the political spectrum to deal with the plight of children of Republicans. Odgers' story is significant as it highlights the central role women played as active humanitarians during the first decades of the twentieth century, particularly in the interests of children. Such war work, precisely because it was undertaken by women, has been undervalued.

---

21 *Woman Today*, August 1937, 4.

22 Henry D. Molumphy, *For Common Decency: The History of Foster Parents Plan, 1937–1983* (Rhode Island: Foster Parents Planning, 1984), 17–35.

23 'Children's Appeal', Spanish Relief Committee, P. Thorne Papers, P15/5/1–88: Circular Letters, Noel Butlin Archives, Menzies Library, Australian National University.

24 Vicken Babkenian 'An SOS from Beyond Gallipoli: Victoria and the Armenian Relief Movement', *Victorian Historical Journal* 81 (2) (November 2010): 250–76.

Odgers' work generated a further significant debate in Australia, her focus on sponsoring children through financial support igniting a crucial discussion about international adoption.[25] Significantly, efforts to support Spanish refugee children led in some quarters to a questioning of the racially defined and inflexible White Australia Policy. Although the international adoption of Spanish children did not eventuate, various organisations fiercely lobbied the government to allow them entry into Australia.

Rarely did humanitarian workers in Australia link the project of the plight of the international refugee to the situation of Indigenous Australians. One of the women who saw common issues of human rights applying to both groups was the activist Mary Bryce. Bryce, together with her husband Ernest Bryce, was a keen advocate for the Armenian Relief Fund in Australia. The Bryces travelled extensively throughout Armenia, Syria and other parts of the world to highlight the genocide inflicted on the Armenian population. Mary became a high-profile speaker on the lecture circuit in the 1920s. But, unlike most of their contemporaries, the Bryces extended their analysis of injustice, racial violence and humanitarianism to local conditions. They saw the two causes—Indigenous rights and the plight of refugees, especially after the Armenian genocide—as linked. In drawing these cases together, the Bryces were unique at this time, and indeed throughout much of the twentieth century.[26]

Newspaper reports described Ernest Bryce's arguments in support of the Armenians:

> He explained the three reasons why the Armenians should be helped; first, because they were the oldest Christians in the world, and were massacred in thousands because they would not give up their religion; secondly, they fought with the Allies and were then forgotten, and they were driven from their own country, and the promises made to secure them independence were not fulfilled; and lastly, they are a good type, sober, brave, industrious, and moral, and their plight since the war has been pitiful.[27]

The Bryces were just as outspoken on Aboriginal rights, 'saying that the lack of sympathy shown generally towards the natives was due to the fact

---

25   *Advertiser*, 13 July 1937, 22.
26   *Sun* (Sydney), 5 August 1928, 51.
27   *Australasian*, 25 February 1928, 15.

that people did not know enough about them'.[28] Ernest Bryce addressed the annual meeting of the Aborigines' Protection Society in London, stressing the claims of natives for better treatment, and commended proposals to establish an Aboriginal state and a royal commission to enquire into the treatment of Aborigines.[29] Bryce joined William Morley in protesting against Indigenous slavery, with Mary Bryce arguing for women protectors in Darwin and Alice Springs.[30] Ernest actively supported efforts for reform and led deputations in international forums such as the Anti-Slavery Society to highlight the plight of Australian Aborigines.[31] Both causes concerned the oppression of colonised peoples. Mary Bryce focused particularly on children and took a special interest in the Australasian orphanage established in 1923 in Beirut. She publicised the plight of Armenian children through the handicrafts they produced, and circulated letters from them. She and her husband also actively engaged in raising funds as this case below suggests:

> An enjoyable "at home" in the interests of the Lord Mayor's Armenian Relief Fund was held on October 15 at Netherby Park Avenue, Concord ... Ernest Bryce, who, with Mrs. Bryce is leaving on the 26th for an extensive tour (including the Near East, Central Africa and Russia) ... Mrs Bryce spoke of her experiences during her time of residence in Armenia telling of the interesting activities in the Australian orphanage, where hundreds of little children are being housed and cared for and equipped for life, in preparation for which they are learning many useful trades and proving themselves worthy in everyway of the kindness that has been shown them. A vote of thanks was proposed to Mrs. Bryce by the Rev. E.B. Reynolds, M.A., B.D., after which a beautiful exhibition of hand-made lace and needle-work by the Armenian girls was viewed, and afternoon tea partaken of. Some extracts of letters received by the Australian committee from the children in our orphanage are appended, which may be of interest to our readers. As it is quite impossible to cope with the utter destitution still existing further help is solicited. Donations

---

28 *Sydney Morning Herald* (*SMH*), 25 May 1934, 4.
29 *Observer* (Adelaide), 16 July 1927, 47.
30 *SMH*, 30 May 1933, 9; Andrew Markus, 'William Morley (1854–1939)', *Australian Dictionary of Biography*, http://adb.anu.edu.au/biography/morley-william-7656/text13391, published first in hardcopy 1986.
31 *SMH*, 10 December 1927, 8.

may be sent to the Lord Mayor or the Armenia Relief Fund, 333 George Street, Sydney.

Drawing on contemporary fundraising images of child refugees as passive, innocent victims, the Christian media published letters of gratitude from some of the orphans to evoke empathy and compassion for the purpose of raising funds as well as promoting Christian ideals:

> My Dear Australian Benefactors, —How grateful we are you are taking care of us these many years.
>
> We are grateful first to God, and then to the people of Australia. We are learning languages and trades here at the Orphanage; every week we are hanging our clothes, and we are taking baths for cleanness.
>
> We are loving you as our benefactors. You do not forget us. We are every time praying for your life and your prosperity. God bless you! I kiss your hands and honour you.
>
> All the orphans are glad that there is someone who takes care of them—thus all the boys go to school and trade joyfully and cheerfully.
>
> We thought that we had no fathers or mothers, but now we have many fathers and mothers. God did not forget the orphans, and gave us good, people like you to care for us.[32]

The Bryces' travels were widely documented through the Australian press, with dramatic and sensational images and photographs of Australian aid efforts for Armenia. Reports covered many of their activities as well as their efforts to discuss Armenians in a positive light as a people who had suffered much. In 1924, the Sydney *Sun* covered in detail a seventeen-month tour the Bryces had undertaken in the Near East. Ernest Bryce

> says that it is a big mistake to imagine that the Armenians are a nation not worth troubling about. Many of the tales that have been broadcasted stating that their moral and intellectual standard is about the lowest In Europe, are erroneous and purely subsidised Turkish propaganda. He says the Armanians are a fine race, well worth saving. In Geneva he met a number of Armenians who were of an extremely high Intellectual standard. One man spoke seven languages. Mr. Bryce declares that since the big persecution of the Armenians in

---

32   *Methodist*, 23 October 1926, 6.

1915, they have had an awful time, and the latest decision of the Turks not to allow any Christians in Turkey has accentuated their martyrdom.[33]

The Bryces' major objective was to engage Australians with their work in the Australiasian orphanage. The Sydney *Sun* reported on the excellent training and assistance it provided for for the Armenian children housed there.

> The orphans are getting exceptionally good training. When the boys become ten or eleven, they are taught carpentering, bootmaking, tailoring; in fact, they make a lot of the material of that description used in the orphanage. The main difficulty is to know how all these boys can be placed when they grow up as the Near East is so full of refugees.[34]

Mary Bryce's outspoken advocacy for Aboriginal communities was forthright and explicit, noting the need for investigations into the position of Indigenous communities. In 1934, she argued that the appalling treatment of Aboriginal Australians was the result of a paucity of knowledge about them.[35]

All four women discussed here—John, Webb, Odgers and Bryce—highlight the place of Australia in international history and provide evidence of the part played by international concerns in Australian history. This has been a central theme pioneered by Marilyn Lake in her work on transnationalism as well as in her studies of the histories of feminism. Women have been crucial in these stories—in fact they have played a central role, and have done so even more emphatically in refugee history. A sustained history of humanitarianism throughout the twentieth century, linking transnationalism, internationalism and gender still remains to be done. The transformative potential of research guided by such an approach will serve to expand methodologies that open up new and dynamic historical perspectives.

---

33   *Sun*, 22 January 1924, 6.
34   *Sun*, 22 January 1924, 6.
35   *SMH*, 25 May 1934, 4.

Chapter 9

IN SEARCH OF EMILY

Mark McKenna

The first time I met Marilyn Lake, around 2002, she attended a seminar I gave at the Australian National University on the need for a reconciled republic. The question she asked me that day has stayed with me. 'What's the source of your emotional involvement in this issue? Why does it matter to you?' I have tried to keep that question uppermost in my mind ever since. So, rather than write a reflective piece on Marilyn Lake's wide-ranging and influential body of scholarship, I decided to write on a matter of importance to me that also highlights at least some of the driving concerns of Marilyn's work.

* * *

It was barely two pages: the story of the murder and midnight burial of a new-born 'half-caste' child on the far south coast of New South Wales in April 1864, witnessed by a fourteen-year-old domestic servant, Emily Wintle (née Gillespie). Of all the histories that I explored while writing *Looking for Blackfellas' Point* (2002), it was this story that continued to unfold long after it was published, unsettling the memories of the families involved, revealing previously hidden details and shifting at the edges as more information came to light. What began as a subject of historical research became increasingly personal. In 2002, I knew little of Emily's background or what happened to her after she gave evidence in court. I had only the fine detail of this one long moment in her life. I had no idea of how the story had resonated in the lives of her descendants or how it had been passed on in family oral history down the years. The story that I originally saw as a metaphor for the 'repression of the memory of Indigenous Australia' became even larger and more mysterious after its telling.[1]

Emily's story

In May 1870, Emily Wintle sat in Sydney's Central Criminal Court, the primary witness in a quite extraordinary case. Barely 20 years of age, she was there to explain events that had taken place six years earlier, late on the evening of Sunday, 9 April 1864. For most of her childhood, Emily had lived at 'Bredbatoura', the Tarlinton family homestead near Cobargo, 40 kilometres north of Bega. Emily had been 'taken in' by the Tarlintons at 6 years of age, after her parents' relationship had descended into endless quarrelling and violence and her mother had decided she could no longer look after her. Like many young women at the time, Emily assisted her foster family with domestic chores in exchange for her board and lodging. On this particular evening in 1864, Mr and Mrs Tarlinton were away in Sydney and would not return for several weeks. Emily was at home alone, together with her sister, the Tarlintons' daughters Elizabeth and Margaret, and the Tarlintons' sons Alexander, James and Thomas. On Saturday evening, 8 April, Emily had gone to bed around 9 pm. In the room next to her, as always when their mother was away, slept the Tarlinton sisters, Margaret and Elizabeth. Shortly after going to bed, Emily was woken by the sound of the sisters moving to an upstairs bedroom. They were forced to pass through Emily's room to reach the stairs. Emily immediately got out of bed and stood at the foot of the stairs, listening to the sound of Elizabeth and Margaret moving about upstairs. They had never slept upstairs before. She waited for around ten minutes and went back to bed. The next day, Margaret Tarlinton was ill and remained in bed. Emily visited Margaret in her room, and tried in vain to comfort her as she 'roared out with pain'. Later that same evening, Sunday, 9 April, Emily and her sister again slept in the parlour where they had slept the night before. After a few hours, she was woken by the sound of a baby crying in the upstairs room. Again, Emily got out of bed and stood at the foot of the stairs. She listened to the baby's cries until she heard Margaret Tarlinton call out, 'You little wretch, you have caused me all this pain'. It was midnight. Emily went back to bed but was unable to sleep, kept awake by Margaret's constant moaning and the cries of the child. 'Just before daylight', Emily heard Elizabeth come downstairs. She lay awake, her eyes closed, her body perfectly

---

1   The italicised telling of Emily's Story is from my *Looking for Blackfellas' Point: An Australian History of Place* (Sydney: New South 2014, first published 2002), 79–83.

still, as Elizabeth stood for a moment over her bed. Certain that Emily was asleep, Elizabeth hurried back upstairs before coming down again, but on this occasion Emily could see she was carrying a 'black bundle'. When Elizabeth had passed through her room and out the front door of the house, Emily got out of bed and looked through the parlour window. She watched as Elizabeth took a spade hidden in the raspberry bushes, walked through the garden and down into the orchard. Alarmed, Emily hurried back to her room, put on her clothes, and walked round the back of the house. As she approached the water closet, she saw Elizabeth Tarlinton digging a hole near the fence. She waited quietly, being careful not to be heard. When Elizabeth had finished digging, Emily saw her place the 'black bundle' in the hole and lay a wooden board on top, before filling the hole with earth. After Elizabeth had gone back upstairs, Emily scratched away the earth with her bare hands. It was now daylight and she was worried that 'the blacks' would see her and think that it was her child. Removing the soil, she found the body of a female infant with black curly hair, its skin dark and yellow. Wrapped in a black silk petticoat, the child had a piece of white calico tied around its neck. Emily washed the child's head with water, wrapped it in the petticoat and reburied it. The next morning, she saw bloodstains on the floor of the upstairs room where Margaret had given birth to the child. They appeared to be smeared, as if someone had tried to wash them away with soap and water. She told the court how two 'darkies', Dick Bolloway and 'Briney', who had been hands on the station for three or four years, were often seen 'skylarking' with the Tarlinton sisters. Mrs Tarlinton had apparently once found Dick's trousers under Margaret's mattress. William Tarlinton, the man who 'discovered' the Bega Valley, had also one day found his daughter Margaret and the 'half-caste' Bolloway 'skylarking'. He threatened to break Margaret's legs if he saw them at it again ... Emily stayed on at the Tarlinton homestead until she was 18, and remained silent. One year later, she married, immediately telling her husband what she had seen five years earlier. In October 1869, her husband supplied the information to local police ...

In court, Emily's evidence was cast in doubt by the counsel for defence ... Remarkably, at the end of the case, the foreman of the jury stated that he did not wish to hear the judge sum up, and found the prisoner not guilty. She could leave the court, he said, 'without a stain on her character'. Reporting the judgment, the editor of the Bega Gazette *expressed relief, claiming Emily's allegations had been little more than a vindictive conspiracy against a 'most respectable resident in the district' ...*

The story unfolds further

I discovered 'Emily's Story' before the digital highways of Trove existed. Newspaper archives for this part of NSW—a narrow stretch of small coastal towns and national parks that extends from Narooma to the Victorian border—were scattered between the National Library, the State Library of NSW, local libraries, historical societies and private collections. No one collection was complete. Winding through reels of microfilm or leafing slowly through originals—their pages could tear easily when turned—there was little rhyme or reason to the search aside from diligently scouring obituaries, 'pioneer recollections', significant anniversaries and following leads found in other sources. Accidental discoveries, usually encountered while looking for something unrelated (and incidentally, the kind of 'find' that is far less likely on Trove's 'search engine') often threw up gems. Working my way through a box of documents collected by local historian W.A. Bayley in the 1920s, I came across the original newspaper report of the trial, which Bayley had cut out and filed. Until then, I had no knowledge of Emily's story. Now I was able to crosscheck the reports in other newspapers, most of which, as I discovered, were syndicated from the report of the trial published in the *Sydney Morning Herald*.[2] In the years after Trove came into being, I uncovered no new details regarding the trial itself, but, by searching the names of Emily, her family and the Tarlintons, I managed to unearth one or two surprising facts that, for me at least, added significantly to the story's allure. But for the moment, these can wait.

Looking at the same reports of the trial more than fifteen years later, it was striking how tiny facts that now leapt out—either for their telling detail or dramatic effect—had appeared less significant at first glance. I was reminded of the time when I lost nearly six weeks of notes while working on Manning Clark's biography in 2009. Returning to the same manuscript files that I had pored over only weeks beforehand, I recognised many of the excerpts I had originally selected. But what alarmed me was the number of things I now saw as extremely significant that I had previously dismissed or missed entirely. Other sections that I had painstakingly transcribed I now decided to leave behind. In the space of little more than a month, my critical judgment had shifted. It was yet

---

2   The Sydney trial at which Emily testified was reported in the *Sydney Morning Herald*, 14 and 16 May 1870, and the *Bega Gazette*, 14 and 24 April, and 26 May 1870.

another reminder of the subjectivity of my 'reading' and interpretation of historical sources. Returning after a fifteen-year hiatus to the evidence presented in the trial of Margaret and Elizabeth Tarlinton in 1870, my interpretation of the evidence remained largely intact, but there were several details I had overlooked that could have made my telling of the story stronger.

By describing Emily's uncovering of the baby's body in the early hours of the morning in the third person, I had deprived the story of the vividness of Emily's voice:

> When I uncovered the child I saw its eyes were only half-closed; the naval string was not tied. I took particular notice of it; I washed the head of the child to satisfy myself; I scratched the earth away with my hands; it was daylight when I did this; I did it in a hurry lest the blacks should see me, and think it was my child; I was then not quite 15 years of age; my sister was with me when I took the water to wash the child's head; it was 12 o'clock at night when I heard the child cry; I struck a match and looked at the clock.

The images are almost photographic in their recall: the umbilical cord untied, the bathing of the cold forehead, the soil on her bare hands, and a few hours earlier, the striking of the match a few minutes before midnight—'I looked at the clock in order to fix the hour at which the child was born'. Told in her own voice, I could feel the intensity of the memory she had carried with her for more than six years. If Emily was concocting the story, potentially as payback for a grievance with the Tarlintons over horses or cattle as the defence counsel implied, she was doing a remarkable job of invention, not only of the tiniest details but also of the emotion in her telling. Her recollections were etched forever in the memory of the teenage girl she then was. Although I had mentioned her recent conversion to the Catholic faith, it now seemed an even stronger catalyst for her to tell the truth when I listened again to her voice: 'I was confirmed about twelve months ago. I partook of the Holy Eucharist sometime before I was confirmed; I took it on the occasion I went to confess, after I had told the prisoner I was going to confession'. She had taken communion to give her strength to confess the knowledge she believed was 'sinful' to withhold. Other details that I had originally passed over now seemed more important. One person who testified, a neighbour of the Tarlinton's, distinctly recalled that about two months before Good Friday 1864, while visiting the family homestead Brebatoura, he had 'remarked to Mrs. Tarlinton that her daughter, Margaret, was getting very fat'. He had also 'frequently seen blacks about Mr. Tarlinton's station'.[3]

Given that Emily's testimony against the Tarlinton sisters was presented six years after the events took place, it was easy for the judge and jury to find the evidence she presented inconclusive. While police had found the bones of a child not far from where she thought them to have been buried, the conclusions of the three medical experts invited to examine them differed substantially. One thought the bones belonged to a child, nine to twelve months of age, another found it difficult to tell. All remarked on the fact that bones were missing and that the calico and black silk petticoat Emily referred to could not be found. Combined with the fact that the police concluded that the stains on the floorboards were caused not by blood but by 'the decay of the board' itself, this cast enough legal doubt for Emily's case to be dismissed.[4] Yet I remain convinced that Emily was telling the truth, especially in light of the family oral history that has come my way since 2002. This is when the story took on yet another inflection, six years after my book was published, when I received a letter from Val Ruttley, in New Zealand.

> Dear Mark,
>
> My name is Val Ruttley and I am the Great Great granddaughter of the Emily Wintle that you mention in your book, *Looking for Blackfellas [Point]*. About 25 years ago, an aboriginal woman told me this story. Her description was very short, but told of how Emily found the baby and was not believed when she went to court. I found your information on the net tonight and am amazed. Thank you for telling the story again, and in such a way, that gave Emily credibility at last. Emily's daughter Jane, who lived until she was 111, is my great-grandmother.[5]

Val told me that she later discovered that Emily Wintle's story had been passed down in other parts of her family for over a century, and, despite the fact that the court dismissed Emily's evidence, declaring the reputation of the squatter's daughters to be unblemished, Emily, she insisted, was telling the truth. The fact that Val claimed to have been told initially by an

---

3   All further details quoted can be found in the report of the *Sydney Morning Herald*, syndicated widely, including for example, the *Monaro Mercury and Cooma and Bombala Advertiser*, 28 May 1870, 6.
4   *Monaro Mercury and Cooma and Bombala Advertiser*, 28 May 1870, 6.
5   Val Ruttley to Mark McKenna, undated, late 2008.

unnamed 'Aboriginal woman' was the first evidence I had of the story's existence in Aboriginal oral history. I would discover more about this side of the story later. But I found it remarkable that the story I had written, based on a newspaper report of the trial in Sydney, now returned to me, verified independently by Emily's descendants' telling of their family history. But something even more remarkable was about to unfold. In December 2009, I met the author and academic Felicity Collins in Sydney and again, six months later, at a conference in Dublin. She had grown up in the Bega Valley, and she explained to me how 'Emily's Story' had affected her more than any other part of my book. It continued to stay with her, but not until several years later did Felicity realise the full import of the story. Her sister, Janene, who had long maintained an interest in their family's history, phoned her unexpectedly: 'Are you sitting down?' she asked Felicity. 'Elizabeth Tarlinton is our great-grandmother.' Felicity was shocked. She could not 'recognise' Elizabeth Tarlinton as part of her family tree. She immediately retrieved the newspaper report of the trial and tried to digest what her sister had told her. Still, she did not experience the moment of 'recognition' until suddenly, some days later, returning from a family barbecue, it finally arrived.

> I realise that Elizabeth Tarlin[g]ton is as close to me, in time, as my mother is to her great-granddaughter, Ivy Elisabeth. A cry of recognition escapes. It's her! It's them! It's me! Great-grandmother Elizabeth's hands held my grandmother. They could have held me. When Elizabeth and Margaret gave birth, when they held their newborns, when they nursed their grandchildren, did a memory flash up of that first birth? If that birth, that baby's first cries, slipped their minds, did their hands remember the black silk petticoat wrapped around her body, the strip of white calico tied around her neck?[6]

Collins's personal experience in coming to terms with her family history, evocatively described in her article 'Tarnished Memory: "Emily's Story" and My Family Tree', points to the difficulties many local communities across the nation continue to face in coming to terms with frontier history. Shortly after *Looking for Blackfellas' Point* was published, a review appeared on Amazon, signed (somewhat incriminatingly) by 'Tarlo', denouncing the book as a 'load of rubbish'. I have often wondered which member of the

---

6   Felicity Collins, 'Tarnished Memory: "Emily's Story" and My Family Tree', *Memory Studies* 6 (3) (2013): 273–85 (276).

Tarlinton family posted the review, long since taken down. More recently, I received an extremely supportive email from another Tarlinton descendant, Christine Goonrey, Elizabeth Tarlinton's great grand-daughter and Felicity Collins's first cousin. While she rightly pointed to one medical expert's conclusion in the trial that the bones found on the property belonged to a child of approximately twelve months age, she also described how 'the accusation of infanticide and the trial was known among our family but never discussed'. 'It was particularly interesting', she wrote, 'to see the phrase "without a stain on her character" in reference to Margaret Gilbert in your book, as it was the phrase my father had repeated to us nearly 100 years later'.[7] The disturbance of Collins's family history caused by the airing of the historical record is something that could potentially happen to many other families in Australia. Yet the Tarlintons' case remains unusual. Settler oral history that tells of frontier violence and mistreatment of Aboriginal people is often generic in form. It speaks of Aborigines being 'mowed down' or 'wiped out', but rarely identifies the names of those responsible. Within the many stories that acknowledge wrongdoing on the part of settlers, there is often an inbuilt protection mechanism, a convenient element of forgetting. Responsibility is rarely claimed. Everyone and no one achieved dispossession.

I had now had contact with the descendants of both families involved in the story and I thought that there was little more to reveal. But there was more to come. In August 2015, I received an email from David Wintle, who had read the book and found my contact details online.

> Dear Mark,
>
> I have an enquiry to make and hope you can assist me please. You have a chapter in the book regarding Emily Wintle. Emily Wintle is my great grandmother and the story of the murdered child had been unspoken family knowledge. The Tarlinton family and mine were close friends but also often adversaries, resulting in Emily's husband Walter Wintle being put in gaol fifteen years later based on Tarlinton's evidence. I noticed a reference you made to true trial transcript and would like to ask if you know how and where I may access the full transcript of the trial or if you have these scanned and available? Any details would be greatly appreciated, thank you kindly. David[8]

---

7   Christine Goonrey to Mark McKenna, 9 May 2017.
8   David Wintle to Mark McKenna, 10 August 2015.

In the months that followed, I met with David several times to discuss Emily's story. As a filmmaker, he was also interested in the story for its dramatic potential. In the course of our conversations, David passed on much of the family history. As I listened, I came to appreciate the deep significance of the story for successive generations of Emily's family. The 'stain' on her reputation that she had felt when her evidence was rejected in court was felt down the years by her descendants, all of whom were convinced, as David told me, that Emily was telling the truth about the events she witnessed in 1864. David was able to tell me much more about Emily's life, both before and after the trial. Her parents, Michael Gillespie and Elizabeth Winter, were of Irish, Scottish and English ancestry. Married in 1844 in Sydney, they had a 'rancorous relationship', separating several times and dividing their children between them. At one point, in the early 1860s, Emily's mother accused Michael Gillespie of abandoning his family and took him to court, after which he was forced to pay a tiny maintenance, which was not enough to sustain the family. Shortly afterwards, Emily was 'bound over' to the Tarlinton family, when her father, Michael, who worked on their property at Cobargo, north of Bega, convinced them to take Emily and her younger sister Elizabeth as domestic help. They would stay on this relatively isolated property for the next thirteen years, doing both household and heavy farm work in exchange for 'good schooling'. Emily's mother, Elizabeth, was traumatised by the separation from her children. Whenever she attempted to visit her daughters at the Tarlinton homestead she was turned away. In 1860 she was driven to attempt suicide, after which she was fined ten pounds in a Bega Court and incarcerated in the 'mental hospital' at Darlinghurst Gaol in Sydney for twelve months. It is not hard to imagine the strain this would have caused for Emily and her sister, as David explained.[9]

> Emily and her sisters and brothers were witnesses to these dramatic events and their mother's suffering, yet they also remained loyal to their father Michael ... [Barely] fifteen in 1864 Emily was a witness to the murder of a "half caste" aboriginal baby at the Tarlintons household. Emily remained adamant of what she saw as a young girl but under threat by the Tarlintons remained silent about what she witnessed being committed by the two Tarlinton daughters. Under duress she stayed silent, still working at the house ... During the

---

9   Emily's mother's suicide attempt and all other details, in David Wintle to Mark McKenna, late 2015.

1860s Walter Wintle appeared in Bega. He was ten years older than Emily, and worked in the area, including the Tarlinton property, stripping and shipping wattle bark up and down the south coast ... Michael Gillespie worked with Walter Wintle and they had a good relationship, yet he disapproved of the marriage between Emily and Walter, a non-Catholic. Walter and Emily eloped in November 1868, and were married in Sydney by a dubious minister named Rev. Bailey who ran a "marriage shop" at his "Free Church of England". Within a few years all the marriages were annulled by the NSW Courts. Emily and Walter returned in December 1868 to Bermagui to build a farmhouse at Camel Rock on land previously in Emily's name, now in the name of [her husband] Walter Wintle.[10]

It was at this time that Emily made the decision to confess her knowledge of what she had witnessed in 1864. She told her new husband, Walter Wintle, who 'convinced Emily to go to the police and reveal she had heard the murder and witnessed the burial of a baby on the Tarlinton property after Margaret Tarlinton gave birth to a half caste child, whilst the Tarlinton parents were away in Sydney'. The pressure on Emily was so great, that in 1869, shortly after she was married, she followed her mother's example and tried to commit suicide. This was one way to relieve herself of the burden of what she had seen. As the local press reported, 'Emily Wintle pleaded guilty to attempting to commit suicide' and was 'bound over to keep the peace towards herself for twelve months, in sureties for 40 pounds'. That Emily recovered her strength of will to go to court only months later and testify to what she had seen is further evidence that she was unlikely to have put herself through such an ordeal if she was not telling the truth.[11]

From what David told me, relations between the Tarlintons and her husband, Walter, continued to be strained long after the trial in Sydney. He was twice accused of 'cattle theft' by the Tarlintons, charged and fined on the first occasion and imprisoned on the second, in 1885. By this time, with her husband in gaol, Emily was bringing up nine children on her own at two farmhouses near Wallaga Lake. Three days after Walter died in 1887, Emily gave birth to their tenth child, a daughter, Elizabeth. Her eldest was then only sixteen. In the late nineteenth and early twentieth centuries, the

---

10   David Wintle to Mark McKenna, late 2015.
11   David Wintle to Mark McKenna, late 2015; Emily's suicide attempt is reported in *Bega Gazette*, 8 July 1882, 2, and *Bega Standard*, 8 July 1882, 2.

south coast of NSW was connected by steamers that plied up and down the coast carrying local produce and passengers to Sydney. The wharves were often hard to reach and subject to storm damage. To support her family, Emily ferried goods across the water from Wallaga Lake to Narooma so they could be shipped to Sydney; she also carted stores and back-loaded railway sleepers with a team of eight horses, and was sometimes seen 'leaving the farm house, riding side saddle, searching for stray calves, and having to camp overnight and return the next day'. At a time when local newspapers regularly lauded the exploits of the 'pioneers', her ability to overcome adversity equalled anything that her male counterparts in the area had achieved. In 1893, another baby arrived in Emily's household, named Amanda. Emily was then forty-five. Although she explained that she had 'taken in' the baby after a 'friend' had been unable to care for her, David believes that Emily was in fact bringing up the child of her eldest daughter, Jane. Ten years later, another of her daughters, Florence, aged twenty-one in 1903, died from blood poisoning after a backyard abortion in Cleveland Street, Sydney, went horribly wrong. 'Flo' was buried in an unmarked grave in Sydney's Waverly Cemetery. Many women of her own generation, and that of her mother's and daughters', whether because of racial and religious boundaries or gendered social mores, were forced to live out their pregnancies in secret, carry the burden of social opprobrium, and risk their lives in the process.

What David had shown me was that Emily's life was not defined by her witnessing the midnight burial of a 'half-caste' child, nor by the trial six years later. Seen in its entirety, despite the fact that we know little more than its bare outline, 'Emily's story' transcended the events that took place that night in 1864. In retrospect, her experience seemed to touch almost every aspect of Australia's history from the late nineteenth to the early twentieth centuries. Fortunately, two of her sons—Alf, who fought in the Boer War and later with his brother Jack in the Dardanelles and on the Western Front—returned home from the Great War, as did Jack. Although Emily continued to run the farm near Wallaga Lake until she was in her seventies, she moved to Bondi with her daughter Dolly and son-in-law Edwin Ward in 1932 and died there in 1937 at the age of eighty-nine.[12]

---

12 All details, David Wintle to Mark McKenna, late 2015; a sketch of Emily's life can also be found in Ron Gaha and Judith Hearn, *Bermagui: A Century of Features & Families* (R.W. Gaha, 1994), 207–08; details of steamers and the south coast, see Lenore Coltheart, *Between Wind & Water: A History of the Ports and Coastal Waterways of New South Wales* (Sydney: Hale & Iremonger, 1997), 51–3, 99–104.

Three years before her death she wrote a brief memoir. There was no mention of the events that surrounded the trial in 1870, only of what had happened when her parents' marriage collapsed, and how she was sent to live at the Tarlintons.

> It was a very cruel time for me as I was bound over to Mrs. W.D. Tarlington. I was there for 13 years under a very severe training where I often sat broken-hearted thinking of my dear mother. I lived there until I was 18 years of age and during that time I assisted scrubbing and clearing timber on the property besides numerous other jobs like chipping corn ... gardening and housework. When my mother used to call to see me I was not allowed to see her and Mother was abused and sent off the property. Mrs. Tarlinton always carried a whip on her belt ... I have been beaten black and blue for nothing and sometimes deservedly.[13]

After one misdemeanour, she described being confronted by Mr Tarlinton: 'he came with the whip'. Emily's experience as a young woman 'bound over' to the Tarlintons was probably not unusual at the time. She would have been told countless times how lucky she was to be 'taken in', regardless of how she was treated.[14] Violence and corporal punishment were a standard means of 'superiors' exerting their control over their underlings. But her memoir of hardship and struggle was given yet another dimension when David sent me what he believes to be the only known photograph of Emily in existence.

Taken by the renowned photographer, William Corkhill, *circa* 1895, it shows part of the congregation gathered for the funeral of 'Queen Narelle' (wife of 'King Merriman') at what was then known as 'the Aboriginal reserve' at Wallaga Lake, the first to be established in NSW by the Aborigines Protection Board in 1891. Emily is on the right of the photograph below, wearing a peak cap. Her farm at 'Camel Rock' was adjacent to the reserve. That she was present for the funeral, and one of only a small number of non-Aboriginal people there, is evidence of her standing within the community. Surrounded by young Aboriginal women and their children, she is one of the few not to look directly at the camera, yet she appears entirely at home. Knowing that Emily's story was passed on by an

---

13 Memoir of Emily Wintle, Photocopy sent to Mark McKenna by Shirley Laird, February 2009.
14 Memoir of Emily Wintle.

The funeral of Queen Narelle, Wallaga Lake, c. 1900
Photographer: William Henry Corkhill (1846–1936)
(Courtesy National Library of Australia)

Aboriginal woman to Val Ruttley some time in the 1980s, it is now clear that she would have been held in high esteem by the local Aboriginal community, who would undoubtedly have respected her for risking everything to take the story of infanticide to court. Living so close to the Wallaga Lake mission over a period of more than forty years as she brought up her family, Emily forged a bond with her Aboriginal neighbours that was likely far deeper than we will ever know. Not only had she testified bravely to what she had witnessed in 1864, but she had also shared her daily existence with Aboriginal people for her entire adult life. The one long moment of Emily's life that I had originally seen as a metaphor for the deep racial divide in colonial Australia, I can now see as something larger and far more hopeful: a life lived across racial boundaries—a life that in so many surprising ways encapsulates Australia's 'shared' histories.

Casting my line in Trove still threw up unexpected and strangely fertile facts. Emily's father, Michael Gillespie, died at the age of eighty-one in 1890. His obituary described how he had lived and worked on the far south coast of New South Wales for fifty years. He claimed to have worked for the Scottish entrepreneur, Ben Boyd, on one of his early dairy farms in the

1840s. As one of the first 'landowners' in the area, he had fathered the 'first white child' born at Cobargo—a crown for which there was always stiff competition among settlers—Emily's brother, John. But there was one detail that I found particularly startling, not only for its resonance, but because is was odd that it should be included in the obituary at all: 'In his youth, [Michael Gillespie] was accidentally speared by a young blackfellow. A small portion of the wood remained embedded under [his] eye which caused a wound, the mark of which he carried to the grave'.[15]

Thinking of the photograph of Emily surrounded by the Aboriginal community at Wallaga Lake in 1895, and her ordeal in a Sydney courtroom in 1870 as she testified to having witnessed the burial of a 'half-caste' child, it was tempting to see the tiny piece of spearhead embedded in her father's eye as a prophecy of a kind, a physical and spiritual omen that would be played out in the course of his daughter's life.

---

15   Michael Gillespie's obituary, 'Death of an Old Resident', can be found in *Cobargo Watch*, 22 March 1890.

Chapter 10

'FOR THE RECORD'

A History of the
New South Wales
Aborigines Protection Board

John Maynard and Victoria Haskins

This joint chapter focuses upon our current research project into a key aspect of the Indigenous history of New South Wales, 'The NSW Aborigines Protection/Welfare Board 1883–1969: A History'. In explaining the project's formation and its background, and offering an overview of some of the issues and insights that have arisen thus far, we highlight our own personal interest in the project and our family connections to early Aboriginal political activism in New South Wales. We speak as two individuals in separate voices—John Maynard as a Worimi Aboriginal historian and Victoria Haskins as a white Australian historian—with a shared opening reflection on the impact of Marilyn Lake and her scholarship upon us both.

The outstanding quality of Marilyn Lake's work constitutes a benchmark against which many judge their work. Marilyn's many and diverse publications have resonated very strongly with our own work and directions: especially her work on transnational racialism, on feminist political activism and, most recently, her reappraisal, with Henry Reynolds and others, of Australia's much-commemorated military past. As a committed collaborative scholar as well as a formidable intellect in her own right, Marilyn is an inspiration and role model to us. We reserve special mention for *Creating a Nation*, which Marilyn wrote with three other giants of Australian history,

Pat Grimshaw, Ann McGrath and Marian Quartly.[1] The book's release in 1994 coincided with John's entry into university as a mature-age student at the age of forty, and became his bible during his Diploma and BA courses. It provided a refreshing perspective, radically different from the dominant trumpet-blowing and drum-banging accounts of Australia's past in privileging the place of women and Indigenous people, previously overlooked in the history of this continent. When Victoria began teaching Australian history in 2000, *Creating a Nation* was the text she set for the incoming tides of wide-eyed first-year students, and it remains on her reading lists today (with a note to students to seek it out in secondhand bookshops). But it was the article Marilyn wrote on the feminist campaigns for women protectors of Aboriginal women in Central Australia, 'Frontier Feminism and the Marauding White Man',[2] that had the most profound impact on Victoria, who first encountered it during her PhD research on Aboriginal rights activism in Sydney in the 1930s. In recent years, Marilyn's transformative impact at an international as well as national level in opening up the field of 'transnational' history has more directly affected our research; her work underpins our exploration of transnational and comparative Indigenous histories, particularly in terms of the parallel experiences of Australian and US Indigenous peoples.

It is not just Marilyn's work but her warmth that has drawn both of us to her. Victoria received a gracious note from Marilyn after the publication of her review of *Faith: Faith Bandler, Gentle Activist*, and ever since then Marilyn has extended a generous hand of help and advice, including introducing Victoria to her networks at Harvard. John recalls bumping into Marilyn unexpectedly at the Library of Congress in Washington DC several years ago. 'We were both on research projects of a transnational nature and headed around the back for a nice Thai lunch. Marilyn is someone who it is enjoyable to just sit down with over a coffee and lunch.' They have continued to correspond with each other, Marilyn passing on some discoveries she thought might be of interest to John, and he, likewise, conveying information that she needed. Marilyn has been a great source of inspiration and support to us both.

---

1 Patricia Grimshaw, Marilyn Lake, Ann McGrath and Marian Quartly, *Creating a Nation* (Melbourne: McPhee Gribble/Penguin, 1994).

2 Marilyn Lake, 'Frontier Feminism and the Marauding White Man', *Journal of Australian Studies* 49 (1996): 12–20.

John Maynard

Our study of the history of the New South Wales Aborigines Protection Board came about through the course of many other projects. Certainly many Aboriginal people and communities have long felt the need for a major study of the Board and its polices from an Indigenous perspective. Of critical importance and understanding is the fact that many of our people who lived under the Board and Act are getting old; we thus need to record their memories to complement the archival study before they and their recollections are gone forever. The team undertaking the study includes five Indigenous members—Ray Kelly, Lawrence Bamblett, Lorena Barker, Jaky Troy and myself. This Indigenous representation was a very significant aspect of the grant application and was complemented by our token whitefella, Victoria. The team has already undertaken research in the NSW State Library, NSW State Archives, and AIATSIS, and conducted Aboriginal community consultations and interviews in La Perouse, Redfern, Newcastle, and Western NSW, and on the South and North coasts. We have had a great response at community level and through Indigenous media.

* * *

From 1883 to 1969, over a period of close on a hundred years, the Aborigines Protection/Welfare Board administered Aboriginal lives and affairs in New South Wales. The impact of the Board's policies of segregation, assimilation, child removal and wage withholding would endure for decades, and the damaging results of those government directives are still visible today. As *The Encyclopedia of Aboriginal Australia* entry on the Board concludes, its principal legacy has been deep bitterness among NSW Aboriginal people over their treatment by those entrusted with their welfare.[3] For many Aboriginal people of those times, the Board was a board not of protection, but of persecution.

The NSW Aborigines Protection Board was established at a time when Social Darwinist theories were hegemonic, and the colony of NSW looked towards a future as part of a federated white Australia. The existence of Aboriginal communities, many of which were then calling for 'land in own

---

3   I. Howie-Willis, 'Aborigines Welfare Board (NSW)', in *The Encyclopaedia of Aboriginal Australia*, Vol. I., ed. D. Horton (Canberra: Aboriginal Studies Press, 1994), 28–9 (29).

country',[4] was a challenge to authorities, and the Protection Board, initially charged with overseeing the gazettal of Aboriginal reserves, quickly took control of them from the missionaries and installed their own managers. Originally headed by a 'Protector', the Board was controlled from 1884 until 1938 by the commissioner of the NSW Police Force. Legal powers first enacted in 1909 were followed by further and more extensive powers in 1915. The following year saw the Board reconstituted, its members being heads of various government departments. Throughout the 1920s and 1930s, as it became increasingly draconian, the Board confronted significant Aboriginal resistance to its policies, with calls for its reform or abolition growing stronger until an enquiry was held in 1937. That enquiry was shelved, then followed by a secret public service review, which ultimately resulted in the passage of the Welfare Board legislation in 1940. Under the head of a new superintendent of Aboriginal welfare, appointed in 1939, the NSW Aborigines Welfare Board continued to exercise unparalleled controls over Aboriginal lives for another thirty years until it was abolished in 1969.

This project holds major importance for Aboriginal communities in NSW. In comparison with other periods and places relating to Aboriginal history, the history of Aboriginal people in NSW during the period of Board control is remarkably under-researched. The period during which state control was most extreme, from the Board's legislated empowerment in 1909 to its reincarnation as the Welfare Board in 1939, when Aboriginal people were largely confined and restrained on the reserves and subject to extremely discriminatory restrictions on their basic civil rights, can be considered a period of erasure and silencing that is perpetuated in historiographical inattention. Yet this was a critical time for Aboriginal communities and individuals as they moved from self-sufficiency through what Heather Goodall has termed 'the second dispossession' into subordination and dependency.[5] Under the regime of the Welfare Board, Aboriginal people were subjected to forced assimilationist programs that perpetuated earlier systems of control and oppression albeit with a new name and with enhanced legitimacy amongst the wider non-Aboriginal population. The result today is a generalised sense of grievance about the past amongst NSW Aboriginal communities but no clear sense of what actually happened and why, and how local experiences of

---

4   Heather Goodall, 'Land in Our Own Country: The Aboriginal Land Rights Movement in South-eastern Australia, 1860 to 1914', *Aboriginal History* 14 (1) (1990): 1–24.

5   Heather Goodall, *Invasion to Embassy: Land in Aboriginal Politics in New South Wales, 1770–1972* (Sydney: Allen & Unwin, 1996), 149.

dispossession, child removal, and employment and educational restrictions fit into larger patterns across the state.

The project holds immense personal importance for both Victoria and me because it contains elements of our long-term studies of her great-grandmother, Joan Kingsley-Strack, and my grandfather, Fred Maynard, in their battles with the NSW Aborigines Protection Board. Recently uncovered material from a 1927 newspaper interview with Fred Maynard indicates the level of intimidation and police harassment he and members of the Australian Aboriginal Progressive Association (AAPA) were subjected to during the 1920s with their challenge to Board control. His defiance is evident:

> he had been warned on many occasions that the doors of Long Bay [Gaol] were opening for him. He would cheerfully go to gaol for the remainder of his life, he declared, if, by so doing, he could make the people of Australia realise the truly frightful administration of the Aborigines Act.[6]

No police records relating to the AAPA during the 1920s remain, despite evidence that suggests large-scale police intimidation and surveillance of Aboriginal activists at the time. Adding further substantiation to the role of the police in the public disappearance of the AAPA, the Australian Communist Party's 1931 *Rights for Aborigines: Draft Program for the Struggle Against Slavery* is revealing:

> the conditions of the Aborigines have not been considered by workers in the revolutionary movement, and the rank and file organisation set up by the [A]borigines was allowed to be broken up by the A.P.B., the missionaries, and the police.[7]

One of the mysteries I hope to solve as part of this study is why none of the prominent 1920s Aboriginal activists in the AAPA were visible in the late 1930s. I am not just speaking here of my grandfather but asking why were John Donovan, Jim Doyle, Sid Ridgeway, Tom Lacey and Dick Johnson missing during the 1930s? We do know that my grandfather and John Donovan's names were put forward during the 1937 government inquiry as important knowledge holders of the conditions of Aboriginal people in NSW, but neither of them was given any opportunity to speak or provide input.

---

6   *Newcastle Sun*, 7 December 1927, 8.
7   *Workers' Weekly*, 24 September 1931, 2.

One of the major features of this project is the importance placed on Aboriginal community testimony about the years under Board control. Thus far we have collected over sixty interviews across the state and have received wonderful support and encouragement at the community level. The power and sadness embedded in these very intimate stories offer personal insights rarely presented alongside the official record. The horrific impact on Aboriginal children and their families was widely evident in these accounts:

> We were taken away at that time in 1942 and that was when dad was overseas in the Middle East [father Jack Patten was fighting in the Australian Army during World War II]. We were coming home from school I was about six and a half ... and the Welfare just came down and grabbed us, took us down to the police station and put us on the train ... When the steam engine was pulling out of the station there I remember looking back and seen mum there crying on the station. This Mrs Healey was one of the officers there I remember. I said "what's wrong with my mum she is crying". Because I had never seen my mum cry always been laughing and joking. Don't worry Pauline she said "she's only got some soot in her eyes". Little did I realise reflecting back that would be the last time I would see her until I turned eighteen.[8]

Auntie Barbara and Uncle Tom Clarke looking back over seventy years of life at Purfleet in Taree spoke of the housing, life and rations. 'Flour, little bit of sugar not much ... There was a lot of sickness going around. It was really hard'. The houses were 'hell, they were just old tin huts. They were really hard times. We were battling'.[9] Colin Jarrett of Nambucca Heads recalled the trauma Aboriginal people faced being moved off their land and forced onto the mission like refugees:

> Twelve houses, just twelve houses made of pine, built pine, cheap pine and mostly fibro and Masonite. Twelve houses in a row ... It was like we lived in third world conditions. When they built the mission they just ah, well built it right out of town away from the white inhabitants. They pushed us way back out of sight ... there was no like tar

---

8   Interview with Pauline Nola Gordon, née Patten, Grafton, 11 August 2017: interviewers John Maynard and Ray Kelly.
9   Interview with Barbara and Tom Clarke, Taree, 24 April 2017: interviewers John Maynard and Ray Kelly.

road or anything like that. Built the houses up there out of sight and out of mind. Moved everybody off where they had lived and moved them all up there.[10]

One of the major surprises of the project was being contacted by David Donaldson, grandson of Robert Donaldson, the sinister and notorious NSW Aborigines Protection Board Inspector. Donaldson had rightly earned the reputation as 'the kids' collector' across New South Wales and was a feared and despised figure among Aboriginal people. Whilst David Donaldson, a man in his mid-eighties, did not carry a lot of memories of his grandfather he did provide an understanding that his was not a close family but one of detachment, a factor that may offer some insight into Donaldson's character.

> There was very little contact I don't recall them [parents] talking about him ... It's that sort of family where we don't actually construct relationships somehow. I only remember one thing about him. It would have been about 1937. I was sent a couple of times perhaps twice to Sydney from Broken Hill. Which in itself was quite an adventure for a kid of that time [age 6 or 7]. The old people had a house on the cliff at Coogee. They had a block there. Today there are three houses ... I only have one memory of him and I don't know whether I spent a week there or a fortnight or what. But all I can see is a fellow sitting in a chair and I think he had a beard and all I saw from my perspective was he was reading the *Bulletin* and it was pink on the outside the *Bulletin* newspaper and I see him sitting there and saying nothing to me. He was a stern person ...[11]

Of even greater importance was the remembering that after Robert Donaldson's death there was a massive dumping of material over the cliff close to the house and into the sea at Coogee. David Donaldson recalled George Donaldson, the brother of Robert, and the event:

> I physically remember George, it seemed to me it was day after day that it just went on and on. He would be taking stuff out of the house walk across the front lawn and tip it into the sea and it seemed to go

---

10   Interview with Colin Jarrett, Nambucca Heads, 8 May 2017: interviewers John Maynard and Ray Kelly.
11   Interview with David Donaldson, Adelaide, 28 September 2015: interviewer John Maynard.

on a long time. It may have been household contents. But I can't help thinking ... Surely in his career, he was an independent member of parliament. Well from quite a time in parliament, which I think could have been close to twenty years and then from 1915 odd, he had this job was it called an Inspector. To I don't know when he retired but it must have been early 1930s. So, he had fifteen years of that work. It's very hard to think that there wouldn't have been papers.[12]

David himself felt the whole business of child removal in which his grandfather was heavily involved smacked of a major cover up:

> I often think of the removal of children, that so many people must have been involved in physically moving the children, or handling the correspondence, the official orders and that sort of thing as clerks, and then people must have been in the towns pretty much conniving at it like ministers of religion and doctors and people who could have spoken up and said what's going on here. What are you doing to this family. And I notice in all the inquiries that there have been in the last thirty years odd there doesn't seem to be any coming forward of people who say I saw this happen or my dad used to tell me about how he agonised about something or other.[13]

The Protection Board had employed in 1910 a home finder for Aboriginal girls in Sydney, a Miss Alice Lowe. The interview with David Donaldson revealed an unexpected link between Robert Donaldson and Lowe.

> Also in Randwick was a lady who I'd thought she was a relative but I don't think so. She was just a family friend. Her name was Alice Lowe and her father must have been a politician or something I suspect. They [the Donaldsons] were in Coogee and she was in Randwick pretty much on the same tramline. And she simply told me that she'd been a form of secretary ... She was a spinster. She said to me when I was about thirteen your grandfather was such a fine man and she was very firm and sincere in that view of him. I always remember the sincerity, she almost admonished me and insisted in this notion that grandfather was a wonderful man.[14]

---

12   Donaldson Interview.
13   Donaldson Interview.
14   Donaldson Interview.

This revelation hints at a much closer relationship between two of the major players at the NSW Aborigines Protection Board. Both Donaldson and Lowe were held in complete contempt by Aboriginal people. My grandfather, in correspondence to the Commonwealth government in 1928, could not constrain his low opinion of Donaldson: 'As for the name of a certain inspector employed by the Aborigines Protection Board, it is passed from one end of New South Wales with all the invectives of a broken hearted despairing people'.[15]

Although the interview material has been rich and rewarding there have been some disappointments connected with the archival research. Mostly these issues arise from the limited access to restricted materials granted and overseen by the Department of Aboriginal Affairs. Before this project commenced, I had heard a number of young Indigenous researchers express frustration and despair that access to records was very, very difficult. Some even complained that, in their own communities, gatekeepers were putting up barriers. It is clear that access to Indigenous records is much easier and more efficient in other states than in NSW. We had hoped when putting our case forward that things might have become easier but that has not been the case. I have hoped for some time that the NSW DAA would conduct a review that incorporated an education program within our own communities on the importance of gaining access to these records. Victoria will elaborate on the archives in greater detail in the second section of this chapter.

Victoria Haskins

I will begin by revisiting the research I did about my great-grandmother's activism before moving on to reflect on the current project John and I are doing on the history of the Board and the problem of its archive.

My father's grandmother Joan Kingsley-Strack—or Ming as she was called by the family—had died years before I discovered her remarkable story hidden in boxes in my aunt's garage. While I was working on my PhD, I spent time with my grandmother, Ming's eldest daughter, picking her mind for memories of Ming that would help me understand her and provide clues for my research. One of those memories was particularly evocative. My Gran described to me how, every evening after dinner, Ming would with great ceremony light her one solitary cigarette, then sit and smoke, delicately tipping her ash into a bronze Indian ashtray she had

---

15   F. Maynard and E. McKenzie-Hatton to Commonwealth government, CRS A659/1, 1943/1/1451, National Archives of Australia.

inherited from *her* grandmother. 'She thought she was very feminist', Gran told me with a mischievous smile—she herself a hardened smoker since the age of fifteen, and inclined to mock both her late mother and feminists. But of course, as it turned out, Ming really *was* a feminist and a pretty committed one at that. As an active member of several key women's political organisations, including the United Associations of Women (UAW) and most importantly the Feminist Club in Sydney, Ming acted as a link between the Aboriginal citizenship rights movement and the women's movement in Sydney, and she and Aboriginal activist Pearl Gibbs spoke together before various women's club meetings throughout the late 1930s. Ming had even contemplated a foray into 'frontier feminism' herself in 1940 when she almost headed off to Central Australia with Olive Pink.[16]

But it was Ming's determination to expose the NSW Aborigines Protection Board—this 'great poisonous fungus' as she described it—and the abuse of the rights of Aboriginal women in removing the girls to be placed in domestic service in Sydney, far from their own communities, that really drove Ming, and was the focus of my work on her. I drew upon Marilyn's concept of 'frontier feminism' to consider the suburban homes where the Aboriginal girls were sent to work as a frontier or contact zone in themselves, where white and Indigenous women encountered each other. On these suburban frontiers, too, we see the rise of 'frontier feminism'—white women's activism for Aboriginal rights.[17] The campaigns of Aboriginal rights activists in the 1930s against the removal of Aboriginal girls and their treatment in domestic service was not widely known when I first uncovered Ming's papers in the early 1990s. Even today the history of these campaigns is not particularly well known. There is the iconic photo of the 1938 Day of Mourning protest, which represents the citizenship rights movement more broadly, but public awareness of the history of the struggle of women (Indigenous and non-Indigenous) for Aboriginal rights is minimal. This is a sobering thought as estimates of the numbers of Indigenous children taken from their mothers

---

16 See Victoria Haskins, 'My One Bright Spot: A Personal Insight into White and Aboriginal Women's Relationships under the NSW Aborigines Protection Board Apprenticeship Policy, 1920–1942' (PhD thesis, University of Sydney, 1998); Victoria Haskins, *One Bright Spot* (Basingstoke: Palgrave, 2005).

17 See Haskins *One Bright Spot*; also Victoria Haskins, 'On the Doorstep: Aboriginal Domestic Service as a "Contact Zone"', *Australian Feminist Studies* 16 (34) (2001): 13–25, 'Domestic Service and Frontier Feminism: The Call for a Woman Visitor to "Half-Caste" Girls and Women in Domestic Service, Adelaide, 1925–1928', *Domestic Frontiers: The Home and Colonization*, special issue of *Frontiers: A Journal of Women Studies* 28 (1–2) (2007): 124–64.

and extended families continue to rise without signs of abating, and the issue of domestic violence against Aboriginal women has again become a front-page story, with little acknowledgment of the long colonial and state history of violence against Aboriginal women. Marilyn raised the question, in her 2013 review of the historiography of women in Australia, of whether the 'cutting-edge' transnational work done by feminist historians today can realise the political ambitions of the nationally focused women historians in the 1970s to reach the national audience (both policy-makers and the public) in order to achieve positive changes and advances at the national level. This remains a key issue, and unfolding events confirm the importance of maintaining our sense of political purpose.[18]

In this regard, the project on the history of the NSW Aborigines Protection and Welfare Board is very close to my heart. It feels like a return to my great-grandmother's story, a continuation of her quest to bring about a wider public awareness of the policies and practices that were operating in her time. When I was doing my doctoral research the discovery of Ming's hoard of papers was a truly remarkable find. But I also needed to get into the official records of the Protection Board, and that is where I struck a problem. It was an experience that I have written about before and will not repeat here.[19] Returning to the records now, however, for this much larger project on the entire history of both the Protection Board and its successor, the Welfare Board, I cannot help but feel a sense of déjà vu.

As Ann McGrath noted in her 2004 submission to the Senate Committee on Stolen Wages, there is scant scholarly work on the Indigenous history of NSW 'due primarily to difficulties of access. Consequently, we have inadequate knowledge of the NSW history of government administration, including Aboriginal Protection, Welfare and Trust regimes'.[20] More than a

---

18   Marilyn Lake, 'Women's and Gender History in Australia: A Transformative Practice', *Journal of Women's History* 25 (4) (2013): 190–211 (202–03).

19   Victoria Haskins, 'Family Histories, Personal Narratives and Race Relations History in Australia', *Canberra Historical Society Journal*, no. 45 (2000): 25–9, and 'Skeletons in Our Closet: Family History, Personal Narratives and Race Relations History in Australia', *The Olive Pink Society Bulletin* 10 (2) (1998): 15–22.

20   Ann McGrath, *Reconciling the Historical Accounts: Trust Funds Reparations & New South Wales Aborigines* (Canberra: ANU, 2004), submission no. 9 to Senate Standing Committee on Legal and Constitutional Affairs.; see also Senate Standing Committee on Legal and Constitutional Affairs, *Unfinished Business: Indigenous Stolen Wages* (Canberra: Commonwealth of Australia, 2006) 3, 88, available at https://www.aph.gov.au/parliamentary_business/committees/senate/legal_and_constitutional_affairs/completed_inquiries/2004-07/stolen_wages/report/index, accessed 6 December 2017.

decade after the publication of the Senate Committee's report, we still have not seen any improvement of access.

John and I applied for access to these records on behalf of our research team, but we have been refused permission to look at significant sections of the material, including the Ward Registers 1916–28, the correspondence files of the Welfare Board 1949–69, and the recently discovered Chief Secretary Records Letters Received relating to Aboriginal matters 1938–49. The grounds on which our access has been declined are 'the personal and sensitive nature' of the records. We are permitted to look at some records, including the Minute Books 1911–1969. We believe that the decision of Aboriginal Affairs NSW in refusing permission stems from their fears of criticism and litigation from Aboriginal community members, rather than because they are hiding anything in particular, and we believe that they are genuine in their concern. There are, certainly, real and powerful issues to be confronted when researchers work with records containing information on Indigenous peoples and communities that has been obtained under coercion and through deceit.[21] However, ongoing secrecy not only makes it impossible to write a full history of the Board but also reinforces the impression that the authorities' actions and policies are being hidden from public exposure.

As a result of the denial of access to the full records, the final part of our study will include a detailed chapter on the history of the records themselves. Ironically, John and I both had greater access to the records back in the 1990s than we do today, so we can draw upon that experience. We have also communicated with a number of scholars who have previously studied the Board records across decades and have generously agreed to share their own personal memories and anecdotes and some of the history of the records' access issues. One of the earliest researchers into the Board records was Heather Goodall, who used them while working on her PhD thesis on Aboriginal land rights activism in NSW back in 1975.[22] This was six years after the dissolution of the Welfare Board, with another six

---

21   I have recently explored key works on this subject and the issues pertaining to my own work: see Victoria Haskins, 'Decolonizing the Archives: A Transnational Perspective', in *Sources and Methods in Histories of Colonialism: Approaching the Imperial Archive*, eds Kirsty Reid and Fiona Paisley (London: Routledge, 2017), 45–66.

22   Heather Goodall, 'A History of Aboriginal Communities in New South Wales, 1909–1939' (PhD thesis, University of Sydney, 1982); also Heather Goodall, *Invasion to Embassy: Land in Aboriginal Politics in New South Wales, 1770–1972* (Sydney: Allen & Unwin, 1996).

years to go before the new Ministry of Aboriginal Affairs would be established. Heather did her research at a transitional time when the Aborigines Welfare Directorate (which was instituted when the old Board was abolished) was about to be absorbed as a branch of the Department of Youth and Community. To our knowledge there was just the one earlier researcher, Susan Johnston, who completed a Master's thesis on early Protection Board policy in 1970 (and thus had presumably undertaken her research while the Welfare Board was still operational); Johnston looked at the Board's minute books, which were then held in the Mitchell Library and open for access, but she stopped at 1909—the period prior to the Board gaining its considerable legislative powers over Aboriginal people.[23]

Heather Goodall has told us the story of her discovery of the Ward Registers. These are two dusty old volumes listing the names and details of around 800 girls and boys taken from their families between 1912 and 1928. The registers were left in a cupboard at the old Directorate, Heather explained. She was told they were on restricted access for 100 years.[24] However, a man involved with the Aboriginal Legal Service, Peter Thompson, organised their deposit in the NSW State Archives under the regular thirty-year access rule, enabling Heather to carry out her doctoral research.[25]

After the Ministry of Aboriginal Affairs was created in 1981, the records of the Board became less accessible. From that point researchers could only look at records with the permission of the individuals mentioned therein, or of their surviving family members. This was the situation in 1993 when I first applied for access. What had happened? Historian Peter Read—whose research into the Board records constitutes the bedrock for the history of the Stolen Generations—speculates that he may be the only historian to have looked at *all* the records relating to Aboriginal people held in the archives (not including the recently discovered Chief Secretary's correspondence files, which turned up around 2008 and are now totally restricted). That was in 1980, Peter recollects, by which time the Board records were at the NSW State Archives repository at Circular Quay. Peter tells us he sought permission to look at them from the Minister for Youth and

---

23 Susan Lindsay Johnston, 'The New South Wales Government Policy towards Aborigines, 1880 to 1909' (MA thesis, University of Sydney, 1970).

24 Heather Goodall, personal communication (email) to Victoria Haskins, 8 August 2016.

25 Peter J. Tyler, *State Records New South Wales 1788 to 2011* (Sydney: Desert Pea Press, 2011), 57. Until 1966 the access period was 50 years; it was reduced to 35 years in 1966, and 30 years in 1972, bringing it into line with international/British practice.

Community Services, the late and 'unlamented' Rex Jackson,[26] who said 'go for it'. There were 22,000 separate files and 'nobody knew what was in them'. Peter 'opened every box and read every one of its contents'. He found 650 personal files of state wards and produced his pamphlet on the Stolen Generations in 1981[27] (the year that a new Ministry of Aboriginal Affairs, the forerunner of the DAA, was established); he was then given $5000 to produce another on the records of Cootamundra and Kinchela Homes. 'Needless to say, that wasn't published', says Peter. His doctoral thesis on the Wiradjuri and the state, completed in 1984, was based on these records and oral histories.[28] It was around this time that the records were closed up, and Peter tells us he has 'always assumed as a direct consequence of my drawing attention to the dynamite they contained'. Since then Peter has also been arguing against 'what seems to be a rational policy' of allowing only family members to look at the files: 'It may sound reasonable but in effect it prevents historians from ever seeing the big picture of the workings of a government department. It's a real disgrace'.[29]

Without being able to go back to the file records that Peter looked at, we do not know how much detail they actually contain. While access to the individual files for Aboriginal descendants may have improved (though this is questionable), it is impossible for historians to get a big-picture view of this history. Keith Windschuttle's very flawed work on the Stolen Generations was based on his limited access to the Board's Ward Registers alone (which were once open to all and have since come under restrictions).[30] But are the records we need actually there? Heather tells us that, when she got to the records in 1975, the correspondence to the Board from Aboriginal people had been 'culled'; today Heather still laments the disappearance (presumed destruction) of what she describes as 'hundreds

---

26 Rex Jackson was Minister for Youth and Community Services between May 1976 and October 1981, then Minister for Corrective Services. He was later charged and convicted for corruption: see 'Mr Rex Frederick Jackson (1928–2011)', *Parliament of New South Wales, Members*, at https://www.parliament.nsw.gov.au/members/Pages/member-details.aspx?pk=1878, accessed 6 December 2017.

27 Peter Read, *The Stolen Generations: The Removal of Aboriginal Children in New South Wales 1883 to 1969* (Sydney: NSW Department of Aboriginal Affairs Occasional Paper No.1, n.d. (1982)).

28 Peter John Read, 'A History of the Wiradjuri People of New South Wales' (PhD thesis, ANU, 1983); see also Peter Read, *A Hundred Years War: The Wiradjuri People and the State* (Sydney: ANU Press, 1988).

29 Peter Read, personal communication (email) to Victoria Haskins, 8 August 2016.

30 Keith Windschuttle, *The Fabrication of Aboriginal History, Volume Three, The Stolen Generations 1881–2008* (Sydney: Macleay Press, 2009), 77.

of letters from Aboriginal people wanting their kids back', writing that she had found lots of letters from Aboriginal people in other official records (for instance, for the State Education Department) so she knew that similar letters would have gone to the Board—but they were 'well and truly vanished [when] I got there ... I looked for years and never got anywhere—and so did the archivists ... who were all just as eager to find them as I was'.[31] Asked about the possibility of gaps in the records he saw, Peter replies, 'Have we got them all? Who knows?', and tells an intriguing story of finding a pile of old records in the government shed at Sheas Creek that were transferred to the archives office after he identified them. But he does not know if they were catalogued.[32] Certainly I was unable to locate my great-grandmother's extensive correspondence in the records, although she had kept copies of her own letters to the Board and official communications to her. Records attesting to protest and resistance concerning Board policies, as well as the Board's maladministration, may well have been destroyed many years ago. Perhaps they ended up in the sea beneath a Coogee cliff ...

The problem with the official archives makes those historical records that have been kept and preserved by Aboriginal individuals and communities even more significant. A large part of our project consists in going to the Aboriginal communities to record their oral histories and memories of life under the Board. This retrieval of Aboriginal experience and recollection is crucial, because we have such limited access to the official record, and we are reasonably sure in any case that that record is nowhere near complete. It is critical, furthermore, that Aboriginal people take the lead in the recording of their history and in the making of it. The future of this history is in the hands of the Aboriginal people.

---

31   Goodall, personal communication (email).
32   Read, personal communication (email).

Chapter 11

GENEALOGIES OF SELF-DETERMINATION

Tim Rowse

As governmental practice, Indigenous self-determination has a social structure: to Indigenous Australians who are literate, numerate and familiar with what anthropologist Victoria Burbank calls 'impersonality', the settler colonial state has delegated powers and resources to administer services to, and to speak on behalf of, other Indigenous Australians.[1] That is, self-determination enacts a difference (not necessarily an antagonism) between Indigenous functionaries (office-bearers and administrative staff in subsidised Indigenous non-profit organisations) and those whom they service and represent. This is the social structure of 'the Indigenous Sector'.[2]

In a recent paper, Elizabeth Watt and I have traced one genealogy of this structure of differentiated Indigeneity.[3] We argue that in northern and central Australia missionaries and pastoralists learned to delegate some colonial authority to certain Aboriginal people whom they believed to be skilful and trustworthy subalterns. They selected and groomed such

---

1   Victoria Burbank, 'From Bedtime to On Time: Why Many Aboriginal People Don't Especially Like Participating in Western Institutions', *Anthropological Forum* 16 (1) (March 2006): 3–20.

2   Tim Rowse 'The Indigenous Sector', in *Culture, Economy and Governance in Aboriginal Australia*, eds D. Austin-Broos and G. Macdonald, Proceedings of a Workshop of the Academy of Social Sciences (Sydney: Sydney University Press, 2005), 207–24; Tim Rowse *Rethinking Social Justice: From 'Peoples' to 'Populations'* (Canberra: Aboriginal Studies Press, 2012), 101–27.

3   Tim Rowse and Elizabeth Watt, '"The North"—Colonial Hegemony and Indigenous Stratification', in *A Historian for All Seasons: Essays for Geoffrey Bolton*, eds Jenny Gregory, Lenore Layman and Stuart Macintyre (Melbourne: Monash University Publishing, 2017), 204–35.

men, usually (but not always) on the basis that, as 'half castes', they were genetically amenable to being socialised away from the milieu of the 'native camp'; such men were given circumscribed powers. The social structure of the Indigenous Sector is in some respects continuous with this older stratification of the remote Aboriginal population by colour/caste and cultural orientation. However, an ideological modification has been crucial to this structure's evolution as 'self-determination'. The terminology of 'half caste' and 'full blood' has been displaced by 'pan-Aboriginal' ideology that declares the language of 'caste' and 'blood' to be a racist precipitate of discredited race science, a language instrumental in dividing a colonised people in order better to rule them. Pan-Aboriginal ideology emphasises the common fate of all Australians of Aboriginal descent as colonised people; asserting the inherent and historic solidarity of Aboriginal people, pan-Aboriginalism helps to legitimise the leadership of people skilled in organisational work, while making them accountable to those whose cultural capital derives from their eminence in the neo-traditional Aboriginal domain.

Pan-Aboriginalism has influenced Australia's post-1960s historiography, engendering uncertainty about how historians should deal with distinctions of 'caste' and 'blood', and even about whether to notice such distinctions at all, when dealing with past discourses in which such distinctions were 'common sense'. For example, in the historiography of British–Australian feminists between the wars, in which Marilyn Lake has been so productive and influential, there has been only a little attention to the significance (if any) that feminist activists attached to distinctions of 'caste' and 'blood'.[4] Indeed, the primary sources on which Lake and others draw do not lead us to think that when the feminist activists protested the abuse of native women they considered 'half-caste' women any more or less entitled to human dignity than 'full-blood' women. Feminist humanitarians used the category 'native women' in an inclusive way when advocating the human dignity of Aboriginal women. On at least one occasion, Mary Bennett explained that when she referred to 'Aboriginal mothers' she intended the category to include 'half-caste mothers, who, in Australia, are deemed to be Aborigines'.[5] This inclusive usage in the primary sources is in harmony

---

4   Alison Holland, in *Just Relations: The Story of Mary Bennett's Crusade for Aboriginal Rights* (Perth: UWA Publishing, 2015), 110, 224, draws attention to the ways that 1930s feminist activists saw the distinction 'half caste'/'full blood'.

5   Mary Bennett, 'The Aboriginal Mother in Western Australia in 1933', excerpt in *Freedom Bound: Documents on Women in Modern Australia 2*, eds Katie Holmes and Marilyn Lake (Sydney: Allen & Unwin, 1995), 61.

with the tendency of Australian historiography to emphasise the shared colonial oppression of Aboriginal people, irrespective of their descent; it is also consistent with the feminist view (which is also mine) that, in sexuality and in mothering, women of Aboriginal descent were subject to patriarchal authorities both Aboriginal and colonial.

However, in some documents, we find a rather different set of terms: 'native and half-caste', 'Aboriginal and half-caste', as if the two were not quite the same. For example, Lake quotes Mary Bennett writing to Sir John Harris of the Anti-Slavery Society in 1935: 'It is the business of Women's Societies to reform the condition of Aboriginal and half-caste women in Australia'.[6] The phrase 'Aboriginal and half-caste women' is either a tautology (if all 'half castes' are considered 'Aboriginal') or it implies that 'Aboriginal women' and 'half-caste women' are distinct categories of women (albeit with much in common in subjection to patriarchy). Mary Bennett wrote to Bessie Rischbieth in April 1932 of 'the loving protection needed by these girls and women, native and half-caste, in the state of transition from native culture to white civilisation'. We find it also in Bennett's 1933 paper, 'The Aboriginal Mother in Western Australia': 'the present iniquitous practice of placing native and half-caste girls and women at the disposal of police officers'.[7]

I will argue in this chapter that we can determine the significance of the distinction 'Aboriginal'/'half caste' if we consider feminist discourse as occupying a position within a field of humanitarian discourse that feminists shared with communist and Aboriginal activists. This 'field' is, of course, my analytic construct, devised to answer the question: what could it have meant then to distinguish the 'half caste' (sometimes 'half-caste') from the 'Aboriginal' or 'native'? By presenting this field, my intention is to reframe the feminist discourse of the 1930s and 1940s—not to replace or to correct the readings offered by Lake and others, but to consider the different ways that it was possible for humanitarianisms—feminist and others—to imagine the Australian Indigenous future. I will contrast the ways that two Australian humanitarianisms—Aboriginal and non-Aboriginal—imagined the role of the more 'civilised' or acculturated Aborigines in the Indigenous future.

---

6   Marilyn Lake, 'Feminism and the Gendered Politics of Antiracism, Australia 1927–1957: From Maternal Protectionism to Leftist Assimilationism', *Australian Historical Studies* 29 (110) (April 1998): 91–108 (95–6).

7   Both Bennett to Rischbieth and Bennett's 1933 paper are reprinted in Lake and Holmes (eds), *Freedom Bound*, 60, 62.

Aboriginal activists of New South Wales and Victoria presented themselves as the more 'capable' Aborigines and thus as the trustees of 'civilisation' who would take over from (or share with) the state and missions the guidance of 'wild' Aborigines and the care of more helpless Aborigines. Communists and feminists, in contrast, saw the remote/tribal Aborigines as having a potential for autonomous development that was lost to those Aboriginal people who had been irreversibly changed by colonial contact—that is, those who were 'detribalised', 'contaminated' and (in most cases) genetically at least half white. The communists and the feminists saw the future of such 'detribalised' Aboriginal people as citizenship in the Australian mainstream, and they reserved to humanitarian whites such as themselves the responsibility to protect and guide the still tribal Aborigines along a more gradual and less pressured path of development whose destination was not clear.

Aborigines and the Communist International

In 1931, the Communist Party of Australia (CPA) published a fourteen-point *Draft Programme of Struggle Against Slavery*. The phrase 'aborigines and half-castes' and 'Aborigines or half-castes' occurred as follows:

> (2) Absolute political freedom for *aborigines and half-castes*; right to membership in, and right to organise, political, economic and cultural organisations, "mixed," or aboriginal. Right to participate in demonstrations and public affairs. Right to leave Australia as full citizens.

> (3) Removal of all color restrictions on *aborigines or half-castes*, in professions, sports, etc. Aboriginal intellectuals, school teachers, etc., not to be prevented from practising because of the "color line."

> (6) Unconditional release from gaol of all *aborigines or half-castes*, and no further arrests until aboriginal juries can hear and decide cases.

> (7) Abolition of Aborigines Protection Boards—Capitalism's slave recruiting agencies and terror organisations against *aborigines and half-castes*.

> (9) Full and unrestricted right of *aboriginal and half-caste* parents to their children, without living in constant fear that the A.P.B. or mission stations will kidnap them to send into slavery.

> (12) Full right of the aborigines to develop native culture. Right to establish their own schools, train their own teachers, for the children of the *aborigines and half-castes*. The Australian Government to make available sums of money for such purposes, to be paid into and controlled by committees comprised solely of *aborigines and half-castes*.[8]

The distinction between the 'Aborigines' and 'half castes' became important to the most prolific CPA theorist of Indigenous liberation, Tom Wright, of the Sheet Metal Workers' Union and the NSW Trades and Labour Council.[9] In correspondence with non-communist activists, Wright asserted that the terms 'Aborigines', 'natives' and 'Aboriginals' should be defined so as to exclude 'half castes and others of mixed blood'. The latter, he said, were better considered as coloured workers who suffered racial discrimination. Their struggle for social advancement was as part of Australia's working class, not as members of a distinct nation or people.[10] According to Wright's 1938 booklet, *New Deal for the Aborigines*, the rights of 'Aborigines proper' who lived on 'tribal sanctuaries' were those of a 'national minority'; their future rested on their strict territorial and cultural segregation from Australian society. Wright was here presenting a version of what the 1931 draft program of the CPA had demanded in its fourteenth point:

> (14) The handing over to the aborigines of large tracts of watered and fertile country, with towns, seaports, railways, roads, etc., to become one or more independent aboriginal states or republics. The handing back to the aborigines of all Central, Northern, and North West Australia to enable the aborigines to develop their native pursuits. These aboriginal republics to be independent of Australian or other foreign powers. To have the right to make treaties with foreign powers, including Australia, establish their own army, governments, industries, and in every way be independent of imperialism.[11]

---

8   *Workers Weekly*, 24 September 1931, 2 (emphasis added), www.reasoninrevolt.net.au/objects/pdf/a000219.pdf, accessed 24 January 2017.

9   Padraic Gibson (per comm.) has studied party archives and not found evidence of 'clear debate within the party over the significance of "caste" in the 20s or 1930s'. Wright's authority within the party was such that his insistence on the 'half caste'/'full blood' distinction seems not to have been challenged, though we should not infer that all communists saw things that way.

10 T. Wright, *New Deal for the Aborigines*, second edition (Sydney: Current Book Distributors, 1944), 30.

11 *Workers Weekly*, 24 September 1931, 2, http://www.reasoninrevolt.net.au/objects/pdf/a000219.pdf, accessed 24 January 2017.

In his 1938 formulation, Wright demanded absolutely inviolable reserves, with tribal ownership of mineral resources. He added that only secular organisations (and not missions) should be allowed to interact with these sovereign reserve owners, who would develop economically, with instruction in their own languages as well as in English. A new Commonwealth department should be established, Wright recommended, with powers to police alien contact with the reserve dwellers. Re-issuing *New Deal for the Aborigines* in 1944, Wright wrote that it would be necessary to exclude 'mixed blood' people from inviolable reserves. People who were of Aboriginal descent but who were no longer 'Aborigines proper' should play no part in the development of reserve residents 'because of the danger of providing focal points for disintegration'.[12]

Wright thought it a mistake to combine people of mixed descent and 'full bloods' in the one organised movement with a single program, as some Aboriginal organisations were beginning to do. As he explained to the Australian Aborigines' League in 1948, the social development of Aboriginal people would proceed along two lines. Some would survive within an evolving tribal organisation; others had lost tribal organisation and thus were a racially oppressed section of the wider Australian working class.[13] Though he often used the racial terms 'full-blood' and 'half-caste', these were shorthand for Wright's distinctions of social organisation and political capacity. The central question for him was whether the 'tribal organisation' of Aborigines still worked effectively. Where it did, Aborigines had a possible future as a distinct people living on their own territory; where it did not, their destiny was as members of the working class. In September 1951 he wrote to the honorary secretary of the Council for Aboriginal Rights (Melbourne) giving the 'half-caste'/'full-blood' distinction geographical expression. New South Wales and Victoria were historically different from the Northern Territory and adjacent areas: 'there is no Aborigine question in Victoria or N.S.W. where few if any aborigines have survived', and the terms 'native', 'Aboriginal' or 'Aborigine' should not 'refer to persons of mixed blood'.[14] Other communist intellectuals made this distinction. Lake quotes Peter Worsley explaining to Jessie Street in 1956 his view that most Aborigines had now become 'workers'; pastoral workers outside the reserves were 'no longer "tribal" people. They are workers again'.

---

12   Wright, *New Deal*, 31.
13   Wright to Curlewis, 13 May 1948, Wright Papers, Box 8, Noel Butlin Archives, Menzies Library, Australian National University.
14   Wright to Wardlaw, 20 September 1951, Wright Papers, Box 8.

Cultural difference had no place in this struggle—'the mythical tribal aborigine ... hardly exists anymore'.[15]

Feminist internationalism and the Aboriginal woman as slave

The 'international' in which some Australian feminists were active was not the Moscow-centred Comintern but the London-centred British Commonwealth League (BCL), formed in 1925 'to deal with issues of Equal Citizenship within the countries ruled under the British flag'. Through membership of bodies such as the Australian Federation of Women's Societies for Equal Citizenship (subsequently the Australian Federation of Women Voters) and several state-based progressive women's associations, women such as Mary Bennett, Bessie Rischbieth, Constance Ternent Cooke, Edith Jones and Helen Baillie were affiliated with the BCL and attended its conferences in London. The third BCL conference, in 1927, tackled the social and industrial position of women who were subjects of British rule but were not of British race.[16] White Australian women activists joined this discussion. Publicising the Aboriginal question from the centre of the Empire, their views were reported in London's press and thus attracted notice in Australia. They also participated in the London-based Anti-Slavery and Aborigines' Protection Society, whose cause resonated with the campaigns against unfree labour pursued by the International Labour Organization (ILO).

Australia's Imperial feminists 'applied equality of rights between men and women to the question of just relations between white and black'.[17] In particular, these women criticised policies that supposed the Aboriginal woman and mother to be defenceless and morally incompetent, and that mandated the supervision of her marital choices and the removal of her children. The feminists upheld the Aboriginal woman as a human with rights, a vulnerable individual to be empowered (as a woman) against sexually predatory, enslaving men and (as a mother and a woman) against crushingly 'protective' bureaucracy. According to Lake, their 'focus on the violated woman and grieving mother as paradigmatic of the oppressed

---

15 Worsley, quoted in Lake, 'Feminism and the Gendered Politics of Antiracism', 106.
16 British Commonwealth League, *A Report of Conference Held June 30th and July 1st, 1927* (London: BCL, n.d.), 5.
17 Fiona Paisley, *Loving Protection? Australian Feminism and Aboriginal Women's Rights, 1919–1939* (Melbourne: Melbourne University Press, 2000), 28.

condition of Aboriginal people ... distinguished feminist discourse from the other Christian and humanitarian discourses current at the time'.[18]

In some of their interventions, feminists distinguished the frontier from the longer-colonised regions. At the 1933 BCL meeting, Mary Bennett explained that 'the study of the Aboriginal mother falls into two parts: (1) dealing with the Aboriginal mother living the wild life uncontaminated by whites; and (2) dealing with the Aboriginal mother living in touch with civilisation'.[19] Women in the first situation were property of men. In the second, 'contaminated' situation (which included but was not confined to the situation of 'half-caste' women) that property had become traded merchandise, as women were driven by hunger to prostitution.

This distinction was about modes of oppression, but it did not *necessarily* give rise, as it did in Wright's view, to distinct corrective policies and scenarios of emancipation. When the anthropologist Olive Pink advocated 'secular sanctuaries', some of them to be administered by a woman, she referred to the needs of the remote and least-disturbed Aboriginal people.[20] However, when Bennett and other feminists demanded the appointment of women like themselves as protectors, they seem to have had in mind the need to protect all kinds of Aboriginal women, not just the most remote. Without distinguishing 'Aboriginal' from 'half-caste' women, Bennett recommended that Aboriginal people be given 'at least fifty native territories ... spaced equitably throughout the state [Western Australia] for the twenty to thirty thousand native inhabitants'.[21] Feminists also endorsed the request for female protectors issued in 1934 by the self-described 'half-caste' women of Broome, who thought that their manner of life should exempt them from the controls applied to 'full-blood' natives.[22]

It was in their projection of the future, rather than in their description of current oppression, that the feminists deployed 'half caste'/'full blood' as a

---

18 Lake, 'Feminism and the Gendered Politics of Antiracism', 100.
19 Lake and Holmes (eds), *Freedom Bound*, 60.
20 Russell McGregor, *Imagined Destinies: Aboriginal Australians and the Doomed Race Theory, 1880–1939* (Melbourne: Melbourne University Press, 1997), 241–9; Julie Marcus, *The Indomitable Miss Pink: A Life in Anthropology* (Sydney: UNSW Press, 2001), 213.
21 Bennett, in *Freedom Bound*, eds Lake and Holmes, 63.
22 Lake, 'Feminism and the Gendered Politics of Antiracism', 95; Marilyn Lake, *Getting Equal: The History of Australian Feminism* (Sydney: Allen & Unwin, 1999), 126–7. Lake and Holmes speculate that this request by the women of Broome 'might have been at the behest of feminist activists in Western Australia'. See Lake and Holmes (eds), *Freedom Bound*, 63.

significant distinction: the former should be assimilated, the latter protected by a high degree of segregation. Thus, in a 1932 letter to Bessie Rischbieth, Bennett distinguished the task of the mission to 'wild natives', such as those in the Kimberley, from the task of the mission serving those who had been '"civilised" or contaminated' by contact with settler society, such as could be found on the edges of pastoral settlement.[23] In editing this document for inclusion in *Freedom Bound II*, Katie Holmes and Marilyn Lake omitted the passage that includes the words '"civilised" or contaminated'. I suggest that these terms are important clues to distinctions that Bennett's humanitarianism sometimes made. According to Alison Holland, 'like many humanitarians of their day', Bennett and her missionary colleague Rod Schenk 'saw in the full-bloods even greater promise than the half-castes, as they were "uncontaminated" by whites'.[24] In her letter to Rischbieth, Bennett contrasted 'practically wild and uncontaminated natives' with 'the broken and embittered remnants of tribes', and she referred to

> these two fine types of mission, the Loves' mission [Kunmunya] for the wild natives, the Schenks' mission [Mount Margaret] for the "civilised" or contaminated ones. Though "contaminated", they are the most magnificent material, and respond splendidly to encouragement to work, and are most industrious and precise.[25]

The notion of 'contamination' in Bennett's typology of native women suggests ambivalence. On the one hand there is an element of moral and physical disgust towards what colonisation has 'broken'; on the other hand, she expresses faith that, under 'loving protection', the contaminated 'remnants' would 'respond splendidly'. In her recent biography of Mary Bennett, Sue Taffe points to the origins of such thinking in Bennett's childhood on her father's pastoral lease; there she was exposed to her father's 'negative stereotype of people of mixed descent being inferior to both races'. As Taffe points out, this view appears in Bennett's admiring biography of her father, *Christison of Lammermoor* (London: Alston Rivers, 1927).[26] Over the course of her activism, this distinction seems to have become less evaluative, and Bennett supported the human rights of both 'Aborigines' and 'half castes'.

---

23   Bennett to Rischbieth, 6 March 1932, Rischbieth Papers, MS 2004/12/23, Box 29, National Library of Australia, and see Paisley, *In Loving Protection*, 89.
24   Holland, *Just Relations*, 224.
25   Bennett to Rischbieth, 6 March 1932.
26   Sue Taffe, *A White Hot Flame: Mary Montgomerie Bennett—Author, Educator, Activist for Indigenous Justice* (Melbourne: Monash University Publishing, 2018), 62, 116–17.

The Garvey-ites of New South Wales

From among those who had been '"civilized" or contaminated' by a century of contact with the colonisers sprang the first wave of Aboriginal intellectuals. A black ('Negro') international movement inspired the Hunter Valley-born Koori Fred Maynard. The Universal Negro Improvement Association (UNIA), led by the Jamaican Marcus Garvey, flourished in the United States after World War I among African Americans for whom post–Civil War Reconstruction had failed. From 1920 Garvey presided over the first of several international conventions of the UNIA. Hearing Garvey's call for global black solidarity, some Aboriginal Australians formed a chapter of UNIA in Sydney in 1920. According to John Maynard they were angered by the NSW government's handing over of much of their reserve lands to returned non-Aboriginal servicemen after World War I. The UNIA activists then established the Australian Aboriginal Progressive Association (AAPA) in 1924, building their platform 'around Garvey's call for pride in culture, solid economic base, and strong association to land of birth'.[27] AAPA referred to Aborigines as 'Australians', and its motto 'Australia for Australians' repeated the Garvey-ite motif 'Africa for Africans'. The Garvey-ite paper *Negro World* reported frequently on 'enslaved and brutalised' Aborigines in the mid-1920s, pointing to the parallel with the 'Red Men' of North America.

AAPA campaigned for four years (1925 to 1929), establishing eleven branches, holding four conferences and demanding: good land in 'fee simple sufficient ... to maintain a family', a 'family life free from invasion', government reserves for 'the incapables of the Aboriginal community', and delegation to 'educated aboriginals' of the supervision of 'Homes, Hostels or Reserve'. Sick of the bullying of the Aborigines Protection Board, AAPA asked that the Board be replaced by a 'board of management comprised of capable educated aboriginals under a chairman to be appointed by the Government'.[28] AAPA's distinction 'capable/incapable' resembles the distinction made in African American political discourse, by black intellectuals, between educated African Americans and those not yet blessed by education. This distinction also appeared in a petition presented by AAPA

---

27 John Maynard, '"In the interests of our people": The Influence of Garveyism on the Rise of Australian Aboriginal Political Activism', *Aboriginal History* 29 (2005): 1–22 (14).

28 John Maynard, *Fight for Liberty and Freedom: The Origins of Australian Aboriginal Activism* (Canberra: Aboriginal Studies Press, 2007), 99–100.

to NSW Premier Jack Lang in May 1927.²⁹ According to a press report of a meeting between Maynard and the chair of the Australian Board of Missions (Reverend J.S. Needham) in November 1927, Maynard envisaged that 'native communities' would be supervised not by white officials of state and church but by 'educated and capable aborigines'.³⁰ John Maynard sees parallels with what Aborigines in South Australia and Western Australia were demanding at this time: governments should acknowledge 'capable' Aborigines as leaders.³¹ A few years later, a deputation of NSW Aborigines, when presenting a long-range policy to Prime Minister Joseph Lyons on 31 January 1938, said:

> In regard to uncivilised and semi-civilised Aborigines, we suggest that patrol officers, nurses, and teachers, both men and women *of Aboriginal blood*, should be specially trained by the Commonwealth Government as Aboriginal Officers, to bring the wild people into contact with civilisation ... While opposing a policy of segregation, we urge that, during a period of transition, the present Aboriginal Reserves should be retained as a sanctuary for aged or incompetent Aborigines who may be unfitted to take their place in the white community, owing to the past policy of neglect.³²

Unlike communist and feminist internationalists, AAPA did not use the language of 'caste' or 'blood' when making distinctions among Aboriginal Australians. The contrast between full-blood/uncontaminated/tribal and half-caste/contaminated/detribalised was useless (and quite possibly offensive) to many emerging Aboriginal intellectuals because, in that way of dichotomising the Indigenous situation, the emerging Aboriginal intellectuals would be marked by what they were not, as the impure, the contaminated, the detribalised, as pitifully damaged and estranged from their authentic being. The articulate urban and rural Aborigines of the southeast and southwest of the continent avoided terms that disqualified their responsibility over and leadership of other Aboriginal people. They were more conscious of what they had achieved than of what they had lost; they

---

29 In Bain Attwood and Andrew Markus (eds), *The Struggle for Aboriginal Rights* (Sydney: Allen & Unwin, 1999), 67.
30 *Sydney Morning Herald*, 15 November 1927, reprinted in Attwood and Markus (eds), 70–1.
31 Maynard, *Fight for Liberty*, 125–30.
32 Attwood and Markus (eds), *The Struggle*, 91 (original emphasis).

sought recognition of their cultural distance from those Aboriginal people who now needed their protection and guidance.

British Aborigines

William Cooper, Yorta Yorta founder of the Australian Aborigines' League (AAL) in 1936, was encouraged by the advance of other native peoples under the proper 'British' tuition that white Australians were failing to give. Like other Aboriginal intellectuals of his time, Cooper believed that the 'half-caste'/'full-blood' distinction was a misleading and harmful way to differentiate the needs, achievements and entitlements of Aboriginal people; 'blood' was neither a determinant nor an index of how far any person had advanced. Instead, Cooper suggested to Joseph Lyons that 'the aboriginal population shall be grouped into classes determined by the stage of their progress and that the policy of the [Northern Territory] Administration shall be the progressive elevation from one class to an higher one till the whole race is fully civilized and cultured'.[33] Cooper classified his Aboriginal contemporaries under three headings: 'primitive aborigines' who needed reserves, rations and special courts based on customary law; 'semi-civilised and detribalised natives' who needed help to turn their land to agricultural use, 'the right to work for adequate remuneration or the provision of full rations and housing' and access to schools and to pensions; and 'civilised natives' (he included all Aborigines of New South Wales) entitled to what the 'semi-civilised' should have and, in addition, to vote and to receive the 'maternity bonus'.[34] The 'civilised'—including Cooper himself—had a duty to defend the 'primitive' and to 'uplift them morally, socially, intellectually and spiritually'.[35] Cooper suggested that the states should cede to the Commonwealth their powers over Aborigines. Whereas Maynard and AAPA focused on New South Wales, Cooper's vision was continental; commenting on 'northern development', he saw a special role for Aborigines in the settlement of northern Australia.[36] In his view,

---

33   In Bain Attwood and Andrew Markus (eds), *Thinking Black: William Cooper and the Australian Aborigines' League* (Canberra: Aboriginal Studies Press, 2004), 65.
34   In Attwood and Markus (eds), *Thinking Black*, 59, 49–50, 65.
35   In Attwood and Markus (eds), *Thinking Black*, 51.
36   In Attwood and Markus (eds), *Thinking Black*, 68, 78, 80, 95, 96, 105.

the proper method of dealing with the primitive people would be to send educated and cultured Aborigines to their own uncivilized people. These men, of the same blood, would understand their people and would be able to suggest to the government means whereby the hardships and sufferings of these people could be alleviated or removed.[37]

A field of distinctions

Although all informed observers in the 1930s agreed that the situations, mentalities and prospects of Aboriginal Australians were differentiated, their loose usage of the terms in which differences were described was a barrier to a clear policy debate. The 'half-caste/full-blood' distinction was entrenched in official statistics and in law. Some policy reformers thought that people's character and outlook were closely correlated with, and substantially determined by, their genetic make-up. Others whose thinking was not so determinist used the terminology of 'blood' and 'caste' as shorthand for sociological distinctions: a 'full blood' was, in most cases, not yet 'detribalised', and a 'half caste' definitely was. 'Aboriginal mother' could be used in a way that included 'half-caste' women, but the same writer could then refer to 'half caste' as if the term designated something different from 'native'/'Aboriginal'. And, as we have seen, some Aboriginal intellectuals avoided using these terms at all.

Obscured by this terminological variety and imprecision was the implicit and largely undebated issue of whether there were two pathways or one pathway forward for the colonised people. Generally, those who used the 'full-blood/half-caste' distinction believed that there were two paths of advancement: 'half castes' should be enabled as individual citizens and absorbed as quickly as possible into the wider society, while 'full bloods' should be enabled as tribal groups to defer indefinitely their engagement with Australian institutions and even to develop themselves, with carefully chosen assistance, along a path to distinct sovereignty or to a high degree of autonomy, in remote regions. In contrast, many Aborigines of south-eastern and south-western agricultural Australia, who understood themselves to be relatively 'civilised', saw themselves as the advance guard in a single line of progression along which all Aboriginal people were moving and must move. Some Aboriginal people, they said, had travelled farther than others

---

37   In Attwood and Markus (eds), *Thinking Black*, 94.

along that path. Those of Aboriginal descent who saw themselves as more advanced said that they merited distinct entitlements and responsibilities as a consequence not of their mixed 'blood' but of their cultural attainments. Some Aboriginal people who claimed this distinction of capability presented themselves as guardians and guides of their less advanced fellows.

Australian political forums did not enable a reasoned confrontation between what I have described here as the two-path and one-path scenarios; on particular issues at particular times, the two sides were in agreement—for example, about the right of remote Aboriginal people to live relatively undisturbed on large reserves. However, the undebated tension between the two perspectives was the role assigned to the 'advanced'/'detribalised'/ 'half-caste'/'contaminated' Aborigines.

On one side of the field that I have constructed, we find communists and feminists. Wright advocated that 'detribalised' Aborigines should play no part in the remote people's future; enlightened government officials should guide the remote, tribal people, he suggested in 1939 and in 1944.[38] The feminists also rested their hopes on appointing a better kind of official (though, in some of their schemes, the female protector might be on the staff of a mission, not necessarily a government employee). The Aboriginal woman needed the empathy that only a female protector could offer.

On the other side of this 'field' we find Aboriginal men (and some women, such as Pearl Gibbs) emboldened by their acculturation. In both Maynard's and Cooper's views, the government officials must step aside so that 'capable' Aborigines' could supervise the 'incapable'—a term broad enough to include many different ways of not (yet) engaging effectively with modern Australia.

Conclusion

Taking a long view (from the late 1920s to the 1960s), Marilyn Lake has persuasively charted the fading influence of a 'maternalist feminism' that distinguished the oppression of Aboriginal women from the oppression of Aboriginal men and the rise, by the 1950s, of a conception of the rights of the Aboriginal Australian as a 'worker'/citizen whose gender was implicitly

---

38   In the 1931 draft policy quoted earlier in this chapter, the CPA did recognise that Aboriginal leaders were emerging. 'Committees comprised solely of aborigines and half-castes' should be given money by the government to 'establish their own schools, train their own teachers'. However, in Wright's exposition of the communist view, Aboriginal leadership would be distributed across two spheres, the 'tribal' and the 'detribalised', that he considered distinct.

masculine. Without seeking to displace or to amend her argument, I have taken an even longer view, informed by knowing what 'self-determination' has turned out to be: a structure that mobilises the distinction between a stratum of Indigenous functionaries (office-bearers and administrative staff in subsidised Indigenous non-profit corporations) and those whom they service and represent. From this posterior standpoint, it has been possible to re-read the Aboriginal and non-Aboriginal humanitarian discourses of the 1920s to 1940s by asking how, in that field of discourse, was the distinction between more and less acculturated Aboriginal people configured in plotting a future? I have argued that the social structure of self-determination has vindicated the vision of the Aboriginal activists, not of the communists and feminists. That is, 'self-determination' has enacted the scenario that Indigenous intellectuals (mostly men) presented to governments in the 1920s and 1930s; the state has delegated to the more acculturated Indigenous Australians certain responsibilities in the 'advancement' of Indigenous Australians generally. I am thus proposing an Aboriginal intellectual and social genealogy of the Australian practices of 'self-determination'.

A theme of Marilyn Lake's scholarship has been the implicit and explicit gendering of 'rights' discourse, and this inspires me to conclude by wondering about the gender of self-determination. I see three kinds of evidence that women have been advantaged by self-determination. First, they seem to be favoured by its employment opportunities.[39] Second, acculturation—under both assimilation and self-determination policies—has imbued three generations of Indigenous Australians with respect for human rights, so that, when they have gathered to design political institutions, they have honoured gender equality. Thus in 2009:

> A national workshop of 100 Aboriginal and Torres Strait Islander people [met] in Adelaide to identify the key elements of a new national representative body. 50 men and 50 women were selected based on merit following a public nomination process, with delegates selected to ensure a gender balance, as well as representation of urban, regional and remote locations.[40]

---

39 For evidence on Indigenous labour force participation, see Tim Rowse, *Indigenous Futures: Choice and Development for Aboriginal and Islander Australia* (Sydney: UNSW Press, 2002), 152–66.

40 Steering Committee for the Creation of a New National Representative Body, *Our Future in Our Hands: Creating a Sustainable Representative Body for Aboriginal and Torres Strait Islander Peoples* (Sydney: Australian Human Rights Commission, 2009), 41.

Third, the Indigenous critique of self-determination since 2000 has made much of the question of the well-being and security of women and children.[41] Self-determination, it seems, stimulates a politics of gender among Indigenous Australians.[42]

---

41 For Indigenous comment, see Tim Rowse, *Indigenous and Other Australians Since 1901* (Sydney: NewSouth, 2017), 391–4, 406–13.
42 For a lively survey of Indigenous views about 'men women and customary law', see Sarah Maddison, *Black Politics: Inside the Complexity of Aboriginal Political Culture* (Sydney: Allen & Unwin, 2009), 185–205.

Chapter 12

FAITH BANDLER
AND THE POLITICS OF RACE

Henry Reynolds

Faith Bandler and Marilyn Lake met at an Independent Scholars Conference in Sydney in August 1998. Marilyn had given an address on the importance of the welfare state. To her surprise Faith invited her to write her biography. It turned out to be an inspired choice. But Faith could have asked any of the country's leading biographers to accept the commission. She was a highly visible celebrity with both star quality and a career of real substance. There was also abundant documentation both public and private on which to base the life story. Faith was obviously attracted to Marilyn's inimitable combination of intellect and elegance. She was no doubt also impressed by her ability to address and engage an audience in a way that she herself had perfected during a long career of public speaking.

It is not clear how much more Faith knew about her future biographer on that August day twenty years ago. But there was much about Marilyn's career that had prepared her, in advance, for the new task. She had conducted research in many areas of Australian history and, like conscientious under-graduate teachers of the time, she had maintained a wide reach across many areas of national life. She was immersed in her work on the first generation of post-suffrage feminist activists, which resulted in the publication of *Getting Equal* in 1999.[1] But she also had her own generation-long experience of community activism, which provided her with an understanding of the challenges and demands that had been an

---

1   Marilyn Lake, *Getting Equal: The History of Australian Feminism* (Sydney: Allen & Unwin, 1999).

inseparable part of Faith's political career. A successful biographer needs more than a series of parallel experiences, however, and a more complex clutch of skills than those required in mainstream history. The summary phrase 'the life and times' may well be over used, but it does encapsulate the demands imposed on the aspiring biographer. First there is the imperative for both insight and empathy, to see the world through the eyes of the central character while appreciating the ancillary roles played by family, friends and other contemporaries. But there must also be an understanding of the social and political milieu, of the intellectual currents swirling around the human actors. And there is the incessant problem of balance between the personal and the public, and between the analysis and the overriding demands of the central narrative.

Marilyn quickly appreciated that Faith's distinctive heritage and childhood were of fundamental importance in any interpretation of her life's work. For a start she was of Pacific Island descent. She was not an Indigenous Australian although she was often mistaken for one. She grew up hearing the stories of the Islander community, of the labour trade that brought the Islanders to Queensland, of the mass deportation of 1906 and the establishment of strong communities in the sugar-growing districts of northern New South Wales and coastal Queensland. The labour trade brought many more men than women to Australia. Islander men married out but brought their wives into their own communities. There were many liaisons and marriages with Aboriginal women, and these unions allowed large numbers of Islanders of Faith's generation to claim Aboriginality on the basis of an Indigenous grandmother. Faith's grandmother, however, was Indian, and this denied her the possibility of passing although she may have chosen not to.

Faith's community had a very distinctive provenance. It was also domiciled in a few specific locations, which had significant influences on its way of life. The sugar industry was a dominating influence. The demand for labour did not lessen when the majority of the Pacific Islanders were expelled. Cane cutting provided the way for many minority communities to bring in high seasonal wages, which enabled Italians and Islanders alike to buy land and set themselves up in the industry. The strong bonds of kinship were the ideal foundation for successful cane-cutting gangs. Four of Faith's brothers appear in the biography in a photo of their own gang. The soil and abundant rainfall that facilitated sugar cultivation also allowed the Islanders to transfer their traditions of gardening to the new land. Faith's memories of childhood are of plain but abundant food either grown on the spot or exchanged in a local system of barter.

The Islanders had become successful settlers by the time Faith was growing up. They still faced discrimination, which she remembered all her life and which encouraged her to empathise with many other black Australians. But the tropical coast also attracted many other people from minority communities, both white and non-European. There were not the sharp and deep lines of racial demarcation apparent in the pastoral districts of the inland. So Faith left the country of her birth and upbringing with a deep hatred of racism but with a belief that the answer to it was solidarity across the colour line. This was as much a feature of her experience as race-based division.

Marilyn creates a vivid picture of Faith's childhood in the Northern Rivers region of New South Wales. Despite the obvious differences in time and circumstances she saw interesting parallels with her own rural childhood in a closely settled community based on one key primary industry that determined patterns of employment and land ownership. In Faith's case it was sugar production; in Marilyn's it was apple and pear growing for export, supplemented by the production of other fruit and vegetables for local consumption.

Faith left her childhood home and, after service in the Women's Land Army during World War II, settled in Sydney, where she lived for the rest of her life. It was an exciting place for young Australians new to the big cities. King's Cross was one of the few places that foreshadowed the country's multi-cultural future. European refugees mingled with artists and intellectuals in exotic coffee shops and wine bars. It was an era of edgy sophistication before its subsequent descent into sleaze. Marilyn remarked that to ordinary Sydney folk the Cross was 'an unkempt, exotic and slightly dangerous place', but Faith 'felt very much at home there'.[2] The political environment that Faith encountered was also distinctive. The federal Labor governments of John Curtin and Ben Chifley were driving forward in an atmosphere of post-war enthusiasm for change. The Communist Party was still a powerful force during that brief period before the full onslaught of the Cold War, when the Soviet Union still basked in the aura of its victory over Nazi Germany. Many of Faith's friends and acquaintances were either party members or sympathisers, and this induction into radical politics influenced her for the rest of her life.

In Marilyn's account, Faith 'heard about communism as a progressive force'[3] and then became involved in the Australian Peace Council, formed

---

2   Marilyn Lake, *Faith: Faith Bandler, Gentle Activist* (Sydney: Allen & Unwin, 2002), 32.
3   Lake, *Faith*, 32.

in 1949. She attended a Eureka Youth League camp in the Blue Mountains and was endorsed as a delegate to the Australian Peace Congress in Melbourne in 1950 where she consolidated her friendship with the formidable activist Jessie Street. Street, Faith declared, didn't see the colour of your skin, and she 'more than any other person on this earth influenced my life'.[4] Faith used the platform provided by the Peace Council to talk about racial discrimination both in Australia and in the United States, her interest in the parallels sparked by reading Howard Fast's best-selling novel *Freedom Road*, first published in 1944. In a speech at a rally protesting about Fast's jailing for 'un-American activities', Faith praised the persecuted novelist for showing that not only could black and white people fight and die together they could also live and work together. In one of her brief, perceptive interventions Marilyn notes here that 'the desirability of Blacks and Whites living together became for Faith a lifelong theme of her public speaking.'[5]

Marilyn's primary focus is on Faith's key role in national politics from the foundation of the Federal Council of Aboriginal Affairs (subsequently FCAATSI) in 1958 to the passage of the constitutional referendum in 1967. Beyond situating her in a narrative linking the principal events, it was essential to analyse Faith's centrality and assess the reason for her great public appeal. There is no doubt that she was a charismatic personality in the true meaning of that over-used term. Having observed Faith's magnetism among family friends and relatives at an event by the Tweed River at Tumbulgum in 1999, Marilyn wrote:

> I was struck by how many were drawn to her presence, wanting to touch her, give her a hug or a kiss, wanting to lay claim to her. Faith exudes a serenity that belies an extraordinary energy. Her radiance commands attention and it is easy to fall under her spell.[6]

Marilyn then teases out some of the underlying reasons for Faith's great charm and effortless elegance. There was the family background of dressmaking and inherited appreciation of fine fabrics, of cut and design. Her training as an opera singer taught her how to speak with precision, to enunciate clearly and to use gesture and pause to increase the dramatic effect of her words. Like the diva she aspired to be she knew how to hold the centre of the stage. Marilyn found a wonderful description of Faith's star

---

4   Lake, *Faith*, 33.
5   Lake, *Faith*, 36.
6   Lake, *Faith*, ix–x.

quality in Bobbi Sykes's autobiography. Faith had travelled to Townsville prior to the referendum and met a gathering of prominent local ladies at the Queen's Hotel. Faith's appearance, Sykes recalled,

> blew me away and still remains in my mind. She was the *most* elegant woman I had ever seen, beautifully groomed and wearing absolutely spotless little white gloves. It was unusual to see anyone wearing gloves in North Queensland's tropical heat, and the difficulty in keeping them so pristine was a feat in itself. When I saw how this room full of white women responded so positively to the manner in which Faith presented herself ... I was completely entranced.[7]

Having herself grown up and been educated in a time when class still had discursive power, Marilyn realised that Faith's quite distinctive personal experience allowed her to reach across the barriers of class and status. She lived most of her life in the upper middle-class suburbs on Sydney's North Shore. Her husband Hans was an engineer refugee from Vienna who shared her passion for classical music and theatre. As a couple they mixed with the cultural élite. At one of the Bandler's new year parties there were fifty or sixty people, and it was a very eclectic crowd. It included 'People from the New Theatre, and from the Labor Party, the Communist Party, and the Schubert Society, from the Bartok Society'. What Faith embodied was the complete rupture of the seemingly cast-iron nexus between class and race. Her performance in Townsville was illustrative of her impact. The ladies of the town were astonished by Faith's bourgeois polish and felt reassured about her leading role in the referendum campaign. For Bobbi Sykes there was a different but still dramatic lesson. In a flash, she recalled, 'all the negative stereotypes of Blacks were smashed down. I had always secretly hoped that it was possible for Blacks to rise above the level at which they were kept in Townsville—and suddenly I knew it was possible!'[8]

Faith was the consummate player of what Marilyn calls coalition politics, which characterised the middle years of the twentieth century. It was a time when white humanitarians were still heavily represented among those fighting for Aboriginal rights. They had done so for generations but, increasingly, Aborigines and Torres Strait Islanders began to infiltrate the movement; this, she explains, 'brought together a real diversity of people', including 'Aboriginal and non-Aboriginal, men and women, university graduates and

---

7   Roberta Sykes, *Snake Dancing* (Sydney Allen & Unwin, 1998), 108.
8   Sykes, 89.

early school leavers, Christians and Communists, members of the Labor Party and trade unionists, working-class and middle-class people'.

One of Faith's talents as an organiser was that she could 'converse with people across these differences of race and class'.[9] She was also able to ameliorate the continuing tensions between the movement's left and right wings, which were sharply aggravated by the Cold War and the unceasing surveillance of ASIO. Research by scholars in recent years has uncovered just how persistent was the infiltration of FCAATSI and kindred organisations. Faith's history of close association with prominent communists made her a suspect fellow traveller but also enabled her to gain the support of still-powerful trade unions. And her charm and exquisite manners disarmed many potential critics, who found it hard to think of her as a subversive.

The most significant development during the era of coalition politics was the establishment of the Federal Council of Aboriginal Affairs in Adelaide in 1958. It was the first such national organisation and soon after became known as FCAATSI (Federal Council for the Advancement of Aborigines and Torres Straits Islanders). Men dominated the leadership positions although, as Marilyn noted, Jessie Street had hoped that Faith would be appointed the national president. She became the New South Wales state secretary, and both she and her Queensland counterpart, Kath Walker (later Oodgeroo Noonuccal), emerged as leading spokespersons for the federal referendum campaign.

The spectacularly successful referendum result of 1967 was Faith's most enduring legacy. Many people have written about it before, but Marilyn's account of the campaign itself and the consequences that followed is hard to beat. The focus on Faith's role helps but so too does the deft handling of the attendant politics, both local and international. The problem most keenly understood by Jessie Street was that it was essential to insist on Australia's conformity with the principles embodied in the Universal Declaration of Human Rights and to establish the fact that Indigenous Australians were members of minority groups as defined in international law. Two steps were essential. Australia needed a national organisation to promote Indigenous rights. It also required a constitutional referendum to allow the federal government to assume responsibility for policies and attendant funding. The creation of FCAATSI responded to the first part of the problem. A constitutional referendum was a much more challenging task, requiring a

---

9   Lake, *Faith*, 73.

powerful campaign to convince the federal government to hold one in the first place and then a crusade, effective and widespread enough to overcome the inbuilt barriers to a successful outcome.

Marilyn appreciated the key role played by Jessie Street in initiating the campaign for constitutional change. Like many feminists of her generation Street was an internationalist. She had significant colleagues in the British Anti-Slavery Society, an organisation that continued to have international standing, and the United Nations. Despite her reputation as a fellow traveller she also retained her high social status, which provided her with important local contacts and the patrician self-confidence to access them. She discussed her ideas for constitutional change with Commander Fox-Pitt, the secretary of the Anti-Slavery Society, and with Paul Hasluck, at the time Minister for Territories. Having drafted her petition, Jessie gave it to Faith confident that her young protégé would carry the campaign forward. But initially Faith was not sure what to do with it and carried it about in her handbag for a couple of weeks because she was ashamed that she did not understand what it was about.

The campaign of persuasion took nearly ten years from 1957 to 1967. FCCATSI assumed the leading role, launching a second petition, 'Towards Equal Citizenship for Aborigines', in 1962. As the campaign intensified it drew on supporters from all over the country. But Faith became, for many, the face and the voice of the crusade. She also did much of the grinding detailed work of organisation in between countless addresses to public meetings and appearances on television and radio. In an important passage of the biography Marilyn asks: Why did Faith identify with the campaign so strongly? What was her personal investment? Her answer is a key passage in the book. 'It is helpful in thinking about this', she observed,

> to remember the emotional bases of powerful political mobilizations. For Faith, the fight to alter the Constitution was a fight for the inclusion of Blacks in the Australian nation on equal terms with Whites. "Let's tell the world there's only One Australian", she proclaimed in an interview with the *Australian Women's Weekly*, "and colour doesn't matter at all".[10]

The referendum held on 27 May 1967 was a triumph, with just under 91 per cent of the electorate voting yes. Marilyn's view is that Faith's role was pre-eminent and it had transformed her into a national celebrity. In

---

10   Lake, *Faith*, 114.

the work of persuasion, in mobilising public opinion, in changing hearts and minds, 'Faith played a key role'. Her magnetism as a speaker and media performer—'together with her sheer persistence—were vital to the successful outcome of the campaign'.[11] But the overall significance of the consequent constitutional change has been much disputed and with it the assessment of Faith's legacy. The actual changes made to the Constitution appeared to add little to Aboriginal political rights. But, as anyone who remembers the campaign will know, the overwhelming vote indicated the desire of the great majority to welcome Indigenous Australians and accord them equal status as members of the Australian nation. The significance of section 127, as Marilyn explained, 'related not to Aborigines' rights as citizens of the state but to their status as national subjects, as members of the imagined community'.[12] But beyond that there was the 'increased discursive power Aboriginal people were able to wield as a result of becoming a national constituency'.[13] As an acute observer of the American scene, she was also able to compare the Aboriginal situation with that of the 550 recognised Indian nations, which have 'no representative voice in the national capital and, relatedly, hardly any presence in the national media'. 'Their impact on public life, national culture and the writing of American history has been minimal.'[14] And the interesting fact is that it was the Civil Rights Movement that influenced Australia, not the political activities of native Americans whose situation had more in common objectively with those of the Indigenous activists who burst onto the political stage in the late sixties and early seventies. These activists are the subject of a perceptive analysis by Marilyn in a chapter called 'The Ambiguities of Black Power'. While important in themselves, they also had a dramatic impact on Faith Bandler's career stripping her, both suddenly and dramatically, of her capacity to influence the course of events in black politics.

Marilyn turns next to the ways, from the mid-1960s, that race relations in Australia began to be transformed by a new confidence in being Black and Aboriginal. The challenge for Aboriginal rights campaigns, 'was to secure recognition for racial/cultural difference as a positive value—and to heed the demand of Aboriginal people to speak in their own voice and elect their own leaders. Self-respect demanded self-determination'.[15]

---

11   Lake, *Faith*, 85.
12   Lake, *Faith*, 67.
13   Lake, *Faith*, 84.
14   Lake, *Faith*, 85.
15   Lake, *Faith*, 120.

Both Faith and FCAATSI itself found it increasingly difficult to deal with the new emerging politics. The 1970 Easter FCAATSI Conference was tumultuous and ended with a devastating split that foreshadowed its eventual demise. Faith's long crusade to lead a movement inspired by the slogan 'black and whites together' had run into trouble. As Marilyn observed, Faith had been inspired by the black power movement, which, as for many others, was 'empowering and constitutive of their political identities'.[16] But the emergent distinction between Indigenous and non-Indigenous became far more important. Faith was often thought to be Aboriginal. Very few Australians were even aware of the existence of the Islander communities, which were concentrated, as we have seen, in a few quite distinct regions in coastal Queensland and the Northern Rivers region of New South Wales. Once her lack of Aboriginal ancestry was realised, Faith's opportunities for employment, even for preferment, were radically diminished. Her influence melted away. It was not just her Islander heritage that handicapped her, however, but also her class. Her lifestyle, along with her tastes and personal style, were far removed from the experience of the new generation of Aboriginal leaders who had grown up in fringe camps, bleak, impoverished institutions, inner city slums or actually on the streets.

Marilyn traces Faith's return to her Islander identity. The communities were in an invidious position. They were excluded from the special benefits that had become available to Aborigines and Torres Strait Islanders as a result of the 1967 referendum. But, as a black minority, they had suffered from the same discrimination and hostility as Indigenous families in a militant white Australia. And, just as history became of central importance to Aborigines, Faith began a journey to retrieve Islander history and to flesh out the stories she had heard as a child from her father and other elderly relatives. Here Marilyn skilfully negotiates a narrow and delicate path among contending interpretations of the history of the labour trade. The position Faith adopted was common among members of the Australian Islander diaspora. Their ancestors had been kidnapped by force or fraud and had been treated like slaves. A bevy of Pacific historians now depict a much more complex picture, with young men shipping voluntarily for Queensland and many of them choosing to return or to stay in Australia. A major point was that the trade changed significantly over the years. Pressure from the Imperial government forced many reforms on the Queensland government, and the Islanders themselves came to know and understand how the

---

16   Lake, *Faith*, 152.

trade worked. The complicating fact was that Islanders who remained in Australia after the mass deportation in 1906 had clearly been determined not to return to the Islands. But in all the extensive debate about this trade there was little recognition of the much more brutal and totally unregulated trade in Aboriginal men and women on the internal, land frontier.

The deft discussion in *Faith* of the historiography of the Pacific Island labour trade illustrates Marilyn's capacity to bring together analysis and narrative, to deal with, and give equal attention to, the life and the times. In dealing with Faith's pivotal role in the evolution of race relations during the middle years of the twentieth century Marilyn provides the reader with sharp insight into the complex political forces at work. But the story of Faith's life obviously takes precedence and that creates its own problems of selection and emphasis. In particular, writing the life commissioned by, and benignly watched over, by the subject herself brings with it demands on the author's tact and discretion. Marilyn clearly admired Faith. But the book is a judicious study and not a hagiography. By the time we reach the conclusion we realise that Marilyn's admiration arose not just from Faith's participation in a multitude of public events but from the ideas and the spirit that sustained her. At the end of the book she reminds us that Faith knew at first hand 'the disabling pain of racial discrimination' but was able to overcome her personal sorrow by translating it into political activism—'into the demand that all human beings be treated with dignity and respect'. In a final moving peroration Marilyn sums up Faith's legacy:

> Her achievements in helping to bring about political and social change was considerable. Now as we look back over the last century and contemplate the challenges of the next one, Faith's example of moral courage and community leadership shines forth like a beacon in a long winter night.[17]

We are left with the inescapable thought that Faith chose wisely at that conference in Sydney in August 1998. She had found both a biographer and a kindred spirit.

---

17   Lake, *Faith*, 209.

Chapter 13

MUSLIMS IN AUSTRALIA

Beyond Narratives of Pioneers and Aliens

Samia Khatun

I first met Marilyn exactly ten years ago. It was at my very first academic conference and it was held at the University of Melbourne in November 2006, titled 'Historicising Whiteness: Transnational Perspectives on the Construction of an Identity'. Towards the end of the conference I asked a question that had been bothering me over the three days: why on earth is no one talking about the role of academic *history* itself in the production of white subjectivities in Australia? Immediately afterwards, on her way to the podium to deliver a paper on W.E.B. Du Bois, Marilyn passed me and said: 'That's a really really good question. You should try and answer it'. It was an invitation to contest Australian history. Today, I want to pick up that dialogue that I began with Marilyn over a decade ago. It is a conversation we have continued in various ways as I worked on my forthcoming book, *Australianama: The South Asian Odyssey in Australia*. Put simply, it is a history of South Asians in Australia during the period 1860–1930, told through non-English language sources.

While some of my questions have changed since then, I have repeatedly returned to the role of history books in the production of human ontologies. History books after all teach us to travel imaginatively through time. In training audiences to travel between the present and the past, historical storytelling can induct publics into axes of temporal movement connecting past, present and future. Particularly as I worked with texts from South Asian knowledge systems and Australian Aboriginal historiographical traditions, my question was in a sense inverted: How do we write histories that do not just reproduce white subjectivities? If history books play a key role in the production of white subjectivities, surely they can be harnessed to the task of the making of non-white subjectivities. As we have been reflecting, Marilyn's scholarship has been crucial in bringing gender relations to the very centre of Australian pasts—a process that has sought to restructure the architecture of historical storytelling itself. In a somewhat parallel vein, *Australianama* was a project that began by trying to narrate the past from the standpoints of people always on the margins of the Australian nation. But it has ended up arguing for the placement of what I would call knowledge-relations at the very centre of enquiries into the past. Here I refer to that tricky relationship between the knower and the known, the historian and the archive or, put even more simply, the relation between a reader and a text—that dynamic relationship that Jorge Luis Borges described as the 'waking dream' of reading.[1] Over the following pages, I will illustrate what I mean by sketching out my own relationship to a particular history book: a Bengali-language text that remains today at a nineteenth-century mosque in the inland Australian town of Broken Hill.

The book I am referring to begins with an account of creation. Around 1268 BS on the Bengali San calendar, or 1861 CE on the Common Era calendar, poet Munshi Rezaulla wrote that history began with the creation of a 'concealed pen and a tablet'.[2] Rezaulla was a poet living in a village in the Hugli district of Bengal—a region today in contemporary India. According to him, a hidden creator used a hidden pen to write seven seas and seven heavens into existence.[3] And, as trees grew into forests, a fist full of dust fleetingly became an earthen statue, and then took the living, breathing shape of Adam.[4] The pages of verse that follow tell the stories of prophets from Adam to Muhammad, from creation to the sixth year on the Hijri calendar (H) of Muslim temporality. This text, which remains in Broken Hill today, is particularly hard to make sense of if we attempt to use the categories that English-language historians today have inherited from British colonial thought. It switches between three different entwined temporalities, it is both 'Indic' and 'Islamic', and it is a printed book that was penned for the purposes of oral performance in front of a gathered

---

1   Jorge Luis Borges, 'Foreword for Leopold Legunes', in *Collected Fictions*, trans. Andrew Hurley (New York & London: Penguin Books, 1999), 291.
2   Kazi Sofiuddin, *Kasasol Ambia* (Calcutta: Hanifia Press, 1895), 3. All translations from Bengali to English are by Samia Khatun unless otherwise stated.
3   Sofiuddin, 5.
4   Sofiuddin, 3.

audience. Nevertheless, however else we might describe the text, it is definitely a book of popular history.

In the 1960s, a century after Munshi Rezaulla put pen to paper, a group of local historians in Broken Hill found Rezaulla's best-selling poetry in the yard of a disused mosque built in the 1880s.[5] It is one of the best preserved of the mosques built during the era of the camel industry between the 1860s and 1930s, when camel transportation formed the arteries of inland mobility in arid Australia. These mosques were built by the South Asian camel owners and workers who are known in Australian vernacular today as the 'Afghans'.

Whilst restoring the Broken Hill mosque in the 1960s, members of the Broken Hill Historical Society labelled the 500-page book as 'the Holy Koran' in English, and placed it inside the mosque. Since then, four different historians have labelled this book as a Quran.[6] In July 2009, when I travelled to Broken Hill, I read the first few pages. These revealed that it was actually a 500-page book of Bengali Sufi poetry translated from Persian into Bengali. The text bears the title *Kasasol Ambia* (Stories of the Prophets). Detailed with the rich imagery of Sufi poetry, it was an instant bestseller in Bengal. The copy that remains in Broken Hill today is an eighth edition and was published in 1895 CE/1301 BS in Calcutta.

The presence of a copy of *Kasasol Ambia* in Broken Hill raises a number of questions. Why have Australian historians mislabelled this text repeatedly? What role can the stories and temporalities that people brought with them to Australian shores play in the histories we write about them? Are colonised peoples' history books of relevance to how we write histories of South Asian diaspora today? If this mosque was built by the camel drivers from Afghanistan, how did a book from Bengal get to Broken Hill? The Bengal delta is not a region known for camels.

---

5   'The Broken Hill Mosque', Information Pamphlet by Ralph Wallace, Item 3, Mosque Records, Broken Hill Historical Society.

6   'The Broken Hill Mosque'. In 1965, A.F. Tylee described the book as 'a translation into the national language of East Pakistan of the Holy Koran' in Mosque Records, Broken Hill Historical Society—see A.F. Tylee, *The Mosque of the Camel-Men* (1965); Christine Stevens' book includes a picture of *Kasasol Ambia* and labels it a Quran—see Stevens, *Tin Mosques & Ghantowns: A History of Afghan Cameldrivers in Australia* (Alice Springs: Paul Fitzsimons, 2002), 84b, 100a; in a Bangladeshi magazine, Australian historian Nahid Kabir from the University of Western Australia likewise referred to the book in Broken Hill as 'translated copy of the Holy Quran'—see Nahid Kabir, 'A History of Muslims in Australia', *Star Weekend Magazine*, 7 September 2007.

Pioneers and aliens

The Australian historians who have mislabelled the *Kasasol Ambia* have structured their accounts of South Asian diaspora around a quite different set of problems. Theirs are works that remain tethered to the dominating question 'were they pioneers, or were they aliens?'—ultimately a question of national border-drawing. Within this tedious mode of thinking, historians never actually ask complex questions about texts such as the *Kasasol Ambia*, systematically transforming dynamic forms of knowledge into dead objects that belong in the 'traditional' past rather then the 'modern' future. To loosen the grip of national border on the questions we ask of archival materials, here I will be using a map showing the Australian mainland in a wider Asia Pacific context. In 1848, Sir Thomas Mitchell, the surveyor general of the British Colony of New South Wales, imagined the slice of the Indian Ocean stretching from South Asia to the Australian colonies as 'the Indian Archipelago'.[7] While this naming did not take hold in settler colonial imaginations, the geography Mitchell's map depicted (see below) was one through which increasing numbers of South Asians began to circulate during the era of camel transportation in Australia.

In the pioneers vs aliens literature on South Asians that narrates the history of the camel industry, the *Kasasol Ambia* at Broken Hill has been repeatedly mislabelled. This reveals something very useful; a crucial part of the insertion of South Asian diaspora into settler narratives of nation-building is the erasure of the stories that they brought with them—the stories that *they* used to make sense of where they had come from and where they were going. I propose that paying closer attention to books like this offers us *one* way out of the accounts of inclusion and exclusion in which diasporic peoples remain trapped in national history books and, more broadly, Anglophone public discourse. So, on a winter day in 2009, as a bitter dust storm was underway outside, I sat down in the mosque at Broken Hill and began to read the *Kasasol Ambia*, deciphering characters I had not read since about the age of eight when I left Bangladesh. It soon became clear that this book is embedded in an entirely different knowledge-system—where knowledge itself operates quite differently from the subject/object divide structuring Enlightenment epistemes.

---

7   Thomas Livingstone Mitchell, *Journal of an Expedition into the Interior of Tropical Australia, in Search of a Route from Sydney to the Gulf of Carpentaria* (London: Longman, Brown, Green and Longmans, 1848), Appendix.

Thomas Mitchell's Map of the 'Indian Archipelago'
'Map 1: The Indian Archipelago' appears in Appendix to Thomas Livingstone Mitchell,
*Journal of an Expedition into the Interior of Tropical Australia,
in Search of a Route from Sydney to the Gulf of Carpentaria*,
London: Longman, Brown, Green and Longmans, 1848

That the stories in the *Kasasol Ambia* were operating according to a schema of knowledge-relations quite distinct from Enlightenment thought was increasingly evident as my literacy in Bengali improved gradually over time. While for a long time I thought that I had found the book in Broken Hill, thereby rescuing it from obscurity, I eventually realised it was *as if* the book had revealed itself to me, binding me into a curious game of revelation and concealment as I slowly learnt to understand the imagery and metaphors it contains. As South Asian cultural historian Aditya Behl writes, a Sufi text is best treated as a sentient being that scripts you into narratives. It is 'aware of misguided attempts at classification and mapping, and resists them successfully, instead positing its own rhetorical enterprise as a form into which the reader/listener is invited, imprinting this form on the reader's consciousness'.[8]

The poet of the *Kasasol Ambia* actually theorises this form of knowledge in an autobiographical section, using a very dense metaphor of a pen. Never having written a book of poetry before, Rezaulla opens his metaphor with the question 'into what form (*rupa*) will I translate'? Realising 'whatever, whoever is searching, to them the protector gives. Placing faith in this hope, I jumped into the sea'.[9] Hewing close to the metaphors of Sufi texts, his body immersed in water evokes the imagery of a pen immersed in an inkwell. Rezaulla wrote 'searching for pearls, I began threading a chain. I named the garland Kasasol Ambia'.[10]

As my Bengali literacy improved, I continued to come across elaborate metaphors contained in the *Kasasol Ambia* that dramatised the poetry's ties to an episteme underpinned by the logic that whatever and whomever you set out in search of, you will find. As I began to wonder whether this was a logic that I could harness to the service of historical research into South Asians in Australia, my relationship to archival materials transformed significantly. My historical methodology came to be structured around a very particular search: who was the Bengali reader who brought the *Kasasol Ambia* from Bengal to Broken Hill, and what was the route s/he travelled across a vast ocean and deserts? These were questions that generated a multiplicity of answers that posed significant challenges to the existing historiography on South Asians in Australia.

---

[8] Wendy Doniger (ed.), *The Magic Doe: Qutban Suhravardī's Mirigāvatī, A New Translation*, trans. Aditya Behl (New York: Oxford University Press, 2012), 30.
[9] Sofiuddin, 6.
[10] Sofiuddin, 6.

Five plausible answers

Could the *Kasasol Ambia* have arrived in Broken Hill with one of the spiritual guides, or mullahs who accompanied the camel merchants? In Australian historiography, it has long been claimed that the most powerful South Asians in the Australian camel industry were from the desert regions of what is today Afghanistan, Pakistan and Northern India. However, searching archives for camel-trading routes connecting Calcutta and Broken Hill revealed an entire trajectory of the trade that is systematically omitted from Australian history books. Mirza Khan was a bookbinder and spiritual leader from Calcutta patronised by one of the most powerful camel owners in Broken Hill. Following Mirza Khan's travels from Calcutta to the Australian colonies and from mosque to inland mosque reveals that many South Asian merchants engaged in the Australian camel trade had in fact been based in Bengal for generations. Tracing their genealogy to Afghanistan centuries earlier reveals that they were part of the community sometimes known as the Afghans of Bengal. However, in step with developments in wider imperial politics, after the drawing of the Durand Line in 1893 demarcating the imperial–national boundary between British India and Afghanistan, the merchants operating between Calcutta and the Australian colonies increasingly began asserting their direct connections to the nation-state of Afghanistan, omitting Bengal from their pasts. The result was that, by the late 1890s, the most powerful South Asians in Broken Hill were themselves effacing Calcutta from the histories they told about themselves. If the *Kasasol Ambia* arrived in Broken Hill with Mirza Khan along camel tracks, it circulated with another story of Afghani nationalism that powerfully shaped how South Asians narrated their past.

Could the *Kasasol Ambia* have arrived in Broken Hill with a sailor? It is now well documented that many Australian shipping companies, like British and European firms, employed South Asians as *lascars*—a term describing the non-white sailors from across the Indian Ocean rim who were contracted at wages significantly lower than those of white sailors. Following Bengali seafarers from Calcutta to Australian ports reveals that in 1896, a few months after the eighth edition of the *Kasasol Ambia* was published in Bengal, the *SS Darius* (owned by a Melbourne-based company) departed from Calcutta for Australian ports with a crew of Bengali *lascars*. On arrival to Port Adelaide, fourteen striking South Asian *lascars* disembarked from the vessel to protest against their working conditions. Anno Khan was one of two sailors who managed to evade customs police, escaping across Jervois Bridge into Adelaide and then into the inland areas. While it cannot be conclusively proved that a copy of *Kasasol Ambia* crossed Jervois bridge in Anno Khan's meagre bundle of belongings, it also cannot be conclusively proved that it did not.

Could the *Kasasol Ambia* have arrived at Broken Hill with a camel driver? Some of the camel drivers who came to be infamously well known at camel communication centres were actually workers contracted in Calcutta, despite being known as 'Afghans' in Australian settler vernacular and 'Abigana' in Aboriginal language archives. Sher Khan, for example, was a camel driver contracted at Calcutta whose failed romance created voluminous archives throughout Australian deserts not just in English, but also in Wangkangarru, Arabunna and Dhirrari—some of the Aboriginal languages spoken in the northern deserts of South Australia. Ben Murray, the son of an Aboriginal mother and a South Asian father, recounted a lengthy story featuring Sher Khan in Dhirarri.[11] As Ben Murray told it in 1980, Sher Khan was a camel driver based in the town of Broken Hill who fell in love with a young woman in the town of Marree—another camel communication centre. While closely examining Aboriginal language accounts of Sher Khan across over seven decades cannot conclusively prove whether a copy of *Kasasol Ambia* was circulating with him, it does offer insight into the workings of Aboriginal historiographical traditions.

Could the *Kasasol Ambia* have arrived in Broken Hill with a hawker? From the eastern ports of Brisbane, Melbourne, Sydney and Adelaide, many Bengali textiles traders built livelihoods selling their wares along the Murray-Darling—a circuit shaped by the topography of eastern Australia.[12] Selling textiles embroidered in the intricate decorative style known as 'chikan', these hawkers whom Australian authorities called 'chikanwallahs' distributed textiles to 'interior towns' along the Murray-Darling system.[13] Abdul Sattar was one of the many chikanwallahs from Bengal who arrived in Australian ports as a *lascar* and worked his way inland hawking textiles, leaving a trace in local historical records in Broken Hill.

Could the *Kasasol Ambia* have arrived to Broken Hill with a woman? Australian historiography about South Asian diaspora is underpinned

---

11   Peter Austin, Luise Hercus, and Philip Jones, 'Ben Murray (Parlku-Nguyu-Thangknyiwarna)', *Aboriginal History* 12 (1988): 145–56.

12   Annette Potts, '"I am a British subject, and I can go wherever the British flag flies": Indians on the Northern Rivers of New South Wales during the Federation Years', *Journal of the Royal Australian Historical Society* 83 (2) (1997): 105.

13   'East Indian Natives in Melbourne', *Age*, 15 June 1885, 5.

by the assumption that South Asian women did not circulate the Indian Ocean, let alone travel throughout Australian interiors. However, searching shipping records for a woman who may have brought the *Kasasol Ambia* from Calcutta to Broken Hill reveals that South Asian women did travel. The largest group of South Asian women arriving on Australian shores were *ayahs*—the domestic servants who accompanied the many white families moving from British India to the Australian colonies. In addition to the constant steady trickle of South Asian *ayahs*, many South Asian merchants arrived accompanied by their wives.[14] As the 1895 edition of *Kasasol Ambia* was circulating though Bengal, for example, 23-year-old Dowlah departed Calcutta for the Australian colonies accompanying her husband and 5-year-old son.[15] The week that Dowlah arrived in Sydney, a debate was underway about the granting of hawkers' licenses to 'female hawkers', confirming that some women were working peddling goods.[16] As the memoirs of Aboriginal writer Ruby Langford Ginibi confirm, South Asian women were present along the Richmond River in inland New South Wales. Reminiscing about her childhood, she recalls that 'we used to row across here to buy lollies from an old Indian woman called Mrs Singh who had a caravan with wheels that was pulled along by a draughthorse'.[17]

Theorising the search

While the reader with whom the *Kasasol Ambia* travelled to the Australian interior remained concealed from view, the search for her or him revealed contours of the architecture of South Asian Muslim knowledge spanning the Indian Ocean during the era of the Australian camel industry. Together they added up to a larger circuit of stories moving across the slice of the Indian Ocean that Thomas Mitchell described as the Indian Archipelago (see Map). It was when my literacy in non-European historiographical discourses began improving that I truly began to understand the implications of what I was doing.

---

14 This is suggested by a photograph of Ashan Bibi and her daughters in 'Ashan Bibi [Also Known as Begum]' (Sydney, 18 April 1929), SP42/1, C1928/10724, National Archives of Australia.
15 Passenger List of *SS Lalpoora*, October 1896, Passengers Arriving 1855–1922, NRS13278, [X242-243] reel 535, Shipping Master's Office, State Records Authority of New South Wales.
16 'Syrians and the Aliens Bill. Female Hawkers', *Sunday Times*, 25 October 1896, 5.
17 Ruby Langford Ginibi, *Real Deadly* (Sydney: Angus & Robertson, 1992), 75.

Let me illustrate with a closer look at the pen with which Munshi Rezaulla claimed that history itself began in the first few pages of the *Kasasol Ambia*. Tracing the genealogy of this pen to a larger discourse of Muslim historiography illuminates the extended architecture of thought to which the poets of the *Kasasol Ambia* claimed a genealogy. I am talking about *ta'rikh*—a historiographical discourse that British imperial forms of knowledge sought to displace in the context of British India. Within South Asian historiography, it is well documented that British colonial regimes comprised a major epistemic invasion into South Asian legal, medical, philosophical and historiographical discourses. British assertions of the superiority of colonisers' knowledge traditions over those of the colonised is perhaps best captured through the figure of Thomas Babington Macaulay, law member in the Indian civil service and influential historian of British nation-building. As Macaulay infamously pronounced in his 1835 Minute on Education, 'a single shelf of a good European library was worth the whole native literature of India and Arabia'.[18]

While Macaulay's Minute marked the beginning of a new era of colonial education that sought to sever élite South Asians from non-European knowledge traditions, the publication of the *Kasasol Ambia* confirms the ongoing popularity and reach of the historiographical traditions that pre-date the rise of European colonial power across the Indian Ocean. With Muslim historical storytelling circulating across the Indian Ocean world since the inception of Islam, scholars today agree that historian Al-Tabari (d. 923 CE) was one of the founding writers in the *ta'rikh* genre of historiography. Writing in tenth-century Baghdad Tabari penned a forty-volume history titled *The History of the Prophets and the Kings*, laying some of the important foundations for the *ta'rikh* genre of storytelling about the past.

Tabari's account of the very first pen highlights some of the methodologies for making truth claims that underpin the *ta'rikh* discourse within which the *Kasasol Ambia* can be situated. Tabari writes that the angel Gibril (Gabriel) said to Muhammad 'the first (thing) created by Allah is the Pen! Allah said to it Write!, and it proceeded at that very hour to (write) whatever is going to be'.[19] In supporting this claim, Tabari cites that Yunus heard

---

18 Minute on Education by Thomas Macaulay (1835), reproduced in Martin Moir and Lynn Zastoupil (eds), *The Great Indian Education Debate: Documents Relating To the Orientalist-Anglicist Controversy, 1781–1843* (Richmond, Surrey: Curzon, 1999), 162–73.

19 Franz Rosenthal, *The History of Al-Tabari, Vol. 1: General Introduction and From the Creation to the Flood* (New York: SUNY Press, 1989), 198.

it from Abdallah who heard it from Muawiyah who heard it from Ayyub who heard it from his father Walid who heard it from his father Ubadah who heard it from Muhammad.[20] Recounting this chain of transmission, Tabari constructs what is known as an *isnad*—a footnoting strategy that underpins truth claims in Muslim historiography. Using slightly different phrasing, next Tabari writes 'The first thing created by Allah is the Pen. Allah commanded it to write everything',[21] supporting this statement with another *isnad*. In his history of the first pen, Tabari lays out ten different chains of transmission, each *isnad* leading back to Muhammad's revelations.

This is followed by a collection of *isnad* claiming that Muhammad said that the first thing created was not the pen, but rather a 'throne'. Next there is a section on all the *isnad* that claim that 'light and dark' were the first entities created. At the end of Tabari's discussion of the debates surrounding the first object no conclusion is reached about whether the first object ever created was the pen, the throne, or light and dark—the reader is expected to come to her own conclusion. However, in collating multiple *isnad* about the first object, Tabari's *History* gives us a detailed picture of the various routes along which manuscripts containing ideas and stories travelled from seventh-century Mecca to tenth-century Baghdad.

In *Australianama*, I argue that the five plausible 'what ifs' that I have presented here can be likened to series of *isnad*—or chains of transmission. It is a collation of the routes along which we *know* for certain that stories, ideas and people, if not a copy of *Kasasol Ambia*, travelled from Bengal to Broken Hill. Together this collection of possible truth-chains tells a much richer history then any singular, definitive route. What I am playing with here is the possibility of locating contemporary history writing within non-European methodologies for claiming historical facticity. I am not trying to suggest here that Tabari's tenth-century use of *isnad* remained unchanged or that Muslim historiography was unalterd by the late nineteenth century CE. However, I do want to suggest that today we *can* read, extend, respond to, and creatively engage and claim continuity with, intellectual traditions that are not those of the colonisers. The purpose is not just to study colonised peoples and the texts they produced, but actually to think using the categories and methodologies of thought that imperial regimes sought and still seek to displace and destroy.

---

20   Tabari identifies each of these transmitters by placing them within a male lineage. See Rosenthal, 198.
21   Rosenthal, 199.

The search for the reader of a book of Bengali Sufi poetry generated something extremely valuable: a rich archive of other non-English language texts that Australian historians simply do not quite know how to deal with—texts embedded in alternative systems of knowledge and operating within alternative philosophies of knowledge. *Australianama* is a history of Muslim South Asian diaspora around the archival base generated by this search. Each of the seven chapters is structured around a text that I came across during the initial search for the person who brought the Bengali book to Broken Hill. And each investigates the architecture of the apparently irrelevant epistemes rendered invisible in the pages of contemporary Australian history books.

Why operate in this mode of historical storytelling? What does it do that Australian history books currently cannot do? Well, first, it offers us an out from the 'pioneers and aliens' framework of storytelling that too often imprisons historical imagination. Second, I have outlined a mode of thinking that directly confronts some of the ways that Australian history books fail migrants today—in particular Muslim migrants. We need history books that tell us something about our own knowledge traditions. We need history books that set precedents for how to engage creatively with the intellectual traditions that colonial regimes have long deemed dead, backward, primitive etc. Particularly at a historical moment when Islam vs the West is the binary that underpins the imperialist logic of contemporary Anglo political regimes across the Indian Ocean rim, *Australianama* makes methodological arguments for strategies of knowledge production about South Asians, Islam and Muslims that sidestep the 'prisonhouse' of orientalist thought.[22]

The very fact that I am able to contribute to this publication is testament to the role that Marilyn Lake and a number of other Australian historians have played in teaching me how to contest Australian history. The snapshot of this project provided here follows a series of questions that it often felt like no one else was asking—questions that sometimes even seemed bizarre. Marilyn in one form or other has always been there saying, 'that's a good question. You should try and answer it'. I hope Australian publics beyond the community of historians will read *Australianama*, because I think it opens up powerful new ways to narrate the past and raises exciting new possibilities about the axes along which we can imagine the future. Since

---

22   Zakia Pathak, Saswati Sengupta, and Sharmila Purkayastha, 'The Prisonhouse of Orientalism', *Textual Practice* 5 (2) (June 1991): 195–218.

James Cook sailed into Botany Bay in the late eighteenth century, founding the Colony of New South Wales, countless settlers have approached Aboriginal geographies with a conviction of the superiority of European epistemologies. My challenge to Australian history is: we don't have to follow this path just because they did.

Chapter 14

TROUBLE IN WHITE AUSTRALIA

Marilyn Lake, Australian History and Asian Exclusion

Sophie Loy-Wilson

In 2001 I was about to vote in my first election when the Norwegian ship MV *Tampa* was refused entry to Christmas Island because aboard were 433 Afghani asylum seekers, rescued from a sinking fishing vessel. Arne Rinnan, the ship's captain, had planned to take the Afghanis back to Indonesia whence they had sailed, but some threatened to commit suicide if he did so. So he set a course for the Australian mainland where, again, he was refused permission to land. These events are now so familiar that they have lost some of their shock value, but I remember debate at the time was furious on all sides of politics.

The Afghanis wanted to be admitted as asylum seekers. Within days it became clear that a majority of Australians opposed their claims. After the Commonwealth government introduced a Border Protection Bill the Afghanis were taken to Nauru (a long-time focus of Australian imperial ambitions).[1] Prime Minister John Howard said: 'I believe that it is in Australia's national interest that we draw a line on what is increasingly becoming an uncontrollable number of illegal arrivals in this country', and that those rescued by the *Tampa* would not be allowed to land in Australia.[2] Australia was criticised for lacking compassion for international refugees

---

1   Victorian Council for Civil Liberties Incorporated v Minister for Immigration & Multicultural Affairs (& summary), FCA 1297 (11 September 2001).
2   John Howard, interview on Radio 3AW, Melbourne, 31 August 2001, *PM Transcripts: Transcripts from the Prime Ministers of Australia*, http://pmtranscripts.pmc.gov.au/release/transcript-12043.

who come by sea and for contravening the United Nations refugee convention ratified in 1954. But domestic support swung behind the government, which soon after was returned to power for a third term.

I was disoriented by the '*Tampa* election'—all explanations seemed to me unsatisfactory. Some commentators referred to Australian racism and nativism, and linked these attitudes to the effects of globalisation on Australia's economy; insecure workers at the margins of first-world societies, coupled with an increase in global migration from the third world, and competition for jobs generated fear and xenophobic nationalism. But what did this mean? How did ideas of race come to be used as expressions of white grievance? What were modern border politics and where had they come from? How did we get to a place where the right to dwell in Australia, and the first world more generally, was a right mostly reserved for those deemed white?

It was at university, in the years following *Tampa*, that I discovered historians blunting the edges of these questions, and followed their research, which injected an illuminating dye through themes of white supremacy, settler colonialism and global migration politics. This chapter charts how the work of Marilyn Lake became a guide through these questions. Lake took Australian race politics at the beginning of this century as a humanitarian challenge of urgent intellectual importance. Her work became a bright line for those seeking to understand Australian racism. At a time when fear of migrants in the West had become so widespread, she reminded me of racism's historical contingency; it did not have to be this way. Looking back, for example, on nineteenth-century Australian border politics from the perspective of *Tampa*, she exposed the racial ideas of the time for what they really were—confronting, extreme, bizarre—and in dire need of better historical explanation. 'The passionate claims made in the name of whiteness were extraordinary', she wrote.[3]

Lake insisted we see Australian racism as part of a larger transnational story, and she explained its twentieth-century emergence as a defensive measure.[4] White men under siege were violently protecting their privileges

---

3   Marilyn Lake, 'White is Wonderful: Emotional Conversion and Subjective Formation', in *Re-Orienting Whiteness*, eds Leigh Boucher, Jane Carey and Katherine Ellinghaus (New York: Palgrave Macmillan, 2009), 120.

4   Marilyn Lake, 'White Man's Country: The Transnational History of a Transnational Project', *Australian Historical Studies* 34 (122) (November 2003): 346–63, and 'From Mississippi to Melbourne via Natal: The Invention of the Literary Test as a Technology of Racial Exclusion', in *Connected Worlds: History in Transnational Perspective*, eds Ann Curthoys and Marilyn Lake (Canberra: ANU ePress, 2005), 209–31.

in the face of non-white activists demanding racial equality and, in the context of global Asian migration to the West, equal rights to mobility. Lake's founding fathers did not give birth to nations, they simply built higher legal and cultural fences, bunkering down against a new 'coloured' political consciousness that terrified them.[5] The 'whiteness' of White Australia, White Canada, White New Zealand had to be understood in a causal relationship with events in the non-west. The anxiety of whites in Australia 'was the anxiety of the colonial apprehending the emergence of a postcolonial world'.[6] Without these encounters between European and Asian peoples, Lake argued, the white-settler nation as a political entity might never have existed.[7] Her intervention led to perhaps the most radical recent challenge to Australian national history: the destabilising of established narratives of the rise of the West. For Lake this meant a shift away from Europe and towards the Asia–Pacific as a context for Australian historical thinking.[8]

Below I explore the consequences of Lake's challenge for my own work on Chinese–Australian history. I make two arguments. First, non-western perceptions of Australia need to be incorporated into mainstream Australian history. For example, Asian-language archives should be used to qualify a record that leans too far towards European intellectual traditions. Second, the periodisation of Australian history should be re-thought to reflect the agency of non-western peoples and events in the forging of the Australian nation. New work on the history of the Asia–Pacific has

---

5 Marilyn Lake 'Mission Impossible: How Men Gave Birth to the Australia Nation—Nationalism, Gender and Other Seminal Acts,' *Gender & History* 4 (3) (1992): 305–22, 'Looking to American Manhood: The Correspondence of Alfred Deakin and Josiah Royle', in *Reading Across the Pacific: Australia–United States Intellectual Histories*, eds Robert Dixon and Nicholas Bird (Sydney: Sydney University Press, 2010), 63–81, '"The Day Will Come": Charles H. Pearson's National Life and Character: A Forecast,' in *Ten Books that Shaped the British Empire: Creating an Imperial Commons*, eds Antoinette Burton and Isabel Hofmeyr (Durham NC: Duke University Press, 2014), 90–112.

6 Marilyn Lake, 'On Being a White Man, circa 1900', in *Cultural History in Australia*, eds Richard White and Hsu Ming Teo (Sydney: UNSW Press, 203), 102.

7 Marilyn Lake, 'The Chinese Empire Encounters the British Empire and Its "Colonial Dependencies": Melbourne, 1887', in Kate Bagnall and Sophie Couchman (eds), 'Special Issue: Chinese Representations in Australia from the mid-19th to the early 20th Century', *Journal of the Chinese Overseas* 9 (2) (2013): 178.

8 Marilyn Lake and Henry Reynolds, *Drawing the Global Colour Line: White Men's Countries and the International Challenge of Racial Equality* (Cambridge: Cambridge University Press, 2008). See also Sophie Loy-Wilson, 'New Directions in Chinese–Australian History', *History Australia* 11 (3) (2014): 233–8; Peter Hobbins and Alison Bashford, 'Rewriting Quarantine: Pacific History at Australia's Edge', *Australian Historical Studies* 46 (3) (September 2015): 392–409.

questioned the exceptional status frequently accorded to Europe in our histories and, in turn, has recast our understandings of the chronology of Australian history.[9] By expanding the boundaries of Australian history to include the archives and agency of Asia–Pacific peoples, we can forge a new historical consciousness in Australian public debate, one tied less to London and Washington, and more to the Asia–Pacific region.

The White Australia Policy as colour bar

In July 2017 the Australian government returned 3300 boxes of archival documents to Japan.[10] Australian officials had confiscated the documents from Japanese businesses during World War II at a time of heightened anti-Japanese feeling that saw over 4000 Japanese civilians placed in internment camps.[11] The documents included a paper trail of Japanese commercial enterprise in Australia since the nineteenth century: journals, catalogues, staff logs, mining minutes, shipping records—materials that show a history of flows, transfers, exchanges between Australia and Asia prior to war and internment, when ports such as Darwin and Broome had Japan communities. They proved what historians of Australia's north had already established; Australia's economic dependence on trade with and markets in Asia had a long history. It dated back at least to the nineteenth century, when Japanese, Arab, Malay, Tamil and Chinese traders dominated the bazaars and shipping routes of the region.[12]

---

9   See Tracey Banivanua Mar, 'Shadowing Imperial Networks: Indigenous Mobility and Australia's Pacific Past', *Australian Historical Studies* 46 (3) (September 2015): 340–55; Marilyn Lake, 'Histories Across Borders,' in *Australian History Now*, eds Anna Clark and Paul Ashton (Sydney: UNSW Press, 2013), 269–88.

10 Tom McIlroy, 'A Unique Gift: National Archives Hands Back Priceless Japanese Records', *Canberra Times*, 20 July 2017.

11 Christine Piper, 'Japanese Internment a Dark Chapter in Australian History', *Sydney Morning Herald*, 15 August 2014.

12 Marilyn Lake, 'Colonial Australia and the Asia Pacific Region', in *The Cambridge History of Australia, Volume 1: Indigenous and Colonial Australia*, eds Alison Bashford and Stuart Macintyre (Melbourne: Cambridge University Press, 2013), 535–60; Julia Martinez and Adrian Vickers, *The Pearl Frontier: Indonesian Labor and Indigenous Encounters in Australia's Northern Trading Network* (Honolulu: Hawai'i University Press, 2015); Claire Lowrie, *Masters and Servants: Cultures of Empire in the Tropics* (Manchester: Manchester University Press, 2016), and 'White "Men" and their Chinese "Boys": Sexuality, Masculinity and Colonial Power in Darwin and Singapore, 1880s–1930s', *History Australia* 10 (1) (April 2013): 35–57; Heather Goodall and Develeena Ghosh, 'Beyond the "Poison of Prejudice": Indian and Australian Women Talk about the White Australia Policy', *History Australia*

While the return of these archives to Japan may have been, in the words of National Archives Director-General David Fricker, a sign of 'enduring friendship' and a way of 'using these records as a cross-cultural cooperation', it was something else as well: a reminder of the war-time xenophobia that brought them to the attention of Australian authorities in the first place. As much as the cache of returned archives represents connections across cultures, it also testifies to the dark currents of racial chauvinism dividing the British Empire in the late nineteenth and early twentieth centuries when white colonial populations moved to block Asian migration. In Australia, the laws enacted under the banner of the *Immigration Restriction Act 1901*, which became known as the White Australia Policy, amounted to a colour bar. This bar remained in place for over sixty years and its legacy continues in Australian immigration policy to this day.

Australia's relationship with the Asia Pacific has been defined by the existence of this colour bar. The Australian nation state was, in Marilyn Lake's words, 'inaugurated in 1901 in a radical act of racial expulsion', and in this seminal act Australia defined itself through a rejection of the Asian region and its peoples.[13] The new Commonwealth of Australia produced a package of legislation through the *Immigration Restriction Act 1901* to mark the racial boundaries of its new political community. It 'prohibited the entry into Australia of any person who, when asked to do so, failed to write out and sign in the presence of an officer, a passage of fifty words in length in a European language'.[14] Australia's decision to introduce a colour bar contravened Britain's international treaties, including with Japan, forcing politicians to cloak their intent, stopping just short of banning non-white immigrants.

White Australia was the culmination of decades of colonial-era legislation. The Australian colony of Victoria was probably the first place in the world to pass legislation making explicit provision for racial discrimination as the basis for immigration restriction following the arrival of tens

---

12 (1) (April 2015):116–40; Regina Ganter, 'Turning the Map Upside Down', *Griffith Review* 9, 'Special Issue: Up North, Threats & Enchantment', 2005, https://griffithreview.com/articles/turning-the-map-upside-down/.

13 Lake, 'On Being a White Man', 101.

14 https://www.legislation.gov.au/Details/C1901A00017, accessed 2 March 2018. By 1905, after representations by the Japanese, the Act was made to seem less racist by dropping a requirement that it should be a European language. In fact, in the Act 'language operated as a replacement for race'. See Jon Stratton, 'The Colour of Jews: Jews, Race and the White Australia Policy', *Journal of Australian Studies* 20 (50–51) (1996): 56.

of thousands of Chinese gold-seekers in the 1850s.[15] Other states quickly followed suit. The federal Act took into account the specific contingencies of each state. Included in the 1901 Act was the *Pacific Islands Labourers Act*, 'which required the Pacific Islanders, or "Kanakas", who have been brought to labour in the Queensland sugar-cane plantations in the late nineteenth century to be deported'.[16] To supply workers for a white population in Queensland, plantation owners had kidnapped and coerced Pacific islanders, depleting nearby islands of their male population. Now they were to be forced out, the first in a series of removals designed *post factum* to both 'whiten' a multi-racial Australian population and assert white colonial rule.

Marilyn Lake pored over debates over the *Immigration Restriction Act 1901*, combing through parliamentary papers, newsprint, and personal archives of politicians. She read the Act in the context of Australia's federal decade, a time when political discussion was suffused with the grand idea that Australia was a social laboratory for the world, a site of radical political experiments and a frontier for new democratic thinking and living. This was, after all, a country in which the world's first basic wage would be introduced in 1907 and the first maternity allowance in 1912, albeit excluding 'women who are Asiatics, or who are Aboriginal natives of Australia, Papua or the islands of the Pacific'.[17] It was also a country gripped by a powerful sense of threat caused by the defeat of Russia by Japan in 1905, the rise of Japan as a world power and Japanese diplomatic manoeuvering for racial equality.

Lake discovered that the practicalities of implementing the Act were left unclear, and the Act itself would later be called 'bad law' owing to its ambiguity. As a technology of border control, the literacy test that underwrote it allowed Australia's leaders to appease their British critics while secretly directing immigration officials to block the entry of non-white immigrants. Lake's research uncovered the remarkable moment Australia's Prime Minister, Alfred Deakin, writing anonymously to the *Morning Post* in London, outlined precisely what the White Australia Policy meant in practice: 'No white men are stopped at our ports for languages or any other

---

15   Marilyn Lake 'Chinese Colonists Assert their Common Human Rights: Cosmopolitanism as Subject and Method in History', *Journal of World History* 21 (3) (September 2010): 381.
16   Lake, 'On Being a White Man', 98.
17   Lake 'Mission Impossible', 306.

tests ... On the other hand all coloured men are stopped unless they come ... merely as visitors'.[18]

For a small nation in the Asia Pacific to pass laws that in effect blocked Asia–Pacific peoples from having any role in its national life—as workers, settlers, spouses, traders—was, as Lake wrote, a 'radical act of racial expulsion'. She formulated three powerful arguments to better explain this racialisation and, more specifically, why race emerged as the fundamental sorting category for territorial entitlement in the modern world. I have grouped these methodological innovations in order under three banners: feminist, transnational, cosmopolitan.

White Australia through a feminist lens

Lake's article 'Mission Impossible: How Men Gave Birth to the Australian Nation', published in 1992, contains a striking criticism of Benedict Anderson's canonical text *Imagined Communities* for overlooking the role of war and military cultures in the creation of nations, focusing instead on 'newspapers, vernacular languages and state bureaucracies'. In Lake's view, this omission:

> compounds the general blindness to gender dynamics that stops Anderson's analysis short, that prevents it from being as illuminating as it might have been. For Anderson never wonders whether men's anxiety about death and mortality and their need for comforting myths of continuity has anything to do with their being men.[19]

Writing from a country steeped in stories about men as frontiersmen, soldiers, statesmen, sportsmen, Lake was familiar with comforting stories told by men about men. She counted the cost to women: 'The discursive emphasis on freedom of men in frontier societies resulted in turn in a heightened perception of women's situation as one of isolation, vulnerability and defensiveness'.[20] Her research into labour history revealed a new female agency in a field written as 'a story of conflict between men'. In Lake's account, women in Australia's labour movement had ideas, men's policies did not

---

18 Marilyn Lake and Vanessa Pratt, '"Blood Brothers". Racial Identification and the Right to Rule: The Australian Response to the Spanish–American War', *Australian Journal of Politics and History* 54 (1) (February 2008): 27.
19 Lake, 'Mission Impossible', 311.
20 Marilyn Lake, 'Frontier Feminism and the Marauding White Man', *Journal of Australian Studies* 20 (49) (1996): 12.

go uncontested by women, and women's involvement in organised labour influenced the creation of the Australian welfare state.

Lake's innovation was to braid feminist theory, tried and tested in a self-consciously masculine historiography of Australian labour history, into the global history of race politics in ways that turned the orthodox explanations for colonial nation-building (some of those comforting stories) on their head. She argued strongly that masculinity was a social construction, a subjectivity that was both raced and gendered; much discursive work went into the making of the 'white man' and therefore the nationalisms they propagated.[21] And she posited a causal relationship between two nineteenth-century institutions that historians had previously viewed through separate frames: the mass Asian migrations of the late nineteenth century from the East to the West spurred at first by the frontier gold rushes, and the rise of a rights discourse that linked good governance to white manhood.

Instead of accepting the growth of anti-Asian attitudes in settler societies as inevitable, Lake looked less at the victimisation of Chinese miners and more at the neuroses of white men. Colonial masculinity was especially vulnerable and in need of much bolstering or 'self-preservation', as she put it. Not only were colonial men considered inferior in their 'mother lands', they had an unstable claim to land ownership and sovereignty in their colonial homelands. Attlee Hunt's papers contained a letter written from London in 1907 to his friend Robert Garran in Melbourne: 'You can hardly conceive what extremely unimportant persons we are in the minds of the Colonial Office', he wrote. Tracing the long friendship between Alfred Deakin and American philosopher Josiah Royce—which had grown in the Australian bush and been sustained across the Pacific for decades—Lake perceived their bond as fearful colonials, burdened with shaping new worlds and better peoples, even as they felt their own inferiority acutely.[22]

Lake saw the *idea* of whiteness and of a 'white' immigration policy as the reaction of anxious men, embarrassed by their subjugated position as colonials, threatened by the idea of racial equality. So the desire to protect their rights as workers and husbands was as one with their white supremacy.

---

21 Marilyn Lake, 'Socialism and Manhood: The Case of William Lane', *Labour History*, no. 50 (May 1986): 54–62, and 'Frontier Feminism', 12–20.

22 Marilyn Lake, 'Looking to American Manhood: The Correspondence of Alfred Deakin and Josiah Royle', in *Reading Across the Pacific: Australia–United States Intellectual Histories*, eds Robert Dixon and Nicholas Bird (Sydney: Sydney University Press, 2010), 63–81.

This ideal of a white nation did not depend on theories of racial difference, or a science of racial classification. It was a counter-mobilisation that 'promised to restore the white man to his rightful place'.

Hitherto, the dominant explanation for Australian race nationalism in the late nineteenth century centred on a 'fear and hatred' of Asian immigrants. I studied anti-Chinese cartoons from the popular *Bulletin* magazine in my first university year in 2004, collecting images of octopuses, hordes, slaves and fiends to demonstrate racist sentiment at the dawn of Australian nationhood. The images were offensive and consistent with the anti-immigration rhetoric of the time but their explanatory power was limited.[23] Bearing witness to racism in the past is not the same as historicising it. And, as I have argued elsewhere, the overuse of such images can work against anti-racist projects.[24] Through her engagement with feminist labour history, Lake took the formation of white men, and not the victimisation of Chinese men, as her starting point. This was not a story of Chinese humiliation at the hands of Australian nationalists—but of white Australian fears of a powerful Asia.

White Australia in a transnational frame

I would like to know when Lake first encountered the work of Charles Pearson—feminist, radical and early proponent of world history. After all, historians had heard of Pearson before Lake began writing about him and had read his famous *National Life and Character: A Forecast*, which foretold the rise of Asia and Africa and an end to the dominance of the white race. But none had read it as a postcolonial text nor embedded it in a series of fateful, interconnected decisions in the late nineteenth century—made by congressmen in the American South, parliamentarians in Melbourne, governors in Papua, race theorists at Oxford, Indian anti-colonists in Durban and Japanese delegates at Versailles—decisions that still shape border politics today. Defending the Immigration Restriction Act in parliament in 1901, Australia's first Prime Minister Edmund Barton held *National Life and Character* in his hands.

At Harvard University in 2002, Lake found Theodore Roosevelt's review of Pearson's work in the *Sewanee Review*, 'a dusty old series located high in

---

23 Sophie Loy-Wilson, 'Peanuts and Publicists: "Letting Australian Friends Know the Chinese Side of the Story" in Interwar Sydney', *History Australia* 6 (1) (2009): 1–20.

24 Hannah Forsyth and Sophie Loy-Wilson, 'Seeking a New Materialism in Australian History', *Australian Historical Studies* 48 (2) (2017): 169–88.

the stacks of the Widener Library'.[25] She uncovered a web of correspondence between Roosevelt and others about the book, and perceived a link between US imperialism in Cuba and the Pacific and Pearson's prophesies. Later, she read W.E.B. Du Bois's 1920s essay on 'The Souls of White Folk' in the *Independent* in the New York Public Library. Reading White Australia from the US, she was struck by Du Bois's sense of whiteness as 'a sudden emotional conversion'. For Lake this was confirmation that the Australian *Immigration Restriction Act 1901* was 'but one expression of a much larger transnational phenomenon; and it was all the more powerful for that'.[26]

The threads of Pearson's own racial ideas mapped the currents Lake and Henry Reynolds would reanimate in *Drawing the Global Colour Line: White Men's Countries and the Question of Racial Equality*. Two threads are vital for our discussion here: Pearson's travels in the Americas, including to San Francisco and the American South, and his exposure to Melbourne's Chinatown. Drawing on the scholarship of Oxford geographer James Bryce, Pearson became convinced that frontier land in the new world was running out. Temperate zones appropriate for white settlement were being ceded to non-whites. New forms of travel were throwing different races together in unprecedented ways: 'Think of the great migration of the Irish to America, of the great migration of the Chinese to Western America and the isles of the Pacific'.[27] Pearson obsessed over census data and birth rates to draw out the implications of multi-racial living, sound the alarm and propose solutions. The 'negro', he argued, was taking over America, and the Chinese were settling the Pacific and Australasia; he noticed thriving Chinatowns in San Francisco and Melbourne and was especially affected by the scale of Chinese settlement of Singapore. These Chinese were no mere 'coolies' or miners, they were co-colonists on their own terms, competitors for the temperate zones with their white counterparts. In the Chinatowns of the West and the booming overseas Chinese colonies of the East, Pearson saw an empire at work.

All this was cause for alarm, and the readers of Pearson's work responded with solutions. One reviewer wrote the 'English race would certainly awake to its duties when the time came and massacre as many Chinese and Hindoos as were found superfluous'. Lake found a letter from Pearson to

---

25 Lake, 'Histories Across Borders', 284.
26 Lake, 'Histories Across Borders', 284.
27 Lake and Pratt, 27.

Deakin at the National Library of Australia responding to this suggestion: 'Can you imagine any European power setting itself to massacre 100 million Chinamen?'[28] Pearson was criticised for betraying his people: for expecting whites 'to vanish before a procession of coffee-coloured, yellow tinted or black-skinned races'.[29]

National Life and Character sparked a conversation between white men in the US, Canada, Australia, New Zealand, South Africa, Rhodesia and Kenya searching for a credo to articulate their claims to colonised lands. Employing new ways of counting and differentiating populations—through the census, for example, and the birth rate—they justified the adoption of key technologies that still underwrite border politics (exemption certificates, language tests, passports), giving concrete form to a growing siege mentality over whiteness and the future of white peoples. These technologies moved transnationally through the friendships and alliances Lake traced, the correspondence they produced, and the comparative mentality this kind of world view encouraged in politicians and legislators.

But what of the many Asians affected by these new immigration regimes? How did Asian migrants appropriate European notions of race and status, and how did they import them into their own self-perceptions? Importantly, how did non-white subjects push back and modify the arguments deployed against them? The insertion of the experience of race from non-white subjects, especially Chinese subjects, has a history of travelling and transformation, which Lake would unpack in subsequent work.[30] She used late–nineteenth century Melbourne as a focal point for posing larger questions about Chinese agency in western historical traditions, and she did so through the re-discovery of a Chinese–Australian historical treatise on migrant rights and human rights by three Chinese community leaders—bankers, missionaries, land owners—Lowe Kong Meng, Cheok Hong Cheong and Louis Ah Mouy's, *The Chinese Question in Australia*, 1879.[31] Before Lake, no one (beyond a few Chinese–Australian researchers) had taken their ideas seriously. Now, in doing so, Lake traced a genealogy that suggested the book's pivotal role in three historiographies typically anchored to European texts and origins: 1) the history of human rights; 2) the history of colonial democracy; and 3) the right to free movement.

---

28   Lake, 'From Mississippi to Melbourne', 223.
29   Lake, 'From Mississippi to Melbourne', 223.
30   Lake, 'The Chinese Empire Encounters', 178.
31   Lake, 'Chinese Colonists Assert', 375–92.

Chinese agency, cosmopolitanism and White Australia

One consequence of the wresting of nineteenth-century border politics from national history was the opening up of the field of overseas Chinese history.[32] New work in Australia suggests there is a vast intellectual reserve of Chinese–Australian writings.[33] Chinese Australians were key contributors to the political and legal debates that were foundational for Australian nation-building. They were often well educated, literate in multiple languages, and wrote books, pamphlets, petitions and letters in both Chinese and English. These Chinese migrants were not a pilloried minority—hapless victims needing recue by white historians—but rather, in Candice Fujikane's words, 'Asian settlers ... active agents in the making of their own histories *and* unwitting recruits swept into the service of empire'.[34]

Once, rifling through old court cases in the Public Record Office Victoria, I had reason to marvel at the empire of Lowe Kong Meng, a man largely forgotten until recently, but whose co-authored text, *The Chinese Question in Australia*, found its way to Marilyn Lake.[35] I found a land deed for Salmon Creek on the Mornington Peninsula signed over by Kong Meng to one of his employees, who had returned from China to claim it years after Kong Meng's death. The deed, in both English and Chinese, confounded Lands Department bureaucrats, not least because detective work revealed the prized land did in fact belong to Kong Meng, whose holdings in the colony had been substantial.

In *The Chinese Question in Australia*, Kong Meng and his co-authors asserted that Chinese migrants had as much right to occupy unsettled parts of Australia as did the British ('Did man create it or did God?'). Lake read

---

32 Mei-Fen Kuo, *Making Chinese Australians: Urban Elites, Newspapers and the Formation of Chinese–Australian Identity, 1892–1912* (Melbourne: Monash University Publishing, 2013); John Fitzgerald, *Big White Lie: Chinese Australians in White Australia* (Sydney: University of NSW Press, 2006).

33 Lake, 'Chinese Colonists Assert', 375–92.

34 Candace Fujikane, 'Introduction: Asian Settler Colonialism in the U.S. Colony of Hawai'i', in *Asian Settler Colonialism: From Local Governance to the Habits of Everyday Life*, eds Candace Fujikane and Jonathan Y. Okamura (Honolulu: University of Hawai'i Press, 2008), 1–42.

35 Marilyn Lake, 'Lowe Kong Meng Appeals to International Law: Transnational Lives Caught between Empire and Nation', in *Transnational Lives: Biographies of Colonial Modernity, 1700 to Present*, eds Desley Deacon and Angela Woollacott (New York: Palgrave Macmillan, 2008), 223–37.

the booklet as a form of activism against the forces of Asian exclusion. She placed it in a longer history of human rights:

> I came across a forgotten tradition of international human rights claims that couldn't be located in the conventional genealogy that sees modern conceptions of "human rights" articulated only in the 1940s. I found moreover that Chinese claims for recognition of their "common human rights" sixty years earlier, in the 1880s, did not emphasize "the sanctity of the individual," but rather the "equality of races." And they were not demanding life, liberty, and the pursuit of happiness—though these were also important considerations for a people who were personally harassed and whose property was routinely confiscated—but freedom of movement, or what one of their Australian supporters, the Liberal politician and lawyer William Shiels, called (possibly with Blackstone's Commentaries on the Laws of England in mind) "the perfect liberty of locomotion."[36]

In 1881 the Victorian government introduced new immigration restrictions, provoked, Lake suspected, by these Chinese–Australian protestations. A poll tax was to be placed on Chinese, and manhood suffrage was to be stripped from any Chinese who might already lay claim to it because of property rights or land ownership.

Charles Pearson well understood Chinese agency. In his work, Lake had uncovered a prophecy. China would inevitably regain its position as one of the great powers. It was a prophecy, she thought:

> that drew heavily—in its cadence, sentiments, and language—on the writings of Chinese themselves, thousands of whom had migrated to Melbourne, and who wrote protest booklets, petitions, and remonstrances that demanded an end to racial discrimination, invoked international law, warned of the global consequences of ill treatment, and called for recognition of their "common human rights".

Lake's white men were weak, neurotic, anxious—her Chinese colonists figures of power rather than fun. The force of their anger and indignation rang through Victorian parliaments as their pamphlets were read out there and their arguments rebutted there by these same nervous white men speaking of 'self-preservation', that 'most basic of human instincts'. Australian

---

36   Lake, 'Lowe Kong Meng Appeals', 379.

history, therefore, needed to be understood in relation to both European and Asian imperial contexts. The Australian colonies, often depicted as isolated imperial outposts, were in fact the site of dynamic encounters between the subjects and officials of different empires (including British and Chinese): 'Australian national aspirations as self-governing communities were fashioned and articulated in the context of these global historic encounters and contestations'.[37]

At the close of the twentieth century, race and culture re-emerged as powerful sites of conflict in global politics, fueling discontent, defiance and violence. Circling back to the *Tampa*, we find in Lake a final explanation for what brought us to that moment. She studied the visit of the Chinese Imperial Commissioners to Australia in 1887 to investigate the discriminatory treatment of Chinese imperial subjects abroad and to demand change. The more the Chinese pressed their claims and the more British authorities attempted to persuade the colonials to conciliate them, the more loudly did local nationalists insist on their status and rights as self-governing colonies. It was in this international context that the Australian sense of national sovereignty was increasingly expressed, in terms of the right to control borders, 'to say who was permitted to join their self-governing community, who was permitted to land and who was permitted to stay'.[38]

David Atkinson has recently critiqued the transnational turn in the history of border politics. He criticises this burgeoning field as overly dependent on 'metaphors of movement and interconnection'. By showing how the campaigns of white activists occurred in response to very specific local concerns and often without any effective support from abroad, Atkinson suggests a tendency amongst some historians to overplay the transnational card: 'Local contingencies were more determinative than scholars suggest'.[39] Any similarity between the campaigns of these 'diffuse coalitions' of 'white activists' in say South Africa, Canada or New Zealand, for example, were 'largely analogous rather than affinitive'.[40] I disagree with this argument, but I find it refreshing, and not a little influenced by Marilyn Lake, who created the intellectual context in which Atkinson stages his intervention.

---

37 Lake, 'The Chinese Empire Encounters', 180.
38 Lake, 'The Chinese Empire Encounters', 179.
39 David C. Atkinson, *The Burden of White Supremacy: Containing Asian Migration in the British Empire and the United States* (Chapel Hill: University of North Carolina Press, 2016), 2.
40 Atkinson, 2.

Whither Australian history? Whether the way forward lies, as Lake suggests, in a greater engagement with the histories and historiographies of other coeval empires and of empires in other historical periods, or in something else, the most important lesson that I take away from her work is precisely this: the openness to revision so as to be constantly vigilant against the drift towards ossified banalities of what were once radical propositions.

Chapter 15

VICTOR SELDEN CLARK'S *THE LABOUR MOVEMENT IN AUSTRALASIA*

Comparative Colonialism and American Exceptionalism

Ian Tyrrell

Marilyn Lake has made key contributions to Australian history, feminist history and transnational history. More recently she has turned her attention to American topics. A large field with many thousands of professional practitioners, it is also one of the world's most heavily published. But Lake has successfully used her Australian perspective as leverage, with great success and promise for the future. Her current work includes essays on Australian–American political and intellectual questions that can be broadly called Progressive reform. This old field is yielding new, insightful results from transnational approaches through her industry. Professor Lake is surely correct that Australian contributions to and connections with American Progressive reform deserve more attention.[1] Federation-era Australia was seen, not only by Americans but also by Europeans, as an advanced social democracy, one that could provide models of reform to the world.

Among the cast of characters in Lake's own work investigating the entanglement of Australian Progressive reformers with American counterparts

---

1   Forthcoming in Marilyn Lake, *Progressive New World: How Settler Colonialism and Trans-Pacific Exchange Shaped American Reform* (Cambridge, MA: Harvard University Press, 2019).

are the familiar Alfred Deakin and H.B. Higgins. On these matters she has written with great distinction, and one finds in a footnote to an *Australian Historical Studies* article and in a web essay references to Victor Selden Clark.[2] With an undergraduate degree from the University of Minnesota, study in Europe (Göttingen and Bern) and a PhD from Columbia University, Clark was a dapper and cosmopolitan young man when he first came to Australia in 1903. Partly for this reason, but also because Australians valued the attention to them given by people on the other side of the world, he was welcomed as, according to one newspaper, an 'exceptionally capable, shrewd and unbiased observer'.[3]

Clark is a forgotten figure. His *The Labour Movement in Australasia: A Study in Social Democracy* (1906) is a book rarely discussed today. An early example of comparative history, this book documented Progressive-era interest in labour relations, arbitration systems, and related questions.[4] His work can be assimilated to the argument that Australasia was a social laboratory, though Clark did not actually use this expression at the time, and it is better attributed to British labour leaders visiting New Zealand.[5]

---

2   See Marilyn Lake, 'Fractured Nation', http://honesthistory.net.au/wp/lake-marilyn-fractured-nation/; 'Challenging the "Slave-Driving Employers": Understanding Victoria's 1896 Minimum Wage through a World-History Approach', *Australian Historical Studies* 45 (1) (2014): 87–102, '"This Great America": H.B. Higgins and Transnational Progressivism', *Australian Historical Studies* 44 (2) (2013): 172–88.

3   *New Ulm Review* (Brown County, Minn.), 21 June 1899, 5, and 17 September 1902, 4; 'New Zealand Notes', *Australasian*, 23 January 1904, 23; *Queensland Times, Ipswich Herald and General Advertiser* (Qld), 3 June 1905, 4 (quote). E. Dana Durand, 'Dr. Victor Selden Clark', *Journal of the American Statistical Association* 41 (235) (1946): 390–2.

4   V.S. Clark, *The Labour Movement in Australasia: A Study in Social Democracy* (New York: H. Holt & Co., 1906).

5   'As Others See Us', *Wanganui Chronicle*, 8 June 1904, 4, regarding the 'canny Scotch Labour leader' who dubbed New Zealand 'an ideal laboratory'. Though Clark did not use the term, a reviewer did. See George B. Mangold, in *Annals of the American Academy of Political and Social Science* 29 (January 1907): 230–2. Victor S. Clark, 'Present State of Labor Legislation in Australia and New Zealand', *Annals of the American Academy of Political and Social Science* 33 (2) (1909): 216–23 (223); Philip Bell and Roger Bell, *Implicated: The United States in Australia* (Melbourne: Oxford University Press, 1993), 39–40; K.R. Howe, *Singer in a Songless Land: A Life of Edward Tregear, 1846–1931* (Auckland: Auckland University Press, 1991), 93; Michael King, *Penguin History of New Zealand* (Auckland: Penguin, 2003), 33; Neville Kirk, *Transnational Radicalism and the Connected Lives of Tom Mann and Robert Samuel Ross* (Liverpool: Liverpool University Press, 2017), 28; 'The Changing Scene', *Dominion*, 6 June 1908; Peter J. Coleman, '"Strikes Are War! War Is Hell!": American Responses to the Compulsory Arbitration of Labor Disputes, 1890–1920', *Wisconsin Magazine of History* 70 (Spring 1987): 187–210; 'New Zealand Notes', 23.

Even as Clark treated Australia as a social 'experiment',[6] he was more impressed by New Zealand's landmark status on arbitration. His research was done before the Commonwealth Conciliation and Arbitration Court was established, and before the Harvester Judgment on a minimum wage in 1907. In this context, it was New Zealand that seemed more important in 1903–06, and it was New Zealand that was given the 'flattering sobriquet of "the Social Laboratory"' in the reception of Clark's work in Australia. Nevertheless, Clark gave attention to the Australian states and the potential of Commonwealth constitutional powers as well. Clark's account of the arbitration system was far more circumspect than the views of pro-labour people, and it was the capacity of Clark's piece to serve as a partial rebuttal to the case for arbitration that attracted much of the extensive press coverage in Australia.[7]

Whatever the bragging rights across the Tasman, Clark's book was not simply part of a transnational discourse over social democracy. Clark's work addressed more fundamentally two interrelated problems raising the question of the place of the United States in the world, and especially its place at an extraordinary historical conjuncture, the emergence of the Great Republic as a world power. The acquisition in 1898–99 of a formal empire overseas spurred this change in consciousness. That included annexation of Puerto Rico, the Philippine Islands, Guam, and Samoa, along with the protectorate over Cuba, the incorporation of Hawaii as a US territory (1898), and the acquisition of the Panama Canal Zone (1903). The Progressive Era (*c.* 1898–1917) was also the period in which a blue-collar American working class reached its demographic high tide and represented a severe political challenge to the American political and social order. The landmark 1902 Anthracite Strike had seen President Theodore Roosevelt take a characteristic Progressive position of trying to adjudicate between capital and labour. Roosevelt's interest was shared by Commissioner of Labor Carroll D. Wright, who sent Clark to the Pacific on a 'roving commission', partly to secure more information on the topic of the arbitration system's 'economic effect'. However it was Roosevelt rather than Wright who was more favourable to arbitration, and his well-known interest in Australia and things Australian suggests that he may

---

6. Clark, *The Labour Movement in Australasia*, esp. 220.
7. Lake, 'Challenging the "Slave-Driving Employers"'; *Ovens and Murray Advertiser*, 16 June 1906, 4 ('sobriquet'); *Queensland Times, Ipswich Herald and General Advertiser*, 3 June 1905, 4.

have been the driving force in adding Australia to Clark's trip.[8] Clark's visit promised to settle the issue over whether compulsory arbitration, rather than merely conciliation, ought to be pushed as part of the president's agenda. That was the practical consideration for the Australian and Zealand leg of his visit.

The underlying intellectual agenda for Clark's 'roving' trip was, however, much more than that; it concerned how the Progressive Era, with its big issues of class conflict at home and imperialism abroad, threatened easy notions of American exceptionalism. On one level the Progressive Era and Progressivism can be viewed as a series of crises in 'exceptionalism', even though that word had not yet been coined to analyse the singularity of the American political and social system.[9] The earlier discourse over the 'exceptional' status of the republic, in which the French traveller and politician Alexis de Tocqueville had played a leading part, was narrowly focused on the meaning of US experience for Europe, and only Western Europe at that. But, as Americans became part of formal imperialism and globally connected via trade and migration in a networked world of telegraphs, railways and steamships, they had to ask how other places, particularly 'white' democracies, fitted into the American narrative of exceptionalism. Interest in Australia was part of this unsettling discourse.

At first glance, Clark was better prepared than most to question the assumptions of American exceptionalism. That was because his training was fundamentally historicist, whereas classic exceptionalism was based on the ahistorical idea of the United States as outside the normal paths of human history. Clark cautiously argued that different conditions and experiences would influence the kinds of social experiments that might succeed. But this historicist methodology meant that Australasian 'lessons' could not readily be applied to the United States. The 'experiments' in social democracy that Clark covered in Australia and New Zealand were considered as subject to historical change, and hence impermanence. This historicism could ironically be used to reinforce an ingrained and anti-historicist

---

8   James Leiby, *Carroll Wright and Labor Reform: The Origin of Labor Statistics* (Cambridge, MA: Harvard University Press, 1960), 179; 'Interview with Victor Clarke' [sic], *West Australian*, 6 August 1904, 7 ('roving', 'effect'); Theodore Roosevelt to Winthrop Murray Crane, 22 October 1902, in *The Letters of Theodore Roosevelt*, vol. 3, ed. Elting E. Morison (Cambridge, MA: Harvard University Press, 1951), 360.

9   Ian Tyrrell, 'From Stalin with Love', *Aeon Magazine*, 10 October 2016, at https://aeon.co/ideas/american-exceptionalism-from-stalin-with-love.

American exceptionalism, as happened with American social science from the 1890s to 1920s.[10]

Clark referred to 'the socialism of Australasia' as 'unique' but knew that there was little point in examining it for the US government if it was truly exceptional. Clark saw Australia as 'worthy of study as a phase—though still incomplete and possibly not abiding—of Anglo-Saxon history'. Clark went on: 'Even more important from a practical standpoint' was 'its revelation of the vital forces directing the labour movement as a world-wide phenomenon'.[11] This was comparative history, engaged with and potentially at odds with American exceptionalism, though Clark was unsure exactly where to place Australasian reform within that existing American understanding of the world.

For Clark and the larger Rooseveltian Progressivism in which he worked, Australia was not a model in itself so much as a link in a larger agenda, the agenda of empire. Specifically this agenda favoured a settler empire grounded in ideas of global Anglo-Saxon hegemony, yet with rational and efficient allocation of natural and human resources at its centre, a possible source of tension. Clark's government work was concerned with more than studying Australia as a unique laboratory of political economy. He went to and reported on other places in a long career, and some of this work is manifest in his book.

Like many Progressive Era 'experts' in the United States, Clark was a globetrotter. As the insightful New Zealand correspondent Edward Tregear stated, writing to him was 'like corresponding with a globule of mercury on a railway train'.[12] Though there is evidence of wanderlust in Clark and a love of tropical, palmy places, he was to occupy positions as a de facto colonial official for the US government on and off over four decades. The areas covered by Clark's research included Puerto Rico, Hawaii, the Philippine Islands, Cuba, Mexico, the Dutch East Indies, New Zealand, Australia and Canada; he also visited Britain, Russia, Spain and, many years later, toured East Africa by motor car. The resultant output was mostly published by the Bureau of Labor Statistics, for which he worked for some years from 1902, but he continued to move in and out

---

10   Clark, *The Labour Movement in Australasia*, 9–10, 111–12; Dorothy Ross, *Origins of American Social Science* (New York: Cambridge University Press, 1991).
11   Clark, *The Labour Movement in Australasia*, ix–x.
12   Edward Tregear to Victor Clark, 3 November 1903, Victor Selden Clark Papers, Box 1, fl. 2, Correspondence 1890–1929, Library of Congress.

of government service for thirty-five years thereafter. He later worked for the Carnegie Endowment and the Brookings Institute, directed a research project (1928–30) on *Porto Rico and Its Problems*, and undertook sensitive and quasi-diplomatic errands on behalf of the US government to the Commonwealth of the Philippines in 1936.[13]

Clark's role was archetypal of an important element in ruling the new American empire. There was little stomach in the United States for extending formal rule over other people beyond the territory acquired between 1898 and 1903. But there was critical interest both in markets for American products in the developing colonial world, and in those places that might provide sources of raw materials for the expanding American industrial juggernaut. Clark wrote reports that were expected to inform American foreign policy, provide models and examples for its new colonial policy, guide business, and develop the intellectual infrastructure for American commercial penetration, particularly in the tropical world. He spent little time administering any overseas territory.

His Australian investigations came in the context of a US Department of Commerce and Labor tour of East Asia and the Pacific in 1903–04. In Queensland, Clark told state government officials and reporters that he had come to study the sugar cane industry 'with a view to furnishing the United States authorities with some points that might be useful ... in developing the Philippine Islands, of which they had then recently become possessed'.[14] From Eastern Australia he went to Java and Manila, then back to Australia to cover the rest of the Australian states before returning to Washington at the end of 1904. Clark was sent across the Pacific to examine not simply Australian and New Zealand labour relations but 'tropical labor conditions' as well.[15] That he wrote highly detailed and insightful reports on Dutch Java, Hawaii, and the Philippine Islands testifies to this function.[16]

---

13   See, for example, *Philippine Herald*, 21 May 1936; *Porto Rico and Its Problems. Survey Staff: Victor S. Clark, Director...* (Washington, DC: Brookings Institution, 1930), vii, ix.; see generally Clark Papers, Box 1, fl. 7, Newspaper clippings, 1897–1910, 1934–1936.

14   *Queensland Times, Ipswich Herald and General Advertiser*, 3 June 1905, 4.

15   'A Finding Aid to the Collection in the Library of Congress', 3 (quote), Clark Papers.

16   V.S. Clark, 'Labor Conditions in the Philippines', *Bulletin of the Bureau of Labor*, no. 58 (May 1905): 721–905 (851–3), 'Labor Conditions in Java', *Bulletin of the Bureau of Labor*, no. 58 (May 1905): 906–54, 'Labor Conditions in Australia', *Bulletin of the Bureau of Labor*, no. 56 (January 1905): 13–247.

Clark got this work because he had served as the McKinley-appointed President of the Insular Board of Education, Puerto Rico, from 1899 to 1900 and Director of Public Instruction from 1900 to 1902, and he also surveyed wage policy in the Cuban protectorate in 1902.[17] Little of Cuba's 'natural resources ... have been exploited', he claimed. Cuban commerce needed 'an American invasion' in the interests of 'industrial efficiency', following and improving on the example of the British Empire, in order to enhance the 'intellectual resources of the people' and spur 'modern inventions, improvements and processes'.[18] Labour conditions and their efficient management were at the heart of his agenda when visiting that island. In line with American colonial policy, Clark encouraged immigration of skilled labour and improvement of infrastructure. This was quite consistent with the view that American officialdom should be an almost invisible hand orchestrating and channelling American economic and missionary penetration abroad, particularly in US colonies and protectorates but also in other places in the tropical world where the government wished to exert informal influence on behalf of business and trade.

Though he was to return to the Caribbean and work for the US government in trying to solve the economic problems of Puerto Rico in the late 1920s, Clark's agenda in the early 1900s led especially to the Pacific. The Roosevelt administration and its intellectual cheerleaders in influential magazines such as *Outlook* and *World's Work* viewed the Asia–Pacific countries through the lens of their potential as tropical colonies and bases, especially those parts of the region possessing strategic assets and resources.[19] This imperialist discourse was at least as important a part of what is today called American Progressivism as social and labour reform.[20] Much is known

---

17   A.J. Angulo, *Empire and Education: A History of Greed and Goodwill from the War of 1898 to the War on Terror* (New York: Palgrave Macmillan, 2012), 36–40; Jose-Manuel Navarro, *Creating Tropical Yankees: Social Science Textbooks and U.S. Ideological Control in Puerto Rico, 1898–1908* (New York: Routledge, 2002), 44; 'Industrial Conditions in America. Interview with Mr Victor S. Clarke [sic]', *Daily Telegraph* (Launceston), 9 September 1903, 6.

18   'Cuban Labor Market', *New York Times*, 24 August 1902, 32.

19   Ian Tyrrell, *Crisis of the Wasteful Nation: Empire and Conservation in Theodore Roosevelt's America* (Chicago: University of Chicago Press, 2015), chapter 3.

20   William E. Leuchtenburg, 'Progressivism and Imperialism: The Progressive Movement and American Foreign Relations', *Mississippi Valley Historical Review* 39 (3) (December 1952): 483–504; Alfred W. McCoy and Francisco A. Scarano, *The Colonial Crucible: Empire in the Making of the Modern American State* (Madison: University of Wisconsin Press, 2009); Fabian Hilfrich, *Debating American Exceptionalism: Empire and Democracy in the Wake of the Spanish-American War* (Basingstoke: Palgrave Macmillan, 2012), 167–8.

about trans-Atlantic social and economic reform in the Progressive Era, but Clark's investigative field was neither that nor Australian–American contacts. We must interpret Clark within a global Progressive Era circulation of theories of social reform and empire building, as does Lake for racial thought and practice.[21]

The Labour Movement in Australasia was an early example of modern historical sociology examining American peculiarities comparatively—leading to and beyond political sociologist Seymour Martin Lipset. Clark's work is subject to criticisms similar to those that faced Lipset and the US social science tradition many decades later—as nurturing an exceptionalist model of social science rooted in normative comparison.[22] Certainly Clark's book contains much recognised as standard exceptionalism. He explored factors that made Australia and New Zealand exceptional in relation to Europe and the United States in the short run but also, somehow, reinforced US exceptionalism in the long run.

Yet in American exceptionalism, either Australia is exceptional or the United States. They could not both be, and, when forced to choose, Clark always chose the latter. Clark conceded that Australasia was leading the world on social democratic initiatives[23] and believed that Europe would ultimately conform to an Australasian social laboratory, but the same would not be true of the United States. Political culture, social traditions and legal structures there would get in the way of adopting Australian precedents.[24] (On the other hand, he stated that if the United States one day *did* adopt such socialist policies it would do so in the manner of New Zealand and Australia, pragmatically and incrementally.)[25] In making his case, Clark deployed significant exceptionalist tropes—especially Frederick Jackson Turner's frontier of pioneers unleashed upon abundant land, and the growth of American individualism. Yet Clark frequently wavered on issues of conventional American exceptionalism. His analysis broke with Social Darwinist themes underlying the frontier thesis and pointed to frontier conditions that defied the supposed unilinear path of

---

21 Daniel T. Rodgers, *Atlantic Crossings: Social Politics in a Progressive Age* (Cambridge, MA: Belknap Press of Harvard University Press, 1998); Marilyn Lake and Henry Reynolds, *Drawing the Global Colour Line: White Men's Countries and the Question of Racial Equality* (Melbourne: Melbourne University Press, 2008).

22 Seymour Martin Lipset, *The First New Nation: The United States in Historical and Comparative Perspective* (New York: Basic Books, 1963).

23 Clark, *The Labour Movement in Australasia*, 303.

24 Clark, *The Labour Movement in Australasia*, 306–07.

25 Clark, *The Labour Movement in Australasia*, 306, 308–10.

the US frontier. This is seen in the way he introduced the concept of a maritime frontier, connected to the expansion of Pacific trade, a theme congruent with his brief to investigate Asia–Pacific societies and their economic potential as matters of interest to the Department of Commerce and Labor. 'The Australians are to some extent a seafaring people', Clark asserted. Though their attention had been turned landward by the 'profitable vocation of developing the country', with longer settlement Australians would

> probably devote their energies more to navigation, and utilise their advantage of position to secure a larger share of the growing commerce of the Pacific. The promise of maritime power might almost be counted among the natural resources of Australasia.[26]

This inconsistency—suggesting the US frontier experience was unique on the one hand but part of a global pattern on the other—is typical of the confusion in Clark's book. It led to fudging on the US prognosis, but there is a more fundamental contradiction. Despite his historicism, Clark insisted conventionally on underlying economic laws governing societies,[27] which meant Australia would one day have to conform to a global standard that the United States already held. In other words, Australia was exceptional, but would not be in the future. These 'laws' concerned the international organisation of labour and trade. Not an exception in labour legislation, the United States is seen as exemplary of the economic laws of the capitalist system. The idea of US exceptionalism could in this context only be maintained by assuming that the United States was the leading capitalist power steering the way and providing a model of an advanced democratic and capitalist society for other nations to imitate, while they could never quite catch up. These ambiguities in Clark's stance over how exceptionalism is to be measured, and what the benchmarks are for judging comparable societies, show how disorienting the introduction of the site of 'Australasia' into the Europe–America dichotomy foundational to American exceptionalism could be.

These disruptions were incorporated within Clark's own world-historical view. Partly the resolution came through the peculiar trajectory of American social science towards a blending of historicism and exceptionalism, a dynamic that has been deftly analysed in Dorothy Ross's work. In

---

26 Clark, *The Labour Movement in Australasia*, 13.
27 Clark, *The Labour Movement in Australasia*, 131, and 'Labor Conditions in the Philippines', 899.

this American social science, the turn-of-the-twentieth-century crisis over American exceptionalism was resolved by adopting the US model of society as coterminous with the universal laws of economics.[28]

Yet Clark's intellectual inspirations were also more specific to the changing political terrain of the administration of Roosevelt, whose views he embraced as a sound but forward-looking Republicanism. Clark's analysis reflected the reconsideration of the US role in the global firmament as a leading power, albeit one that could no longer rely on the old exceptionalist verities of the frontier and individualism. Because Clark wrote originally for the government, his reports reflected the Roosevelt agenda—of rationalised resource management and reorganisation of the state to reflect these new (truly) world-historical conditions. Clark saw these problems of labour and empire as internationally shared problems and historically contingent. This Progressive Era context included an important interest in resolving labour conflict in the interests of efficiency and progress, and in promoting tropical development, especially where likely to provide the United States with new resources.

For Clark, natural resources were foundational to both Australian and American development and their degrees of exceptionalism. The foundations of prosperity and therefore empire and permanency were, in the estimate of most Progressives, material, not the nation's supposedly 'chosen' status favoured by modern evangelical versions of American exceptionalism. Clark's trip was part of a much larger and characteristically Progressive mapping of these resources. Labour was considered one, since Progressives had begun to pioneer the inclusion of human health and worker safety within conservation's remit.[29] More important still was a second issue, race. Clark saw Australians as Anglo-Saxon cousins, a common cliché at the time. Widely discussed was the idea of a global chain of white settlements providing hegemony and economic progress under future US leadership.[30]

To achieve the US geopolitical agenda, race was tied to a third issue: the future of tropical agriculture in the service of empires or colonial peoples. Such discussion occurred in the works of Benjamin Kidd, modified in the United States by William Eliot Griffis.[31] Here, labour was put in the context of specifically tropical resources that must be developed, yet most likely not

---

28   Ross, *Origins of American Social Science*.
29   Tyrrell, *Crisis*, chapter 9.
30   Tyrrell, *Crisis*, chapters 10, 11.
31   William Eliot Griffis, *America in the East: A Glance at Our History, Prospects, Problems, and Duties in the Pacific Ocean*, 2nd edn (New York: A.S. Barnes, 1900).

with white labour, though under white supervision.[32] Clark saw Australia as an experiment in racial exclusion because the nation had embarked upon complete exclusion of non-whites—'literally' white, as Clark conveyed it.[33] Here again it was the United States that was unexceptional. But, as already stated, Clark believed that Australia would likely have to obey the rules of supply and demand in the long run and adhere to the standard of the United States on this score. The lily-white experiment would fail, he feared, unless new technological conditions intervened. This last point involved more hedging, but Clark showed his true colours when highlighting how racial exclusion meant non-development of the tropics and a 'waste' of resources because not utilised for a needy world. Through the refusal of cheap Asian labour,

> Australians [were] not making an aggressive effort to bring into use the natural resources of their tropical empire. They seem content to wait *if necessary forever* rather than seek another solution for the problem than the one they have adopted.[34]

This 'future of the tropics' and occupation of 'waste lands' debate was a major theme in Progressive geopolitical discourse—and a matter of intense interest to the United States in view of its newly acquired imperial possessions and informal empire. If the Australian experiment of high-wage policies and white labour failed to develop the 'torrid zone', it would undermine the search for a rational and fair global allocation of resources, and hence the new empire that Roosevelt and his advisers were bent on creating. Australia provided interesting evidence for this debate and on the wisdom of not giving priority to white settlement over economic development; racial exclusion seemed a 'laboratory' not so much for industrial issues as for white control of the tropics.

In Clark's work Australia was certainly injected into a world-historical problematic. But that perspective was as a laboratory of empire. This judgment is reinforced by Clark's subsequent career, including as Commissioner for Immigration, Labor and Statistics in the Territory of Hawaii, 1910–13. With 'Oriental' Japanese migration increasing into Hawaii, the US government gave Clark the task of trying to expand the supply of 'white' labour, to prevent 'the progressive orientalization of these Islands, leading

---

32   Clark, *The Labour Movement in Australasia*. 127–35.
33   Clark, *The Labour Movement in Australasia*, 132.
34   Clark, *The Labour Movement in Australasia*, 132 (italics added).

them towards dependency instead of statehood'.[35] This geopolitical manoeuvre was linked to Roosevelt's idea of empire founded on white leadership. Implementing federal objectives rather than territorial pressures, Clark sought Spanish, Portuguese and, more quixotically, Russians from Siberia, before World War I shut down the trade. But the example of Australia could not be applied any more than on the arbitration question.

In his Hawaiian policy, Clark declared Australia's racial exclusion to be economically impractical. Clark saw Australia as a luxurious experiment, impractical in the larger world with its laws of supply and demand. Unlike some other admirers of Australian social democracy, he did not accept the idea of government control over wages. It was on race, not the arbitration question, that his views came closest to those of Australian experimenters, though the outcomes were different in Hawaii. Reinforced by Australian precedents it may have been, but his settler-based labour policy for the tropics was actually based on his earlier Cuban work.[36] His approach in Hawaii was pragmatic and economically oriented. It was grounded in white ownership and control of plantations but with imported labour that would be a mix of whites favoured for small-scale settlements and 'Asian' labour on plantations. In practice he sought a middle way between exclusion of 'coloured' labour and use of it; he opposed removal of existing Chinese workers, in contrast to Queensland's treatment of Pacific Islanders at Federation. For this reason, the 1916 report on Hawaii, which he researched and largely wrote, actually called Hawaii, not Australia, a 'laboratory' on race relations, and declared the Australian alternative certain to cause 'an enormous depreciation of existing investments'.[37]

Behind his reservations on Australian political economy was his assessment of American exceptionalism. Despite vacillation over this matter, and the existence of a geopolitical agenda, his book does not expunge exceptionalism from its frame of reference. Social science evidence was never going to be enough to do so without re-examining the tropes of American exceptionalism and the methodologies of comparative history, which was beyond Clark's scholarly apparatus.

---

35 'Clark Speaks Plainly', *Pacific Commercial Advertiser* (Honolulu), 30 September 1910, 1.
36 'Cuban Labor Market', 32; Victor S. Clark, 'Labor Conditions in Cuba', *Bulletin of the Department [sic] of Labor*, no. 41 (July 1902): 663–793.
37 *Labor Conditions in Hawaii*, Fifth Annual Report of the Commissioner for Labor Statistics, Washington, DC, 1916, 5 ('wrote'), 62 ('laboratory'), 63 ('depreciation').

The resilience of American exceptionalism in the face of mere empirical 'facts' is revealed in Clark's use of personal experience as a reference point for the study of comparative social mobility. As a New Zealander reported of one of Clark's talks during his tour there:

> In America, among the personal acquaintances of the writer is a man high on the judicial bench who worked at a carpenter's bench till he was 35; a successful newspaper man who made barrels in a cooper's shop till he had boys of high school age; a well-known scientist who was a farm labourer till he was nearly 30; a prominent insurance man who began as a section hand on a railway. The frequent advance ... from the bottom to the top of society appears not to be so common in New Zealand.[38]

This was social science as personal identity forged in anecdotal experience. It remains how many Americans think about their national exceptionalism.[39]

The book's impact for Americans was slight. Certainly, it was respectfully reviewed by the standards of Scientific History—but rarely was there explicit reference to the difficulties the Australasian material posed for American exceptionalism. The *Journal of Political Economy* alone raised the exceptionalist challenge only to dismiss it: namely,

> the Australasian regards with perfect equanimity a country of immense natural resources, which are, as yet, quite undeveloped and vast territories as yet unpopulated. It is the price, [Clark] thinks, of social progress. To Americans, who do not regard economic progress as inconsistent with, but rather as essential to, social progress, this attitude of mind appears inexplicable.[40]

This is exactly the emphasis that Clark struck.

The geopolitical and imperial context that informed the book was not favourable in the longer run either. After 1917, the Antipodes slipped in importance to the United States, but Australasia's long-term significance as cognate democracies on the strategically significant Pacific Rim and at the edge of a restive tropical world remained as an undercurrent. Despite professions to universalism, the geopolitics of American foreign policy today rely upon a far-flung network of like-minded Anglosphere societies. Clark glimpsed the importance of this region to the growth of a globalised society

---

38 'New Zealand Notes', 23.
39 'New Zealand Notes', 23.
40 John Cummings, review in *Journal of Political Economy* 15 (April 1907): 243.

under American aegis, but he wondered if Australia was up to the task of 'world-wide competition, from which no country can escape'.[41] That is still true today. About the USA he had no such doubts, for it led the alternative model.

---

41   Clark, *The Labour Movement in Australasia*, 133.

Chapter 16

AMERICAN EXCEPTIONALISM SUBTRACTED

Taking on Transnational History from an Australian Stance[*]

Warwick Anderson

Most who write United States history from abroad seek to add to the national story; some of us try to diminish it. Others, such as Marilyn Lake, attempt to connect American figures with other histories, to tether them to transnational networks, thus challenging conventional national narratives. Transnational histories of this sort can circumvent or transect tales of national exceptionalism, whereas comparative history, shaped along national contours, often merely denies or supplements standard nationalist claims. Accordingly, thinking transnationally is not just another way of writing US history; rather, it allows us to subtend or even subvert the nation, to render more porous its constructed boundaries, to undermine assumed national sovereignty. It requires us to study 'the ways in which past lives and events have been shaped by processes and relationships that have transcended the borders of nation states'.[1] Inasmuch as this is

---

[*] I am grateful to Marilyn Lake, Clare Corbould, Ann Curthoys and Julia Martinez for their critical engagement with earlier drafts of this chapter. I would also like to thank James Dunk for research assistance. My research was supported by the Australian Research Council (FL110100243).

[1] Ann Curthoys and Marilyn Lake, 'Introduction', in *Connected Worlds: History in Transnational Perspective*, eds Curthoys and Lake (Canberra: ANU E-Press, 2005), 5–20 (5). Ironically, those of us studying the history of science and medicine rebelled against older universalist or diffusionist assumptions in the field and wrote instead

a means of doing US history from abroad, the results turn out decidedly un-American—or at least, they reveal the brittle fabrication of border protection and national sovereignty. In considering 'the inter-relationship of British and American racial regimes in the same analytic frame', Lake shows us the white nationalist outcomes of transnational processes.[2] Thus 'transnational networks and exchanges were crucial, not just to social and political movements, but to the processes of nation-building itself'.[3] This is not the national history to which we have become accustomed.

In this chapter, I want to consider Lake's distinguished career as a case study in why and how one might undertake transnational—or trans-Pacific—research into our shared past. In particular, I would like to trace her passage from narratives oriented around, or featuring, the nation toward more dispersed and connected histories—in a sense, from typological fixations to deracinated racial subjectivities. At the turn of the last century, Lake, inspired in part by feminist scholarship and critical race studies, took the turn toward the study of widely distributed historical networks and relationships spanning the Pacific.[4] Many feminist, Black and labour historians had already explored transnational themes, but Lake chose a different direction, examining the fashioning of white men's inter-subjectivity between Anglo settler societies, emphasising connections between the US and Australia. This should be distinguished from comparative history, retaining customary national substrates, and from new imperial histories, which constrain networks within the boundaries of empire, usually omitting the US. Nor should it be confused with inclusive, though largely systemic, 'world history', still often a pedagogical innovation, with few scholarly tools for illuminating historical connectivity.[5] Lake's transnational studies of the invention of

---

nation-centred histories during this period: see Warwick Anderson, *The Cultivation of Whiteness: Science, Health and Racial Destiny in Australia* (Melbourne: Melbourne University Press, 2002).

2   Marilyn Lake and Henry Reynolds, *Drawing the Global Colour Line: White Men's Countries and the International Challenge of Racial Equality* (Cambridge: Cambridge University Press, 2008), 8–9.

3   Marilyn Lake, 'White Man's Country: The Transnational History of a National Project', *Australian Historical Studies* 34 (122) (October 2003): 346–63 (348).

4   A likely model is Daniel Rodgers, *Atlantic Crossings: Social Politics in a Progressive Age* (Cambridge, MA: Harvard University Press, 1998).

5   Michael Geyer and Charles Bright, 'World History in a Global Age', *American Historical Review* 100 (4) (October 1995): 1034–60. See Kenneth Pomeranz, *The Great Divergence: China, Europe, and the Making of the Modern World Economy* (Princeton: Princeton University Press, 2000); and C.A. Bayly, *The Birth of the Modern World, 1780–1914* (Oxford: Blackwell, 2004).

white men's countries and Anglo-Saxonism vividly reveal the interpretative benefits, and occasional difficulties, of such connected or entangled histories. Moreover, they force us to question what it means to do, or to propound, national histories, whether of Australia or the United States, from whatever stance.

* * *

At the end of the twentieth century, after the Cold War, the perceived amplification of mobility of persons and things, together with the increasing flux of ideas and practices, concentrated the minds of humanities scholars and social scientists. In anthropology, intensive studies of isolated communities fell out of favour as theorists came to promote 'multi-sited' ethnography or the mapping of global 'scapes' of one kind or another.[6] Diffusion and contact, migration and diaspora, all demanded explanation. In history, national stories seemed ever more old-fashioned and nostalgic, especially those predicated on idiosyncrasy or genius or exceptional virtue or some other family romance. The genealogy of our increasingly mobile and interconnected world needed more rigorous and critical investigation. We even came to wonder whether intellectuals in the past could have been as cosmopolitan as us. Thus, historians schooled in nationalist modes of inquiry sought more encompassing analytic frames. Many took up studies of the British world, connecting particularly the scattered settler societies of the former empire.[7] Those committed to the 'new' imperial history looked critically at colonial entanglements and linkages more generally, often focusing on the metropole–colony dyad.[8]

---

6   George E. Marcus, 'Ethnography in/of the World System: The Emergence of Multi-sited Ethnography', *Annual Review of Anthropology* 24 (October 1995): 95–117; and Arjun Appadurai, *Modernity at Large: Cultural Dimensions of Globalization* (Minneapolis: University of Minnesota Press, 1996).

7   J.G.A. Pocock, 'British History: A Plea for a New Subject', *New Zealand Journal of History* 8 (1) (1974), 3–21; and Carl Bridge and Kent Fedorowich, 'Mapping the British World', *Journal of Imperial and Commonwealth History* 31 (2) (May 2003): 1–15. See Kirsten McKenzie, *Scandal in the Colonies: Sydney and Cape Town, 1820–1850* (Melbourne: Melbourne University Press, 2004); David Lambert and Alan Lester (eds), *Colonial Lives Across the British Empire: Imperial Careering in the Long Nineteenth Century* (Cambridge: Cambridge University Press, 2006); and Duncan Bell, *The Idea of Greater Britain: Empire and the Future of World Order, 1860–1900* (Princeton: Princeton University Press, 2009).

8   Catherine Hall, *Civilising Subjects: Metropole and Colony in the English Imagination 1830–1867* (Chicago: University of Chicago Press, 2002); Antoinette Burton (ed.),

Some historians fixed on exchanges and interactions between Australia and Asia or the Pacific.⁹ Early this century, Ann Curthoys and Marilyn Lake led the push in Australia for a more eclectic and expansive transnational framework, even as Curthoys observed, somewhat regretfully, that national self-assertion had been a latecomer to our historiography.¹⁰

Lake's sensibility, training and early intellectual pursuits rendered her sympathetic to transnational methods and feminist themes. Her teachers at the University of Tasmania influenced her later trajectory. Michael Roe was tracing, in a quirky fashion, connections between Australian reformers and American Progressives, or 'vitalists' as he called them. Thus F.M. Alexander, the posture fanatic from Tasmania, had shaped the thought of John Dewey and other élite figures along the Northeast corridor of the US.¹¹ In the early twentieth century, the actions and convictions of Progressives like Theodore Roosevelt (who Roe believed was 'the forerunner of Mussolini') and the direct intervention of Victor G. Heiser of the Rockefeller Foundation had stimulated the establishment of the Australian Department of Health. 'The Australian health reformers belonged to the Progressive–Fabian surge', wrote Roe, soon after Lake finished her MA

After the Imperial Turn: Thinking with and through the Nation (Durham, NC: Duke University Press, 2003), and 'Getting Outside the Global: Re-positioning British Imperialism in World History, in *Race, Nation and Empire: Making Histories, 1750 to the Present*, eds Catherine Hall and Keith McClelland (Manchester: Manchester University Press, 2010), 199–216; Kathleen Wilson (ed.), *A New Imperial History: Culture, Identity and Modernity in Britain and the Empire, 1660–1840* (Cambridge: Cambridge University Press, 2004); and Antoinette Burton and Tony Ballantyne (eds), *Moving Subjects: Gender, Mobility and Intimacy in an Age of Empire* (Champagne-Urbana: University of Illinois Press, 2009).

9   David Walker, *Anxious Nation: Australia and the Rise of Asia, 1850-1939* (Brisbane: University of Queensland Press, 1996); Regina Ganter with Julia Martinez and Gary Lee, *Mixed Relations: Asian-Aboriginal Contact in North Australia* (Perth: University of Western Australia Press, 2005); and Julia Martinez and Adrian Vickers, *The Pearl Frontier: Indonesian Labor and Indigenous Encounters in Australia's Northern Trading Network* (Honolulu: University of Hawai'i Press, 2015). See also Donald Denoon, *Settler Capitalism: The Dynamics of Dependent Development in the Southern Hemisphere* (Melbourne: Oxford University Press, 1983), 'The Isolation of Australian History', *Historical Studies* 22 (87) (October 1986): 252–60, and 'Remembering Australasia: A Repressed Memory', *Australian Historical Studies* 34 (122) (April 2003): 290–304; and Patrick Wolfe, 'Land, Labor, and Difference: Elementary Structures of Race', *American Historical Review* 106 (3) (June 2001): 866–905. Denoon's career in Africa and Papua New Guinea, as well as Australia, made him acutely sensitive to south–south connections.

10   Ann Curthoys, 'We've Just Started Making National Histories and You Want Us to Stop Already?' in Burton (ed.), *After the Imperial Turn*, 70–89.

11   Michael Roe, 'F.M. Alexander: A Prophet from Australia', *Journal of the Royal Australian Historical Society* 60 (2) (June 1974): 117–23.

thesis in his department.[12] Much earlier, Roe had speculated on Australia as 'a useful case study on which to test the validity of the Turner [frontier] thesis', and he had urged Australian historians to 'widen our sympathies and research so far that all new world countries come within their range'.[13] Meanwhile, Malcolm McCrae was teaching magnetically the nationalist version of Australian history, focusing on the convict legacy, the labour movement and Russel Ward's Australian legend.[14] But Kay Daniels, who arrived in Hobart in 1967, was perhaps the most appealing figure for Lake. In particular, Daniels helped her 'to understand the difference that a feminist framework of analysis might make to our understanding of the past'. Daniels showed how 'women's past experiences were integral to the basic social processes that comprised history', and she suggested 'the gendered nature of men's historical experience and related national mythologies'. 'My study of nineteenth-century Australian nationalism as a masculinist project', Lake recalled, 'clearly drew inspiration from Kay's earlier critique'.[15] During the following two decades, while based at Monash and then La Trobe universities, Lake's studies in feminist history and Black Australian history would further sensitise her to long-distance international influences, connections and relationships.[16]

---

12   Michael Roe, 'The Establishment of the Australian Department of Health: Its Background and Significance', *Historical Studies* 17 (67) (October 1976):176–92 (185, 184). See also Michael Roe, *Nine Australian Progressives: Vitalism in Bourgeois Social Thought, 1890–1960* (Brisbane: University of Queensland Press, 1984). On Heiser and US Progressivism in the colonial Philippines, see Warwick Anderson, *Colonial Pathologies: American Tropical Medicine, Race, and Hygiene in the Philippines* (Durham, NC: Duke University Press, 2006).

13   Michael Roe, 'An Aspect of Australia's Place in World History', *Melbourne Historical Journal* 1 (1961): 34–37 (34, 37). Roe, whose PhD supervisor had been C.M.H. Clark, also expressed admiration for the cosmopolitan historical research (though not the personality) of Stephen H. Roberts at the University of Sydney. Lake acknowledges Roe's influence in her first book, based on her Tasmanian MA thesis—*A Divided Society: Tasmania During World War I* (Melbourne: Melbourne University Press, 1975).

14   Russel Ward, *The Australian Legend* (Melbourne: Oxford University Press, 1958).

15   Marilyn Lake, 'Kay Daniels as Feminist Historian', *Women's History Review* 12 (2) (2003): 149–51 (149, 150). Daniels arrived fresh from completing her DPhil thesis at Sussex with Asa Briggs.

16   Patricia Grimshaw, Marilyn Lake, Ann McGrath and Marian Quartly, *Creating a Nation* (Melbourne: McPhee Gribble, 1994); and Marilyn Lake, 'Frontier Feminism and the Marauding White Man', *Journal of Australian Studies* 20 (49) (1996): 12–20, *Getting Equal: The History of Australian Feminism* (Sydney: Allen & Unwin, 1999), and *Faith: Faith Bandler, Gentle Activist* (Sydney: Allen & Unwin, 2002).

By the turn of the century, Lake's research was becoming expressly transnational in orientation. Her critical inquiry into the conceptual categories and intimate experiences of race and gender persisted, but new studies increasingly recognised instrumental connections beyond national borders.[17] 'I suggest that the founding idea of Australia as a "white man's country"', Lake wrote in 2003, 'can only be fully understood in the context of the trans-national circulation of knowledge in the late nineteenth century, especially historical knowledge'.[18] She explicitly distinguished her transnational project from the analytic oscillations of comparative history, and from the new imperial history, which seemed merely to 're-inforce the old imperial hegemony'. Obsession with metropole and colony had obscured other significant entanglements. In particular, it disguised the trans-Pacific ways 'in which the emergent identity of the "white man" began to complement, and then displace, the figure of the Britisher in Australian cultural and political discourse'.[19] 'In addressing the new global history of the races', she wrote in 2004, 'Australian colonial leaders came to identify as white men under siege'.[20] Initially, Lake focused on the intellectual salons of Melbourne, Boston, New York and Washington DC, in the late nineteenth century, elucidating the personal bonds and shared conceptual repertoires of Australians such as Charles Pearson, Alfred Deakin, H.B. Higgins, and American Progressives and reformers, including Theodore Roosevelt. Additional trans-Atlantic figures, like British scholar–diplomat James Bryce and Oxford historian E.A. Freeman, trod the boards. With each staging, the cast expanded. Lake showed how these votaries in the cult of the white man formed sentimental attachments and intellectual associations, sharing racial anxieties and apprehensions under their confident white carapace. During the following years, she would let fly a series of fusillades into the fretful and edgy, yet

---

17 But not comparative history such as Andrew Markus, *Fear and Hatred: Purifying Australia, 1850–1901* (Sydney: Hale & Iremonger, 1979); and David Goodman, *Gold-Seeking: Victoria and California in the 1850s* (Sydney: Allen & Unwin, 1994). Markus and Lake were both at Monash University in the 1970s.

18 Marilyn Lake, 'White Man's Country: The Transnational History of a National Project', *Australian Historical Studies* 34 (122) (April 2003): 346–63 (346). See also her 'On Being a White Man, Australia, circa 1900', in *Cultural History in Australia*, eds Hsu-Ming Teo and Richard White (Sydney: UNSW Press, 2003), 101–12.

19 Lake, 'White Man's Country', 349, 350.

20 Marilyn Lake, 'The White Man Under Siege: New Histories of Race in the Nineteenth Century', *History Workshop Journal* 58 (1) (January 2004): 41–62 (59).

also insufferably proud and puffed-up, figure of the transnational white man.[21]

Lake's commitment to tracking down the transnational career of white masculinity culminated in *Drawing the Global Colour Line* (2008), written with Henry Reynolds. Ambitious in scale, their book charts 'the spread of "whiteness" as a transnational form of racial identification that was ... at once global in its power and personal in its meaning, the basis of geopolitical alliances and a subjective sense of self'. Taking the lead of African American scholar W.E.B. Du Bois, Lake and Reynolds observe that 'the assertion of whiteness was born in the apprehension of imminent loss'; it was a defensive, defiant mode of subject positioning.[22] While most studies of whiteness—indeed, of racial thought and practice—have been constricted by a national frame, they write, 'we trace the transnational circulation of emotions and ideas, people and publications, racial knowledge and technologies that animated white men's countries and their strategies of exclusion, deportation and segregation'.[23] Nineteenth-century opposition to Chinese immigration to the Australian and Californian goldfields sets the scene, leading to studies of conceptual responses to the Russian–Japanese war of 1904–05, early twentieth-century Asian settlement on the Pacific slope of North America, the Pacific tour of the American Fleet in 1908, the South African war, and major international conferences and institution building after World War I. Lake and Reynolds argue that Australia came to represent a model for 'coming out' as a white man, the paradigm for defensive racial profiling. Although the spotlight is on the anxious assertions of white male intellectuals and politicians in Anglo settler societies, challenges from Asian actors, such as Lowe Kong Meng in Australia and Mohandas K. Gandhi in South Africa, are also treated seriously. Much of the narrative concentrates on the intellectual entanglements of Australia and the US, whose stories previously had 'remained parallel,

---

21   For example, Marilyn Lake, 'From Mississippi to Melbourne via Natal: The Invention of the Literacy Test as a Technology of Racial Exclusion', in *Connected Worlds*, eds Curthoys and Lake, 209–29; '"The brightness of eyes and the quiet assurance which seem to say American": Alfred Deakin's Identification with Republican Manhood', *Australian Historical Studies* 38 (129) (April 2007): 32–51; 'Fellow Feeling: A Transnational Perspective on Conceptions of Civil Society and Citizenship in "White Men's Countries"', in *Civil Society and Gender Justice: Historical and Comparative Perspectives*, eds Karen Hagemann, Sonya Michel, and Gunilla Budde (New York: Berghahn Books, 2008), 265–84; and '"This great America": H.B. Higgins and Transnational Progressivism', *Australian Historical Studies* 44 (2) (2013): 172–88.

22   Lake and Reynolds, *Drawing the Global Colour Line*, 3, 2.

23   Lake and Reynolds, *Drawing the Global Colour Line*, 4.

rather than dynamically interconnected and thus mutually formative'.²⁴ As Antoinette Burton noted, this constituted 'a truly unparalleled form of transnational history', while Jonathan Hyslop confirmed 'this book is one of the few that genuinely moves beyond thinking within the framework of the nation-state'.²⁵

* * *

In advocating transnational history in the early years of the twenty-first century, Curthoys and Lake had recourse to a debate on how to write the history of the United States. 'Earlier interpretations of American history and culture ... emphasizing uniquely American experiences and habits of mind, served largely to mislead us', Laurence Veysey wrote in 1979. 'American history has been viewed far too often as if it were autonomous, a theme entirely unto itself, rather than in enormous measure a reflection of forces operating throughout the modern world.' Instead, Veysey recommended an approach 'centering upon the way that ideas travel across borders, mainly within the milieu of cultivated elites'.²⁶ According to Dorothy Ross, millennial and republican investments had led to the fable of American exceptionalism, the sense that the country possessed a unique mission and special virtue, separate from other nations. From the late nineteenth century, the notion of some essential distinction gained a racial or naturalistic gloss, as historians such as George Bancroft and Herbert Baxter Adams (who had studied in Germany) proclaimed the republic as the finest expression, or highest stage, of Teutonic liberty. During the Gilded Age, historicist explanations like Frederick Jackson Turner's 'frontier thesis' tended to displace providential and naturalistic claims.²⁷ The justification may have varied, but the nationalist tone of American history writing had proven durable. However, in 1991, Ian Tyrrell, based

---

24 Lake and Reynolds, *Drawing the Global Colour Line*, 6. See also Paul Giles, *Antipodean America: Australasia and the Constitution of U.S. Literature* (Oxford: Oxford University Press, 2014).

25 Antoinette Burton, *International History Review* 33 (4) (2011): 744–6 (745); and Jonathan Hyslop, *Journal of Global History* 4 (1) (March 2009): 175–7 (177).

26 Laurence Veysey, 'The Autonomy of American History Reconsidered', *American Quarterly* 31 (4) (Autumn 1979): 455–77 (455–6, 472).

27 Dorothy Ross, 'Historical Consciousness in Nineteenth-century America', *American Historical Review* 89 (4) (October 1984): 909–28.

in Australia, declared that the American 'paradigm of national history must be rigorously scrutinized from the perspective of alternative transnational approaches'. He urged US historians to try 'a global focus more attentive to historical specificity', to look for the transnational connections of environmentalism, economics, organisations, popular movements and ideologies.[28] In making this plea, Tyrrell pointed out that some scholars like Randolph Bourne and Du Bois during the past century already had provided compelling models for such transnational inquiry.[29] A few years after Tyrrell's intervention, David Thelen edited a special issue of the *Journal of American History*, promoting transnational approaches. Rather than taking for granted the nation, historians, according to Thelen, should concentrate 'on individuals and debates that were constructing national policies and nationalist ideas'. In particular, historians ought to examine the 'interactions, exchanges, constructions, and translations that people made as they engaged each other across national borders'.[30]

Evidently, Lake was paying close attention to specific discussions of American historiography—but this was part of a broader conversation, just one segment of the general trend away from national narratives. Thus, Lake might also have referred to Sanjay Subrahmanyam's proposal for 'connected histories', his call for tracing networks, flows, circulations, and other modes of interaction across Asia. 'How were these myths and ideas carried', he asked in 1997, 'and did the channels by which they circulated also serve as the sluices for convention of other "technologies"'? He protested that until now 'nationalism has blinded us to the possibility of connection'.[31] Similarly, Ann Laura Stoler around this time was favouring

---

28   Ian Tyrrell, 'American Exceptionalism in an Age of International History', *American Historical Review* 96 (4) (October 1991): 1031–55 (1038, 1044). See also his 'Making Nations/Making States: American Historians in the Context of Empire', *Journal of American History* 86 (3) (December 1999): 1015–44, and 'Beyond the View from Euro-America: Environment, Settler Societies, and the Internationalization of American History', in *Rethinking American History in a Global Age*, ed. Thomas H. Bender (Berkeley: University of California Press, 2002), 168–92.

29   See Robin D.G. Kelley, '"But a local phase of a world problem": Black History's Global Vision', *Journal of American History* 86 (3) (December 1999): 1054–77.

30   David Thelen, 'The Nation and Beyond: Transnational Perspectives on United States History', *Journal of American History* 86 (3) (December 1999): 965–75 (972, 973). See also Jane C. Desmond and Virginia R. Dominguez, 'Resituating American Studies in a Critical Internationalism', *American Quarterly* 48 (3) (September 1996): 475–91.

31   Sanjay Subrahmanyam, 'Connected Histories: Notes Towards a Reconfiguration of Early Modern Eurasia', *Modern Asian Studies* 31 (3) (1997): 735–62 (761). For a consideration of the 'hydraulic turn' in global histories, see Warwick Anderson,

comparative and connected histories of the intimate and affective domains of imperial governance—colonialism as a sentimental education, in effect. She was examining racial formations and gender imaginaries at a number of sites, 'to illustrate the value of looking comparatively at circuits of knowledge production, governing practices, and indirect as well as direct connections in the political rationalities that informed imperial rule'.[32] 'As North American history is becoming more international', Stoler argued in 2001, 'the imperial politics of intimacies begs for broader comparison as well'. Too often, she wrote, we 'have subscribed to models that privilege metropolitan–colony exchanges rather than circuits of people, produce, and narrations that might track common gendered principles of governance through this broader global frame'.[33] As it turned out, the work of Subrahmanyam and Stoler would prove either redundant or extraneous to Lake's purposes; after all, Subrahmanyam mostly limited himself to Asia, while Stoler still was engrossed in the Dutch East Indies, despite gestures toward North America, and her preferred style of comparison remained static and sociological, not realistically connective.

Lake's initial focus on white masculinity in her transnational inquiries seems especially apposite. Anne McClintock has claimed that women became the boundary markers of European expansion, but so too surely did nervy white men.[34] In 1910, as Lake points out, Du Bois had wryly remarked that 'the world in sudden emotional conversion has discovered that it is white, and by that token, wonderful'.[35] 'Whiteness' in the late nineteenth and early twentieth centuries developed into a particularly labile and recursive category of distinction in settler societies and administrative colonies, functioning as a boundary subject or edge effect of empire and

---

'Waiting for Newton? From Hydraulic Societies to the Hydraulics of Globalization', in *Force, Movement, Intensity: The Newtonian Imagination and the Humanities and Social Sciences*, eds Ghassan Hage and Emma Kowal (Melbourne: Melbourne University Press, 2011), 128–35.

32 Ann Laura Stoler, 'Tense and Tender Ties: The Politics of Comparison in North American History and (Post)colonial Studies', *Journal of American History* 88 (3) (December 2001): 829–65 (831). For an implied critique of this project, see Warwick Anderson, 'Racial Hygiene and the Making of Citizens in the Philippines and Australia', in *Haunted by Empire: Geographies of Intimacy in North American History*, ed. Ann L. Stoler (Durham, NC: Duke University Press, 2006), 94–115.

33 Stoler, 'Tense and Tender Ties', 837, 840. Another multi-sited model is Philippa Levine, *Prostitution, Race, and Politics: Policing Venereal Disease in the British Empire* (New York: Routledge, 2003).

34 Anne McClintock, *Imperial Leather: Race, Gender, and Sexuality in the Colonial Conquest* (New York: Routledge, 1995), 24.

35 W.E.B. Du Bois, 'The Souls of White Folk', *Independent*, 18 August 1910, 339.

nation.³⁶ That is, as Homi K. Bhabha put it, whiteness served as a 'strategy of authority', more than as any 'authentic or essential "identity"'.³⁷ A flexible yet durable artifice, whiteness worked best on the borderlands, at sites of perceived weakness or vulnerability, whether social or environmental. No coincidence then that Lake's and Reynold's case studies of transnational white men often involved war, invasion, migration, travel or secondment—displacements and threats of one sort or another, stuff happening in liminal places. The agitated assertion of whiteness on these sites constituted a powerful biopolitical interposition, unlike more culturally expressive identifications such as 'British', 'English', 'Scottish', 'Irish' and 'American'. The white man emerged as an adaptable boundary subject, an incarnation, a lively form of what sociologists describe as a 'boundary object'. According to Susan Leigh Star and James R. Griesemer, such

> boundary objects are both plastic enough to adapt to local needs and constraints of the several parties employing them, yet robust enough to maintain a common identity across sites. They are weakly structured in common use and become strongly structured in individual-site use.³⁸

As Lake astutely recognised, there is a certain flatness in the terrain of white men's countries that makes them readily connected, multiply articulated, translatable, suited to transnational analysis.

* * *

In the ten years since publication of *Drawing the Global Colour Line*, Lake has been inclined to substitute the Anglo-Saxon for the intriguing figure of the white man. It might be, as she claims, that 'the "white man" was the Anglo-Saxon rendered into vernacular', but each category seems to possess

---

36   Warwick Anderson, 'Traveling White', in *Reorienting Whiteness*, eds Leigh Boucher, Jane Carey and Katherine Ellinghaus (Basingstoke: Palgrave Macmillan, 2009), 65–72, and 'Edge Effects in Science and Medicine', *Western Humanities Review* 69 (3) (2015): 373–84.

37   Homi K. Bhabha, 'The White Stuff', *Artforum* 36 (9) (May 1998): 21–4 (21). See also Ann Laura Stoler, *Race and the Education of Desire: Foucault's History of Sexuality and the Colonial Order of Things* (Durham, NC: Duke University Press, 1995).

38   Susan Leigh Star and James R. Griesemer, 'Institutional Ecology, "Translations", and Boundary Objects: Amateurs and Professionals in Berkeley's Museum of Vertebrate Zoology, 1907–39', *Social Studies of Science* 19 (3) (August 1989): 387–420 (393).

a distinct genealogy and purpose; each implies a different mode of being in the world.[39] Lake has chosen to explore the Anglo-Saxon and Teutonic enthusiasms of historians such as Freeman in England and Adams in the United States, scouting out their influence in dispersed settler societies at the turn of the nineteenth century. Freeman's historical theories flourished, she writes, 'in the democratic New World societies of America and Australia, which were keen to locate themselves in, and provide their new societies with, a long and illustrious "race history"'. Moreover, 'the discourse on Anglo-Saxonism also enabled Australian federal fathers to identify with the United States without appearing to be disloyal'.[40] Certainly, Lake adduces plentiful evidence indicating that luminaries like Teddy Roosevelt and Alfred Deakin fetishised the rude, democratic Anglo-Saxon male. But as she suggests, the widely dispersed figures of the Anglo-Saxon male and the white man were made to perform disparate tasks—just as an Anglo-Saxon Australia policy would have been incommensurate with the white Australia policy, and probably unimaginable in the circumstances. The Anglo-Saxon appeared to frequent the intellectual salons of the northeast United Sates, southern England and southeast Australia (to which Lake has returned)—his conceit gave way to real white men at times of stress, confronting Asians and Africans and Indigenous people, and in menacing places such as tropical Australia or the colonial Philippines.[41] When Paul A. Kramer influentially attempted in 2002 to place 'histories of U.S. race making … in a transnational frame', he turned to the 'complex invocations … of racial Anglo-Saxonism'.[42] Kramer believed that 'the success of the Anglo-Saxon as a racial-exceptionalist bridge between the United States and the British Empire was due in part to the social, familial, intellectual, and literary networks that tied élite Americans and Britons together'. The 'élite' in his formulation does a lot of work. As Kramer admitted, in the colonial Philippines 'the formal rhetoric of Anglo-Saxonism was notably

---

39   Marilyn Lake, 'White is Wonderful: Emotional Conversion and Subjective Formation', in Boucher, Ellinghaus and Carey (eds), 119–34 (131).

40   Marilyn Lake, '"Essentially Teutonic": E.A. Freeman, Liberal Race Historian. A Transnational Perspective', in Hall and McClelland (eds), 56–73 (62, 68), and 'British World or New World? Anglo-Saxonism and Australian Engagement with America', *History Australia* 10 (3) (February 2013): 36–50.

41   This is implied, too, in Peter Mandler, *The Idea of Greater Britain: Empire and the Future of World Order, 1860–1900* (Princeton: Princeton University Press, 2007), chapter 4; and Bell, 114.

42   Paul A. Kramer, 'Empires, Exceptions and Anglo-Saxons: Race and Rule Between the British and United States Empires, 1880–1910', *Journal of American History* 88 (4) (March 2002): 1315–53 (1319, 1318).

absent'; he conceded the 'limited Philippine relevance of Anglo-Saxonism', compared to whiteness.[43]

The apparently irresistible rise of the Anglo-Saxon male in recent transnational histories causes me to question the broad analytic utility of the historiographic frame. In subjecting some phenomena to transnational analysis, one might distort them or, rather, leave out key features. Clearly, whiteness has proven to be a sensitive transnational sampling device, an effective means of gauging a specific racial inter-subjectivity and dispersed biopolitical subject positioning. In Kramer's words, such a mode of subjectification 'highlights race as a dynamic, contextual, contested, and contingent field of power'—therefore it makes possible compelling connected or transnational histories, like *Drawing the Global Colour Line*.[44] But my impression is that Anglo-Saxonism is a configuration that exudes intellectual dependency and cultural cringe. It seems less a transnational pattern than an imperial or derivative phenomenon, perhaps replacing greater Britain with greater America, and inadvertently recapitulating US sovereignty. It might thus constitute a story of national expansion more than transnational relatedness. There is significant asymmetry in interaction, a failure of reciprocity in exchange, that conventional transnational analysis does not readily capture. In a world of flows and circulation and connections how does one detect and explain persistent dependency and exploitation?[45] Might a transnational approach gloss over tenacious imperial structures and relations? Are some matters, some racial concepts or formations, more amenable to critique by the new imperial history or postcolonial methods—in this case, targeting the US? It is a tribute to Marilyn Lake's questing historical intelligence that we are stimulated to ask such questions. Through her further studies of the dissemination, as it were, of élite Anglo-Saxonism, Lake no doubt will continue to illuminate these and other conundrums in writing history beyond the nation

---

43   Kramer, 'Empires, Exceptions and Anglo-Saxons', 1326, 1345.

44   Paul A. Kramer, *The Blood of Government: Race, Empire, and the United States in the Philippines* (Chapel Hill: University of North Carolina Press, 2006), 2. Kramer was referring to his project generally, not to Anglo-Saxonism or whiteness.

45   David Washbrook makes a similar point in postulating that connections and networks now stand in for force and coercion—'Problems in Global History', in *Writing the History of the Global*, ed. Maxine Berg (Oxford: Oxford University Press, 2013), 21–31 (27).

Chapter 17

SETTLER COLONIALISM AND AFRICAN AMERICAN HISTORIOGRAPHY

Reflections on Marilyn Lake's Contribution to Transnational Histories of Race

Clare Corbould

Scene: 22-year-old PhD student, green as, staffing the registration desk of the 1998 Sydney AHA conference in order to earn her entrance fee.

Enters from offstage: Professor Marilyn Lake. A buzz goes around the group of postgraduate students. Nervous, agog, as the author approaches; she of the ripping articles, 'Female Desires' and 'Mission Impossible', and co-author of the signal *Creating a Nation*, all of which we had read as undergraduates. None has the courage to talk to her directly, but her confident presence alone inspires. Wow! If that's what feminist history looks like, our young faces signal, SIGN. US. UP.

Scene. Fifteen years later. Not-so-young couple buys a house in Melbourne after moving from Sydney, and it turns out to be just around the corner from one Professor Lake. The proximity facilitates a growing and warm friendship, based in part on their shared experiences of being out-of-staters who have moved to the city. Some years later still, the elder of the two begins to cull her research materials to prepare for the loss of her office upon retirement. The younger can hardly believe her luck as the professor begins to hand them over. On one occasion she even returns home to find four ring-binders of material on Faith Bandler sitting in plastic bags on her doorstep. Jokes to her spouse: better research assistance than she could ever dream of.

* * *

Australian historians of the United States have long enjoyed an elevated reputation in the US itself—burnished especially by Rhys Isaac's groundbreaking work on colonial Virginia, Ian Tyrrell's path-setting work on transnational history, Shane White's dogged work in the archives of nineteenth-century New York, and Patrick Wolfe's articles in *American Historical Review*, still regularly set on graduate student syllabi—and helped along since the early 1990s by efforts in American organisations and institutions to 'internationalize' American history.[1] In fact, the historiographies of the United States *and* Australia through the middle decades of the twentieth century were unusually parochial, and both have benefited from consideration of the relationship between one another (and other places). To be sure, approaches taken to United States and colonial American history among Australian-based scholars have varied and not all have used a comparative or transnational lens. Some, rather, have written history indistinguishable from that of their US-born-and-trained peers.[2] Even then, Australian-based scholars have often asked questions, used methods, or drawn conclusions

---

1 Key among the efforts were the *Journal of American History*, published by the Organization of American Historians, and the multi-year 'Project on Internationalizing the Study of American History', hosted by NYU at its Tuscan villa and known thereafter as 'The La Pietra Project'. See David Thelen, Willi Paul Adams, Honoré Mobonda et al., 'Toward the Internationalization of American History: A Round Table', *Journal of American History* 79 (2) (September 1992): 432–542. See also the special issues of *Journal of American History* in March, September, and December 1999, introduced in 'A Note to Readers on Internationalization of the *JAH*' 85 (4) (March 1999): 1278–9. On La Pietra see Thomas Bender (ed.), *Rethinking American History in a Global Age* (Berkeley: University of California Press, 2002); and Robert Shaffer, 'The "Internationalization" of U.S. History: A Progress Report for World Historians', *Journal of World History* 20 (4) (December 2009): 581–94.

2 There are more than a dozen articles on 'doing' American Studies in Australia in the *Australasian Journal of American Studies* alone, not including those on teaching. All are authored by male historians. See, for example, David Goodman, 'Location, Location—American History in Australia', *Australasian Journal of American Studies* 23 (2) (December 2004): 55–64; and Ian Tyrrell, 'From the Wet and Mud of Newcastle: Reflections on ANZASA and U.S. History in Australia, 1974–2012', *Australasian Journal of American Studies* 32 (1) (July 2013): 62–79.

that reflect preoccupations particular to their place in the world, or that derive from a set of institutional demands quite foreign to the United States.[3]

The most significant impact Australian-based scholars have had on the field of United States history has been in the realm of settler colonialism (and perhaps to a lesser degree in feminist history—more on this later). This is hardly a surprise, given what the two nations share: a history of British colonialism (if also French and Spanish in the United States) and dispossession of native peoples from their lands; a language; and close political connections. But where Australian historiography in the past forty years has been transformed by the activism of Indigenous Australians, the same has not quite been the case in the United States. The social movements of the 1960s and beyond have resulted there instead in a massive outpouring of work on slavery and its aftermath, so much so that slavery is very often referenced casually as America's 'original sin'. Settler colonialism and its long effects are yet to be integrated into historical enterprise in the United States to the extent that has been the case in Australian scholarship.

This impact is evident in responses to Marilyn Lake and Henry Reynolds's important transnational study of the making of 'white men's countries' in *Drawing the Global Colour Line* (2008). While Australian reviewers tended not to spend much time discussing the book as an example of a settler colonial perspective, or even to mention it—perhaps taking that point so for granted it did not require attention—several American reviewers emphasised the innovation of a settler colonial approach to questions that US historians had long dealt with. Likewise the blurbs by Americans on the book's back cover, presumably targeting a US audience, emphasised this point.

Such variance was also evident to me during a 2011 conference titled 'Beyond Freedom: New Directions in the Study of Emancipation', hosted by the Gilder Lehrman Center for the Study of Slavery, Resistance, and Abolition at Yale University. Although the bulk of the conference dealt with the middle decades of the nineteenth century, it was one of those frustrating American affairs in which the few foreigners in the audience wondered if any of those participating had even heard of convict labour,

---

3   For a recent discussion of how 'positionality' and location affect the questions, approaches, methods, and conclusions of non-US-based historians, see Nicolas Barreyre, Manfred Berg and Simon Middleton, 'Straddling Intellectual Worlds: Positionality and the Writing of American History', in *Historians Across Borders: Writing American History in a Global Age*, eds Nicolas Barreyre, Michael Heale, Stephen Tuck and Cécile Vidal (Berkeley: University of California Press, 2014), 75–92.

transportation, or any other form of unfree labour besides American slavery and its aftermath.[4] The 'new directions' were exciting in and of themselves, and the papers excellent, but they were also limited to questions that could be answered wholly within the borders of the United States. (In a recent and otherwise outstanding book on the same topic, the editors state they hope that the book's questions will 'point to as-yet-unrealized possibilities for transnational, comparative, and global history', noting the potential for comparative studies of governance in the late nineteenth century, in particular.[5]) Two papers on the end of slavery elsewhere did not tip the balance. One exception came in the opening session, when Eric Foner, distinguished United States historian and now emeritus professor at Columbia University, spent five of his seven allotted minutes talking excitedly about a recent book: *Drawing the Global Colour Line*. As I sat in the audience, I reflected on just how rare it was to hear a speech like that, not only for its enthusiasm but also for its recognition of the novelty of Lake and Reynolds's insights. Not least is it rare to see a woman's work treated that way. Foner was excited because *Drawing the Global Colour Line* brought something fresh to United States history: a perspective steeped in settler colonial history that achieved what few transnational histories of the United States had until then managed, an account of the genuine back-and-forth that took place in ideas about race, governance, borders.[6] Lake's forthcoming work, which extends that settler colonial framework into the interchange between Australia and the United States in the era of Progressivism, promises to have an even greater impact on US historians.[7]

Partly inspired by that experience, partly by Lake's work itself, I recently shifted focus, too, to try to engage US history from a more explicitly Australian standpoint, and vice versa. For the remainder of this essay, I will reflect on the direct and indirect ways Lake's work has influenced mine. As a foreign-born and foreign-trained historian in a huge intellectual

---

4   For another example, from the title onwards, see Lisa Lowe, *The Intimacies of Four Continents* (Durham: Duke University Press, 2015).

5   Gregory P. Downs and Kate Masur, 'Introduction: Echoes of War: Rethinking Post-Civil War Governance and Politics', in *The World the Civil War Made*, eds Gregory P. Downs and Kate Masur (Chapel Hill: University of North Carolina Press, 2015), 16–17.

6   Eric Foner, 'Prologue', in *Beyond Freedom: Disrupting the History of Emancipation*, eds David W. Blight and Jim Downs (Athens: University of Georgia Press, 2017), xv.

7   Marilyn Lake, *Progressive New World: How Settler Colonialism and Transpacific Exchange Shaped American Reform* (Cambridge, MA: Harvard University Press, 2018).

marketplace such as the US and, as an employee in a system that for better or worse measures its academics' outputs and impacts, I have had cause to consider what I might bring to American history that is worthwhile and noteworthy. The answer lies in my outsider's perspective, which has in recent years led me to the study of the transnational creation of ideas from below about the nature and extent of the British world.

Specifically, I have so far examined the way that African Americans reimagined their own position by comparing it to that of Indigenous and local populations in settler colonial and colonial polities worldwide. I have also written about the converse scenario in which Indigenous Australians and Australian South Sea Islanders identified with African Americans in the late 1970s and 1980s.[8] Such work might seem to reify that unreflexive tendency to assume, as Patrick Wolfe observed in 1991, that race and blackness are somehow equivalent on both sides of the Pacific.[9] On the contrary, as my recent work with Hilary Emmett suggests, when either African Americans or Aboriginal Australians made these links across the Pacific, they did so in ways that were clearly cognisant of the different regimes of racial meaning that the distinct histories of each place had foisted upon them. In fact, any assertions of an alliance between the two groups made use of those supposed differences. Our investigation of the afterlife of Atlantic slavery in Australia and the Pacific owes much to Lake's groundbreaking work on labour, race and narratives of slavery.[10] Such deliberate, transnational efforts to make race were in some ways a response to the devastating efforts among the élite white men of Lake's work, and of the settler colonial state that those men staffed. While they sometimes used the techniques of those élite men—meetings, letters, legislation, legal apparatus—more often they did not, as they were shut out of the institutions of the state. Instead, the subaltern form of transnational race making took place through newspapers, public protest, and popular culture.

---

8   Clare Corbould, 'The Struggle for Land Rights Will Not Be Televised: Settler Colonialism and *Roots* Down Under', *Transition: The Magazine of Africa and the Diaspora*, no. 122 (2017): 79–97.

9   Patrick Wolfe, 'Land, Labor, and Difference: Elementary Structures of Race', *American Historical Review* 106 (3) (June 2001): 866–905.

10   Marilyn Lake, 'The White Man under Siege: New Histories of Race in the Nineteenth Century and the Advent of White Australia', *History Workshop Journal* 58 (1) (January 2004): 41–62; Marilyn Lake and Henry Reynolds, *Drawing the Global Colour Line: White Men's Countries and the Question of Racial Equality* (Melbourne: Melbourne University Press, 2008); Marilyn Lake, 'Challenging the "Slave-Driving Employers": Understanding Victoria's 1896 Minimum Wage through a World-History Approach', *Australian Historical Studies* 45 (1) (2014): 87–102.

***

Reading microfilm of African American New York newspapers of the 1920s and 1930s in the basement of Harlem's Schomburg Center for Research in Black Culture, my attention was often caught by references to Aboriginal Australians or 'native Australians'. I was too inexperienced to realise I could be collecting such mentions alongside material for my PhD thesis about black Americans' ideas about Africa, but I nevertheless kept note of a few instances. In any case, examples cropped up whenever black internationalists enumerated the list of subjugated people worldwide with whom they identified. Digitisation of many of the key national African American newspapers has enabled me to conduct systematic research. It reveals that throughout the 1910s, 1920s and 1930s, African American reporters and opinion columnists all stressed with reasonable frequency an imagined alliance with Indigenous Australians, among others.

By linking their own experiences to the travails of colonised people in Australia, as well as those in India and other parts of Asia, South America, Africa and the Caribbean, African American activists cast their own situation as that of a colonised people. This in turn recast white Americans as part of the British world and called into question the idea that the Revolution had rendered them a uniquely democratic people and nation.

Newspapers were key resources for colonised people worldwide, including in this case African Americans, to co-create a sense of shared blackness or at least of a shared condition. Scholars have long observed the role that print culture has played in connecting people who are physically removed from one another. While the black American press of the early and mid-twentieth century is not a transparent window into the thoughts and feelings of all African Americans, it was utterly integral to black political and cultural life. This was true at the local, national and international level, including a distinct emphasis on the black diaspora. African American publishers built businesses in cities in all the nation's regions, the biggest with several city editions. The circulation of these newspapers, which peaked in the 1940s, was wider still, with stories abounding of the papers being transported by railroad porters to rural areas of the South, being passed on from person to person as a matter of course, and being read aloud in communal spaces such as barber shops and front porches.[11] Black American newspapers had subscribers in the Caribbean, and Caribbean migrants remained loyal purchasers of their hometown newspapers, which were shipped to Brooklyn and other port cities.[12] In addition to local and national news, each paper printed international news, news of migrant communities, and news reprinted from newspapers worldwide.

The imagined connection between African Americans and Indigenous Australians reached its peak in the black American press when it seemed that white Australians were enslaving Aboriginal people. In the early 1930s, revelations from the Anti-Slavery and Aborigines' Protection Society made for sensational headlines. The northern Australian cattle industry, the society charged, relied on forced labour. Two African American newspapers reproduced 'a photo of some black Australian natives in chains, being held captive by two white men standing over them with guns'. The picture, said an African American columnist in a competing newspaper, 'looked like the slave system brought down to date'.[13] (He admonished the competitor for printing such a degrading image.) This was part and parcel of the treatment

---

11   According to Washburn, after a peak circulation of 250,000 in four editions in 1937, and distribution in every state and abroad, the *Pittsburgh Courier* dropped to about 149,000 for the rest of the 1930s, with local city circulation at 20,000: see Patrick S. Washburn, *The African American Newspaper: Voice of Freedom* (Evanston, IL: Northwestern University Press, 2006), 133–5. Andrew Buni writes that the *Courier* outsold other black newspapers from 1937 to 1945, reaching a high point in 1947 of 357,212, which decreased to 280,000 by 1950: see Andrew Buni, *Robert L. Vann of the Pittsburgh Courier: Politics and Black Journalism* (Pittsburgh: University of Pittsburgh Press, 1974), 325. On the *Chicago Defender*'s circulation, see James R. Grossman, *Land of Hope: Chicago, Black Southerners and the Great Migration* (Chicago: University of Chicago Press, 1989), 74, 76–80, 302 n32, 344 n68; Ethan Michaeli, *The* Defender*: How the Legendary Black Newspaper Changed America* (New York: Houghton Mifflin, 2016), 256. For more general figures, see Roland E. Wolseley, *The Black Press, U.S.A.*, 2nd edn (Ames: Iowa State University Press, 1972), 10. On the post-purchase circulation of black newspapers see Grossman, *Land of Hope*, 78; Mary G. Rolinson, *Grassroots Garveyism: The Universal Negro Improvement Association in the Rural South, 1920–1927* (Chapel Hill: University of North Carolina Press, 2007), 72–102, 119–20; Kim T. Gallon, 'Between Respectability and Modernity: Black Newspapers and Sexuality, 1925–1940' (PhD dissertation, University of Pennsylvania, 2009), 32; Ula Yvette Taylor, *The Veiled Garvey: The Life and Times of Amy Jacques Garvey* (Chapel Hill: University of North Carolina Press, 2002), 77.

12   Lara Putnam, 'Circum-Atlantic Print Circuits and Internationalism from the Peripheries in the Interwar Era', in *Print Culture Histories Beyond the Metropolis*, eds James J. Connolly et al. (Toronto: University of Toronto Press, 2016), 215–39.

13   'Calvin's Digest', *Pittsburgh Courier*, 23 January 1932. I use this example and the next several in Clare Corbould, 'Black Internationalism's Shifting Alliances: African American Newspapers, the White Australia Policy, and Indigenous Australians, 1919–1948', *History Compass* 15 (5) (May 2017): e12366. For details of international

all people of colour could expect, the newspapers pointed out, in a 'white man's country' or 'white Australia'.[14]

African American reporters, editors and cartoonists continued to excoriate the policies of a government committed to White Australia for decades, taking only a brief hiatus during the time when black American GIs found themselves stationed up and down the east and west coasts of Australia. After those troops arrived in 1942, the black American press fell oddly silent on the conditions under which Indigenous people lived. Instead, those newspapers reported frequently on the surprisingly warm welcome with which white Australians greeted the US forces, including its African American servicemen. Cartoonists took up the theme, with one depicting the arrival of the first of the African American troops. A huge ship lingers at the dock in the background as the soldiers march onto land, four-abreast. Illustrator Jay Jackson sketched the black GIs as literally taller and broader than the white Australian men standing on the sidelines. Each carries a large rifle on his shoulder and all are dressed in the eye-catching uniforms, including long pants, that distinguished American servicemen from the drab Australian troops in their shorts.[15] One such Australian soldier stands between the marching African Americans and the rope that has been strung up to hold back the surging crowds. He leans backwards, arms outstretched, in a vain attempt to restrain white Australian women who are leaning forward to reach and touch the newcomers. The crowds on either side clap, cheer and hold aloft both Australian and American flags.[16]

Positive accounts of white Australians appeared in the black press throughout the time black troops were stationed 'down under', because they were a useful counterpoint to racism and discrimination prevalent in the United States. Newspapers used these reports to show that white people's nature could change; that racism was neither natural nor immutable. That Australians were a white people with whom white Americans felt a

---

attention to Aboriginal labour at the time, see Fiona Paisley, 'An Echo of Black Slavery: Emancipation, Forced Labour and Australia in 1933', *Australian Historical Studies* 45 (1) (2014): 103–25.

14   Such phrases appeared often in the African American press, including the quotation marks to indicate the disdain of the authors for a nation that had deliberately constructed itself as such, e.g., 'The Week', *Chicago Defender*, 19 August 1922; 'Tan Americans Unwittingly Capture Women of the World', *Baltimore Afro-American*, 7 October 1944.

15   Marilyn Lake, 'The Desire for a Yank: Sexual Relations between Australian Women and American Servicemen during World War II', *Journal of the History of Sexuality* 2 (4) (April 1992): 621–33.

16   Jay Jackson, 'To the Rescue', *Chicago Defender*, 18 April 1942.

natural affinity—hence the new use of the affectionate monikers, 'Aussie' and 'downunder'—made this case even more persuasive. Fondness for white Australians did not last long; in 1945 the African American press reverted to the kinds of accounts of Australia that had dominated until 1942.

With an eye on the peace and especially on the drafting of the UN charter of human rights, the black press redoubled its efforts to show that colonisation and imperialism were the root of war, maintaining a steady critique of the British Empire even as the Allies rejoiced at the defeat of fascism. Australia was once again criticised as a 'white man's country', an outpost remote from the heart of the British Empire but nevertheless typical of it. 'Australia', an unnamed *Chicago Defender* journalist remarked in 1947, 'keeps its native dark-skinned population (called Aborigines) on reservations that have been described as comparable to concentration camps. They also segregate the men from the women in order to prevent their breedings and kill off the original Australians'.[17] The phrase 'concentration camp' would immediately have conjured up for readers the policies of genocide in Nazi Germany, serving to link the imperial efforts to control Indigenous people to fascist policies. Black newspapers also resumed criticism of Australian unions and the federal government for their policies regarding labour and immigration. When Canada hosted a conference of Commonwealth Labour Parties in Toronto in 1947, the Associated Negro Press provided a report that appeared in varied versions in many of the black newspapers. These articles singled out the white Australian representative who affirmed 'that Australia's Labor government believes in a "white Australia. Other people may have different opinions, but we will never allow colored peoples into Australia", he said'.[18] The *Chicago Defender* condemned Australia for shirking its duties to displaced people, especially after relying on protection from black American servicemen during the war.[19] As they continued to fight at home for justice—even after hundreds of thousands of black men served in the armed forces to defeat fascism—African American activists likewise continued to draw parallels between the Australian state, the US state, and the British Empire.

---

17   'The Land Down Under … Way Under', *Chicago Defender*, 6 September 1947.
18   'Australia Bars All Non-whites', *Norfolk Journal and Guide*, 20 September 1947.
19   'Yank-sparked Aussie Race Hate Stands Firm at Labor Conference', *Chicago Defender*, 20 September 1947.

***

Much of what appeared in African American newspapers about Indigenous Australians and about the shared experiences of racism and colonialism was theoretical and abstract rather than based on direct connections between the two groups of people. There were occasional exceptions, as historian John Maynard has noted, such as when the black nationalist newspaper of the Universal Negro Improvement Association, the *Negro World*, published a letter from Indigenous man Tom Lacey.[20] For reasons described above, the black American press neglected to report on Indigenous Australians during the war, when members of both groups certainly met.[21] Perhaps, too, the differences between the groups became apparent upon meeting: one descended from transported and enslaved people from Africa, the other a native group whose politics were inseparable from claims to land. Certainly, when groups of Indigenous people and African-descended groups in the US and Caribbean gathered in the late 1960s and 1970s, they recognised very clearly what they shared *and* how they differed, as work by many scholars on this side of the Pacific has shown.[22]

Just as African Americans asserted their affinity with colonised Australians in the 1920s and 1930s, so too did Indigenous Australians make use of a relationship with a 'black' world from that period forward. Maynard's work has shown the inspiration early Aboriginal activist organisations took from African American political groups. Into the 1960s and 1970s, as Kathy Lothian and Tracey Banivanua Mar's research has proven,

---

20 John Maynard, '"In the Interests of Our People": The Influence of Garveyism on the Rise of Australian Aboriginal Political Activism', *Aboriginal History* 25 (2005): 1–22.

21 For evidence of relations between African American servicemen and Aboriginal women, see Karen Hughes, 'Mobilising Across Colour Lines: Intimate Encounters between Aboriginal Women and African American and Other Allied Servicemen on the World War II Australian Home Front', *Aboriginal History* 41 (2017): 47–70; Stephen Kinnane, *Shadow Lines* (Fremantle: Fremantle Arts Centre Press, 2003).

22 For studies that include Australian activists in such networks, see Marilyn Lake, *Faith: Faith Bandler, Gentle Activist* (Sydney: Allen & Unwin, 2002), 144–58; Tracey Banivanua Mar, *Decolonisation and the Pacific: Indigenous Globalisation and the Ends of Empire* (Cambridge: Cambridge University Press, 2014); Angelique Stastny and Raymond Orr, 'The Influence of the US Black Panthers on Indigenous Activism in Australia and New Zealand from 1969 Onwards', *Australian Aboriginal Studies* 2 (2014): 60–74; Alyssa L. Trometter, 'Malcolm X and the Aboriginal Black Power Movement in Australia, 1967–1972', *Journal of African American History* 100 (2) (Spring 2015): 226–49; Jon Piccini, *Transnational Protest, Australia and the 1960s: Global Radicals* (Basingstoke: Palgrave, 2016).

Indigenous groups throughout Australia and the Western Pacific took up the compelling rhetoric encapsulated in the phrase 'Black Power' and, by yoking it to claims for self-determination, land rights and spatial autonomy, made it their own.[23] Definitions of Indigeneity also altered. Partly in response to decades of state-sponsored efforts to 'breed out' Aboriginality, men and women who could claim any Indigenous forebears could now proudly claim an Indigenous identity.[24] In an article written with Hilary Emmett, I have taken Lake's observations about Faith Bandler as a point of departure in order to examine how activists for racial justice in Australia took up tropes and rhetoric from slavery and its aftermath in the United States South.[25] In 1977, after two decades of full-time activism, Bandler wrote a novel she based on the life of her father, Wacvie Mussingkon, who had been transported to Queensland to work in the sugar trade. 'The cover of *Wacvie*', wrote Lake, 'would show a Black man with a chain around his neck'.[26] Bandler's book, as Hilary and I have observed, takes all kinds of tropes from nineteenth-century slave narratives and twentieth-century neo-slave narratives published in the United States. Bandler by that time had been shut out of the Indigenous activism of which she had long been part, and her identification with narratives of enslavement in the United States followed an obvious logic.

But so too did the affinity that Aboriginal activists had for African American activism and history, with the most prominent examples being the Freedom Rides Charles Perkins organised in northern New South Wales, the Australian Black Panther Party, and Gary Foley's reminiscences of scouring Sydney bookshops for works by prominent African American activists such as Malcolm X.[27] It was no doubt expedient for Aboriginal

---

23 Banivanua Mar, *Decolonisation*, 183–215; Kathy Lothian, 'Seizing the Time: Australian Aborigines and the Influence of the Black Panther Party', *Journal of Black Studies* 35 (4) (2005): 179–200.

24 Emma Kowal, 'Descent, Classification and Indigeneity in Australia', in *Mixed Race Identities in Australia, New Zealand and the Pacific Islands*, eds Kirsten McGavin and Farida Fozdar (New York: Routledge, 2017), 19–35.

25 Clare Corbould and Hilary Emmett, 'Australian Afterlives of Atlantic Slavery: Belatedness and Transpacific American Studies', *Journal of American Studies* 52 (3) (2018): 602–17.

26 Lake *Faith*, 158.

27 Ann Curthoys, *Freedom Ride: A Freedom Rider Remembers* (Sydney: Allen & Unwin, 2002); John Maynard, 'Marching to a Different Beat: The Influence of the International Black Diaspora on Aboriginal Australia', in *Indigenous Networks: Mobility, Connections and Exchange*, eds Jane Carey and Jane Lydon (New York: Routledge, 2014), 262–72.

activists to link their own efforts to a group whose profile was so high. But, as the examples above show, this link had a longer history, with African Americans since the early twentieth century joining forces, at least theoretically, with colonised people. In the era of Black Power, moreover, African Americans had made extensive claims that the Atlantic slave trade and its aftermath constituted a kind of genocide, making an explicit link with the spatial removal and racial assimilation practised on native people by settler colonial states. Such rhetoric took the masters' tools—the regimes of racial management designed to expropriate land and labour—on both sides of the Pacific to build an altogether new house, with new residents.

* * *

Denouement (deus ex machina?): These days, on her frequent trips to the United States, the middle-aged researcher is happy at conferences when the locals say not only: 'oh, wow, you're Australian, do you know Shane White/ Ian Tyrrell', but also now: 'do you know Marilyn Lake?' Unfortunately, when I reply I live around the corner from her, I do somewhat confirm Americans' stereotypes about Australia being distant and small, but that's a small price to pay.

TRIBUTES FROM AFAR

A number of Marilyn's friends and colleagues were unable to attend the Festschrift celebrating her career and achievements. Some of her Australian colleagues were located overseas at the time but were eager to send tributes, while many of those comprising her international scholarly friendship circle also expressed a desire to have their accolades and reminiscences made public on the occasion of Marilyn's retirement. We are delighted to be able to publish their brief tributes in this final chapter. They come from the following:

Sally Alexander, London
Alison Bashford, Cambridge, UK
Eileen Boris, Santa Barbara
Antoinette Burton, Urbana-Champaign
Dipesh Chakrabarty, Chicago
Nancy Cott, Harvard
Karen Hagemann, Chapel Hill
Catherine Hall, London
Barbara Hobson, Stockholm
Dane Kennedy, Washington
Linda Kerber, Iowa
Alice Kessler-Harris, New York
Ann McGrath, Durham
Mae Ngai, New York
Penny Russell, Harvard
Glenda Sluga, Vienna
Ellen Boucher, Amherst

Sally Alexander, Goldsmith's, London

Marilyn's history is truly radical: she has pressed British and European historians to think about race as well as gender in the making of national identity, she has reconstructed the formative role of international human rights in shaping twentieth century liberal democracies, and she has laid bare the transnational processes of making 'A White Australia'. Her essay, for instance, about the historians who influenced the making of White Australia (*History Workshop Journal* 58, Autumn 2004) is at once dramatic in its choice of imagery and precise in its attention to detail—the finer qualities of what we used to call 'close reading'. Charles Pearson, historian (with the help of the census) of the global political demography of race towards the end of the nineteenth century, unnerved the psyche of the white imperial class with his vision of the black and yellow races multiplying in their millions, ruling independently, seizing and monopolising European trade. This gentle, scholarly, peripatetic historian was 'the prophet of decolonisation' whose racial thinking underpinned government thinking in Australia, where white governing men identified with white Americans in the aftermath of civil war and with the European governing classes—all those white races who lived in 'temperate' climates, whose superior intellects and liberal institutions made it imperative for them to govern. The attention to the political fantasies and nightmares of her subjects, as well as to the development of policy and law, distinguishes Marilyn's thinking. A passionate feminist, she pushes her historical curiosity as far as it will go.

Marilyn and I met through Catherine Hall, historian of gender and empire, in London. Marilyn invited me to give a plenary lecture to the AGM of the Australian Historical Association in the early 1990s. I spoke about sexual knowledge among mothers and daughters in London between the two world wars—about subjectivity as well as the emotional economy of the family and moral authority of sexology and feminist research. When I looked up, Marilyn's smile, her mop of blonde hair and the light in her blue eyes were deeply reassuring as she deftly summarised the paper and spelled out the significance for the histories of subjectivity, in which of course, she was very skilled!

She's a brilliant friend. 'Stimulating, sharply intelligent', as she described Faith Bandler, Gentle Activist, the Aboriginal human rights activist about whom she wrote a biography, given to me on one of her London visits. (Marilyn always arrives with gifts, usually also a carrier bag with some delicious garment inside for herself or one of her daughters). We don't meet often enough, but when we do we pick up the threads as if we left them off only last month. She's the best conversationalist, always challenging and fun, warm and sympathetic. And she loves to talk history, over a glass of wine and a good meal, in the interstices of a seminar. I'm happy to celebrate her, and would love to be there in person.

Alison Bashford, Cambridge, UK

I'm very sorry not to be at this celebration of Marilyn's work and her remarkable influence in our field. This is the closest I've ever come to writing a wedding telegram.

My first memory of Marilyn Lake—in person—is in the Melbourne University History Department's common room. A few of us had just produced a *Lilith* issue. I was a graduate student, talking—I think with Di Hall—about a group of 1920s women pledging to uphold the brotherhood of man. Marilyn was in the adjacent conversation but I remember her suddenly turning, and listening intently. I have a strong memory of wondering how it was possible to listen so ferociously.

But then—and again, I remember thinking this quite explicitly—this ferocious listener was the one who wrote 'The Politics of Respectability' and 'Mission Impossible'. It all made sense. For me, as I'm sure for many of us, those articles heralded a wholly new kind of intervention into the Australian history project. All kinds of new prospects unfolded. The clarity, the surprising twists and turns, the unpredictability and boldness of Marilyn's scholarly work have been enormously influential. Australian history would look wholly different had she not written these early essays.

As I ventured into various US conferences over the mid and late 1990s, Marilyn was always there! At that point when so many were thinking through the history of internationalism through the history of feminism, she put Australia firmly into that conversation, and at the same time brought a gendered international history back. It was quite a moment in women's history, probably unrepeatable.

Personally, Marilyn has been an inspiration from the beginning. And an active mentor. She took time early on in my career—after I'd written 'Is White Australia Possible?', I think it was—to send a written note of appreciation for that article. That vote of confidence and interest was much appreciated, and certainly spurred me on. Her talks after the Harvard Australian Studies year, including descriptions of the Cambridge bookshops and exciting conversations, made me aspire to that post as well. She was right. It was remarkable.

But teaching these last few years in the other Cambridge, it's quite clear that *Drawing the Global Colour Line* is what defines Marilyn's work internationally—at least thus far. British students here are often entirely unfamiliar with Australian history. It is interesting and surely important, that these days it's through a Lake-inspired transnational Pacific history, not an older British imperial history, that many British students come to Australian history for the first time.

Congratulations, Marilyn. I wish I was there to celebrate. With warm thanks for the ideas, the conversations and the inspirations over many years.

Eileen Boris, Santa Barbara, President of the International Federation for Research in Women's History

It's easy to talk intersectionality, but, in her beautifully crafted and impressively researched books, Marilyn Lake has paved the way to writing history that accounts for race and whiteness, gender and femininity, settler colonialism and indigeneity, class and large social structures—without neglecting culture either. Whether viewing Australia through the lens of women's history, explicating the travels of British and US feminist texts, or giving us a transnational understanding of white men's nations, Marilyn has transformed how we think. I'll never think of the minimum wage the same way after your recent reconsideration! We couldn't ask for a better colleague or sister in the struggle. We honour you and hope we can entice you to still visit our meetings!

Antoinette Burton, Urbana-Champaign, Illinois

What I most admire about Marilyn's career-long work is the pattern we see of critical engagement with the question of women and gender and with the protocols of traditional history writing itself. She has always been invested in tracking gender as a field of power, the nation as a constructed object, and politics as a contingent though decisive force in the making and unmaking of historical interpretation. Whether it's Faith Bandler or the white and Chinese men who make up the story of 'the global colour line', Lake has exhibited a keen eye for subjects above and below the threshold of History, aiming to restore 'minor' figures to our vision and to reorient 'major' players in new interpretive contexts. In step with many feminist historians of her cohort, she was a champion of Aboriginal histories as right and proper Australian histories. And as a 'women's historian' from the start, she has taken a genuinely intersectional approach to gender, race and class in ways that not all her peers, male or female, necessarily did. Lake's work has been published in nearly every possible genre imaginable—monograph, biography, edited collection, jointly written work, book chapter, refereed journal article, encyclopaedia entry—and in venues too numerous to count. She has also been an inveterate public intellectual, doing op-eds and radio shows and film and television bits and public talks. As anyone who has been in her company will know, Marilyn is a most articulate **and** entertaining interlocutor: serious and passionate and dedicated to the production of new historical knowledge in many contexts and dimensions.

What is perhaps most impressive about Marilyn is that she has been incredibly productive and influential as a scholar, yet she has never shirked institutional work. Whether as (twice) president of the Australian Historical Association or as an associate dean at La Trobe, she has brought her intellectual agenda to the table in various organisational venues and thereby done what we are all charged to do: make the academy a place that is run by ideas that emanate from engaged and enterprising faculty. I cannot think of a more hard-working, intellectually lively or dedicated historian than Marilyn, whether in Australia or beyond. On a personal note, I am most grateful that she took me so seriously when I was a young scholar. She encouraged and debated and outright fought with me, challenging me and keeping me sharp intellectually at every turn. By the sounds of it, the projects she has planned for her 'retirement' will keep her at the centre of the dynamic transnational histories and historiographies she has helped to bring into being across the course of her whole career. I can't wait to see what she does next, and I send all warmest wishes and love at this celebratory moment.

Dipesh Chakrabarty, Chicago

I am very pleased to know that colleagues at Melbourne University are celebrating the work of Marilyn Lake. Marilyn has not only been a very productive and prolific historian and a leader of her profession; she is also an evolving intellectual whose researches have increasingly addressed new questions and charted out new paths of inquiry. My earliest memories of

Marilyn go back to the mid-1980s when I first met her in Melbourne—she was then an up-and-coming historian with strong interests in feminist critiques of patriarchy and nationalism. She went on to become, unsurprisingly, an internationally prominent historian of the nation, war, race, and gender in Australia. But then I watched with delight how her interests took yet another, a global, turn when she co-authored with Henry Reynolds an imaginative and innovative book offering a transnational history of the 'colour line' as it figured in the making of the modern world. It would not be an exaggeration to say that Marilyn—and Reynolds as her co-author—pioneered the turn towards 'transnational' histories. As someone who has benefited from her academic presence, I join my colleagues in Melbourne in their celebrations and wish Marilyn many, many productive years that bring joy and intellectual stimulation to her friends, colleagues, students and admirers, who are now spread throughout the world.

Nancy Cott, Harvard

Ever since I met Marilyn at a wonderful conference in Wellington, New Zealand, in 1993—when it was easy to see that she was a vital intellectual who liked to have fun, as well as to engage seriously in feminist scholarship—I have looked forward to her visits to the US so that I can keep up with her ever-widening and deepening range of interests and writings. Brava to Marilyn, who crosses oceans regularly with seeming ease, and whose originality and productivity in writing history have made her name well known on at least three continents.

Karen Hagemann, Chapel Hill

I would love to be in Melbourne to celebrate your retirement with you on 8 and 9 December 2016. But unfortunately that is not possible. So I can only write that your work was, since 1995, when we first met for the conference on 'Gendered Nations' in Berlin, a great inspiration for me. It was an honour and pleasure to work with you on several projects, including your chapters for the books *Gendered Nations* (2000), *Masculinities in Politics and War* (2004) and most recently for the *Oxford Handbook on Gender, War and the Western World since 1600* (2017–18).

For your retirement I sent you from Chapel Hill one of my favorite poems by Emily Dickinson: 'We Turn Not Older with the Years, but Newer Every Day'.

Catherine Hall, UCL, London

I first met Marilyn in 1992 when we established a connection that bloomed into a friendship that has been with us ever since. The occasion was a symposium in the amazing Rockefeller Center in Bellagio focused on the then new topic of gender, nation and national identities. The organising group came from the UK but we made efforts to identify feminist scholars who were taking up these issues in other parts of the world and invited Marilyn and Ann Curthoys to bring Australian perspectives. It was a memorable occasion—from which much work flowed. *Creating a Nation* was one of the most exciting projects coming out of that shared political moment—that need to re-write national histories from a raced and feminist perspective.

Since then I have met with Marilyn over the years—in Melbourne, in London, in Berlin, in Oslo and elsewhere and have kept in touch with her work and her writing. We have had many memorable walks—in Melbourne's Royal Botanic Gardens, round Viking exhibitions, in the grounds of Potsdam—always talking about work, life and politics, sharing joys, sorrows and intellectual excitement. As one of the editors of Cambridge University Press's 'Critical Perspectives on Empire', I was proud to be able to publish her outstanding book, the fruit of her collaboration with Henry Reynolds, *Drawing the Global Colour Line*. That book—an exemplary transnational history—explored the construction of white solidarity and white privilege as a response to the threats posed by migrant labour and anti-colonialism to the established order of the early twentieth century. Marilyn was able to draw on her body of research and writing—on gendered national identities, white masculinity, Australian feminism and Aboriginal activism—and take it in new and demanding directions. Her current work on the international history of Australian democracy promises to be an important intervention, not least in the entangled histories of the US and Australia. Marilyn has also done an enormous amount to develop feminist scholarship internationally and support critical intellectual work. I am delighted to be able to add my voice to this celebration of her and only wish I could have been there to share it.

Barbara Hobson, Stockholm

I am pleased and honoured to write this for Marilyn Lake's Festschrift, who has travelled with me in my journey as a scholar in gender studies, a colleague in research projects and as a friend. Dating to 1994, she came to Stockholm to attend an international conference bringing gender scholars from around the globe together—Marilyn had come from the continent furthest away. The title of the conference, 'Crossing Borders: International Dialogues on Gender, Citizenship and Social Politics', signified not only the geographical spread but the crossing of disciplinary boundaries and new frontiers in gender research. The conference was celebrating the launching of a new journal: *Social Politics: International Studies of Gender, State and Society*, founded by myself, Ann Orloff and Sonya Michel—still going strong with Oxford University Press after twenty years. Marilyn Lake became a player, serving as a board member for seventeen years, but also as editor of the agenda-setting thematic issue, 'Citizenship: Intersections in Gender, Race and Ethnicity', one of the most cited in our journal. As this thematic issue highlights, Marilyn has been at the forefront of crossing borders, anticipating the flowering of research in intersectionalities and revealing how these intersections are bound up with histories of nationhood, colonialism and citizenship.

Her direct influence on the paths that I have taken is apparent in the project where I was PI and the book that followed, *Recognition Struggles and Social Movements: Contested Identities, Agency and Power* (published by Cambridge University Press, 2002). The genesis of this project emerged from dialogues at the Crossing Borders conference and, in particular, from Marilyn's work on feminist politics and national/racial identity. She became part of the core team of renowned scholars in gender—to name a few: Myra Marx Ferree, Fiona Williams, Susan Gal, Daine Sainsbury. We met for four years, thanks to the generosity of the Bank of Sweden Tercentenary foundation, which allowed us to spend days together thrashing out the complexities in the tensions within the inter-relationships in recognition and redistribution, our conversations spilling over into dinners at outdoor restaurants, where we would be sipping wine in the twilight of the land of the midnight sun. We became friends, as colleagues do who are involved in research where there is passion and intellectual synergy.

Marilyn's contribution, 'Women, Black, Indigenous: Recognition Struggles in Dialogue', took up the key dimension in the book: that recognition struggles are not only between élites and marginalised groups, but also between groups themselves engaged in recognition struggles. Through her historical lens, we see how white feminists, in their own narrative of oppression, appropriated the frame of being colonised: for white women, 'the colonisers were men; the territory colonialised women's bodies'. In asking, will the real colonisers stand up, Marilyn not only reveals the ire of Aboriginal women activists, but also their awareness of the larger issue, that who speaks on behalf of women reflects differences in power. Hence recognition means more than white women acknowledging that Aboriginal women have a different history and agenda from white women, but that white women have to own up to their role in the oppression of Aboriginal people. Reflecting her engagement in the feminist project, Marilyn speaks to the crisis in identity around race and ethnicity in the feminist politics of recognition. She affirms that feminists need Aboriginal women to teach them about the centrality of race and identity, but also to affirm the legitimacy of the feminist project.

Marilyn has made important contributions to feminist research that resonate beyond the borders of Australia and are salient for current debates in gender research, based on an understanding that nation-building is a gendered and racialised endeavour and that intersections in the multiplicity of gendered identities need to be understood in terms of complex inequalities.

In celebrating her, we all recognise the crucial role that she has played in the project of revisioning gender.

Dane Kennedy, George Washington

It's been a real privilege for me to get to know you over the past decade or so. I've long marvelled at your remarkable combination of talents—intense intellectual curiosity, a relentless work ethic, a wide-ranging historical imagination, and a fierce commitment to women's rights and social justice more generally. You've written history that *matters*, and there can be no greater accomplishment than that.

It may be customary on an occasion such as this to congratulate you on a remarkable career, but I know it would be premature to suggest that it is coming to a close. I'm sure you'll continue to do interesting and important work for a long time to come. So, for now, let me simply say I've learned a lot from your scholarship and count myself lucky to know you.

Sorry I can't attend the celebration, but I'll be sure to hoist a glass in your honour.

Linda Kerber, Iowa

When I think of Marilyn, we are all twenty-five years younger, and we are walking on the street in Hyde Park with Leora Auslander, heading for an Italian restaurant. It is a beautiful fall day (in my memory—maybe it wasn't!), and Marilyn is at the University of Chicago to offer an early version of 'A Desire for a Yank' to our Gender Studies Reading Group. I am stunned by Marilyn's combination of brilliance, historical depth and laugh-out-loud wit. This Americanist feminist is feeling suddenly cosmopolitan, engaged as I am with Marilyn and with Leora (a historian of France).

A few years later, I am back in Iowa, and I invite Marilyn to a seminar I'm conducting at the College of Law. I don't quite remember what you are presenting; I do remember that it was something of a move to make a historian a guest of the law school, and she does not disappoint, giving me (a courtesy colleague there) fresh credibility. Over the years we continue to read and savour each other's work; we stay in the same conversation. We continue to meet serendipitously—when she presents papers at the AHA and the OAH, when she spends a year as Visiting Professor of Australian Studies at Harvard, and, quite wonderfully, when Dick and I turn up in Melbourne and we all go to the beach together, and to museums, and just wander around.

Marilyn's mind works fast; she has no fear. In the 1980s, when everyone was calling for a feminist history of men *and* women, and wringing their hands about how hard/impossible it will be to accomplish that, Marilyn has already embarked on *Creating a Nation* (with three others), and publishes it in 1994, while everyone else is still dithering. Everyone calls for authentically transnational histories but almost no one writes them. Marilyn is ahead with *Connected Worlds* in 2006, followed virtually instantly with the deeply researched *Drawing the Global Colour Line* (2008, with Henry Reynolds)—books that crack open the naive assumption that it is possible to write the history of one nation at a time. And now, when most of us would still be catching our breaths, she has embraced the largest, most wide-ranging subject yet—the international history of Australian democracy!

As I pause to write these words, I realise that my good resolutions about turning up in Melbourne again have not been fulfilled. And I resolve, once again, to try, once again, to settle myself and Marilyn on opposite sides of a café table, on one side of the Pacific or the other, so that I can, once again, absorb a fresh infusion of your determination, your belief in the importance of historical perspective and of what we can learn from the hard lessons of the past, and of the solidarity of our international feminist community, now challenged as never before in our lifetimes. I end with gratitude for the good fortune that brought us into each other's orbit a quarter-century ago.

Alice Kessler-Harris, New York

I've met Marilyn in many corners of the world, and each time with delightful anticipation. She always has a sparkle in her eye, a new project on the table, an important issue to confront. She commits herself to unceasing work, and yet is always ready for a drink or a coffee. She is endlessly curious about how others receive her work. These qualities make not only for great conversation but for challenging encounters as well. Every meeting is a provocation; every provocation an intellectual exercise. I will miss her when I round the next corner.

Ann McGrath, Durham

I wish I could be there to celebrate but I am overseas in wintry Durham, UK. Let me first address Marilyn and say THANK YOU for everything.

Thanks for being part of a team that shifted the world off its usual rotation point. Yes, you intervened and changed things and the history landscape now looks different.

My first memory of meeting Marilyn was at Monash University. I remember the seminar room in the Menzies Building and I recall she was visiting the campus to give a paper. I think it was on soldier settler families.

Being at Monash as a tutor was a wonderful time for me. It was a real change from working in the Darwin Community College where I was either berated in unpleasant ways or not heard at all. For example, I'd just started up in my first position as a lecturer and I was asked: 'Do you have a problem with men?'

Me—a little aghast. 'Oh. Why are you asking that?'

'I've seen the feminist stickers on your car [a VW Beetle of course]. It appears that you <u>are</u> a feminist. Could you confirm if that's true?'

Outed by the bumper stickers. That was my boss talking. A psychologist. Clearly he saw being a feminist as a <u>pathology</u> that could possibly be fixed with some 'conversion therapy'.

So, anyway, here I was at Monash. What a contrast. Melbourne. So cultured and sophisticated; hell—people even talked about the opera. Senior male historians offered you SHERRY in their office—or *'A* <u>sherry</u>, I should say', and there were inspiring feminist historians too—men and women genuinely interested in women's history and, fortunately, in mentoring a young scholar like myself in the final throes of a PhD.

Before Marilyn arrived for the seminar, however, it was noticeable that the air had changed. It was like a troubling weather event was brewing.

Indeed, Marilyn whooshed in like a major storm cell. When she gave her paper, it was clear that she had this startling incisive mind, a cleverness, a strength and a confidence, plus a no-holds-barred willingness to confront the historical status quo. In the seminar, she showed herself capable of slicing through masculinist history—if not the whole male domination of the academy thing—and doing this with a razor sharp mind. You knew in that seminar room that the men, even *the good men*, were frightened. And after Marilyn left, they virtually said so.

After this, our first meeting, I recall worrying whether this woman would ever be able to get a job. Well of course the wisdom of teleology! The profession needed someone of her calibre—and needed her badly. And we all know now, not only did she get a job, she did an astonishingly good job. She proactively grabbed every chance for breakthroughs with both hands—whether opportunities were offered or not. Deservedly, Marilyn got the very best jobs and many accolades. I recall one AHA Conference where it was announced that she had obtained a Personal Chair. The thunderous clapping at the news showed what the younger generation thought about her work. She took on the highest echelons of leadership. Her work has been a great influence on many.

Marilyn has not only put her feminist politics into practice, she has also written them into history. And through her AHA work and advocacy, she has written them into the way our profession works. Marilyn's work to date leaves a sweeping, lasting and profound legacy. I won't go through all her prolific publications, as I'm sure many other speakers will be doing that. Of special note for me personally was her wonderful study of masculinity and the bush, her path-breaking work on whiteness and transnationalism, and her absolutely courageous co-authored work on *What's Wrong with Anzac?* Working with Henry Reynolds was a very productive move for scholarship. The quality of their jointly authored work is exceptional too, and rightly recognised in major book prizes.

When Marilyn speaks on Radio National and in other public venues, she's nothing less than stellar, cutting through all the crap with strong evidence and powerful argument. Cutting through all the supposed 'common sense' myths most Australians don't want disputed.

A great highlight for me personally was when I was invited, not that long after I arrived at Monash in the 1980s, to join her and the talented team of Marian Quartly/Aveling and Pat Grimshaw to write a feminist history of Australia. I was flattered and excited. Despite its being such an ambitious enterprise, we worked together well, and we got *Creating a Nation* done. Afterwards, Marilyn took the helm, doing the publicity, which she did magnificently. I saw her in action once during a Melbourne interview with Peter Mares. She was great on TV too. Not too many general histories garner that sort of attention. And, when the book was attacked, she took on the warrior role, astutely defending it.

Marilyn has written the major history of the Australian feminist movement. She was an exemplar of taking Australian history overseas—ensuring that the Americans and British could not ignore it. In fact, several high-flying stars in the US and UK have commented to me over the years that Australia was way ahead of other countries in feminist history. Marilyn—along with a couple of others I suspect are in this room—deserves much praise for forging empowering networks for all of us and getting our scholarship out there. Marilyn wrote across nations to find the links and common threads that explain what we are today. A pioneer in the transnational turn, she made it a feminist turn, a race turn and a settler coloniser turn—with great success.

Earlier this year she kindly launched my latest book. I wanted to ask Marilyn to do this as she'd encouraged me from early in my career and she had helped to urge me to the finishing post. I was extremely moved by her generous comments and her careful engagement with the book's ideas. She is both conscientious and generous. So basically, as my piece started off, it's a GREAT BIG THANK YOU and a WARM CONGRATULATIONS to Marilyn on an astonishing record of achievement. You have been a great companion along history's gendered paths. You're a role model for today and the future.

Mae Ngai, New York

I am sorry that I cannot be in Melbourne to celebrate Marilyn Lake's wonderful career. Her contributions to history are numerous, but from my vantage point the most meaningful are those that have contributed to our understanding of the Pacific World, Australia's place as an imagined white men's country in Asia, and its connections to the United States as well as to China. Her works, including *Drawing the Global Colour Line*, written with Henry Reynolds, and her more recent article on 'Rethinking Labour Rights through the "Coolie" Question', are path-breaking in the knowledge they've produced. They have inspired historians like myself who attempt work in these fields. I also want to thank Marilyn for her generosity to other scholars. Over the years she's taken time to meet with me, in both Melbourne and New York, to talk about our respective interests. Congratulations, Marilyn, on your retirement.

Penny Russell, Harvard

Marilyn was my tutor for one term at Monash University in 1981, in a class on 'Class' as a special theme in Australian History. The tutorial was dominated by young men with loud voices and strongly expressed opinions on class in general and Marx in particular, and I sat through them all without, to my recollection, opening my mouth once. At the end of the year there was a party for History students, and there, for the first time, I had something approaching a conversation with Marilyn—though again I don't remember saying a great deal. She observed, to a small group of us, that age and gender both influenced people's willingness to speak up in tutorials. Young men and older women spoke freely; older men and young women were more inclined to say little or nothing at all. Relieved, I blurted out, 'Ah, then I have an excuse!' Marilyn glanced at me, not unkindly. 'It's an explanation', she said. 'It's not an excuse.'

That remark effectually shut me up for the rest of the party—but the exchange stayed with me, and is still my sharpest memory of Marilyn from Monash days. I can't say that from that day forward I began to dominate tutorial discussions, but I did begin to see my habitual silence as a self-imposed limitation: one that was not helpful to myself or anyone else, and that was in my power to change.

I think the memory is so clear because it encapsulates Marilyn's influence on me as a feminist scholar and mentor. It's all there: on the one hand, the sharp recognition of the gendered subjectivity of young women and the challenges it imposed; on the other, the equally sharp insistence that those young women had the capacity—and the responsibility—to rise to the challenge. And though at the time I felt rebuked, I came eventually to recognise the implied compliment. By that time Marilyn had read my essay for the class and liked it. If she thought I should speak up more, it was because she thought I had something worthwhile to say.

That is the only time in my life that Marilyn was formally my teacher. She did not supervise my honours thesis, nor my PhD. But she was at Melbourne University while I wrote my thesis and she formed, with Pat Grimshaw and Marian Quartly, a triumvirate of historians who throughout the eighties were building a powerful network of feminist historians across Melbourne. Marilyn's scholarship—bold, acerbic, astute and expansive—pressed insistently at the boundaries of feminist history, continually extending the parameters of what it was and what it could be. At the same time she became, for me, a stringent critic, a rigorous interlocutor, a generous mentor, and a valued friend. Often intimidating but always inspiring, she instilled in me a desire to measure up to her expectations—an ambition that I am still conscious of as a motivating force.

Glenda Sluga, Vienna and Sydney

I can't remember when Marilyn came into my life. I remember sitting across a desk from her. She was blonde and backlit, a glamorous scary thing, giving me work. I went to Canberra with her mission, I took notes, but most of the time I thought how much I hated doing research for anyone—libraries/archives could be boring. I remember still feeling I had cheated her of the research she deserved. Somewhere it's written up on those blue lined cards we used to use. I learnt a lot about Australian women, but she probably got short-changed; I should have listened to her more.

I remember her kneeling on the floor next to me at a talk in the western tower building in that bridge area of the John Medley Building, listening to someone, was it Dipesh? I had a question I told her, she told me to ask it. I did the girl thing (what would I know?) and kept quiet. I should have listened to her and asked the question. Always ask the question.

I remember Marilyn at an AHA, where was it? We were all on buses being transported to dinner, and Marilyn strode on owning the world, still backlit, a scary gifted intellectual. And she does, own the world. Still the Australian historian the world reads on Australia. The historian who keeps being relevant, whose work keeps reminding us about the relevance of women. While we still can, we should all listen to her more. I'm sorry I can't be there. Add it to the pile of Marilyn regrets.

Ellen Boucher, History, Amherst College

I first met Marilyn in 2007, when I came to Melbourne on a short-term fellowship that she and some colleagues at La Trobe had created for postgraduates applying for ARC grants. I was already a huge fan of her work, having discovered *The Limits of Hope* when I was just beginning to conceptualise my dissertation research on British child migrants. Its impact on my thinking had been profound. Marilyn's study offered a wonderful model of how to write about a political topic—in this case, the role of soldier settlement in the Victorian government's post–World War I reconstruction efforts—in a way that foregrounded the real-life impact of these policies on the men, women, and children who experienced them firsthand. *The Limits of Hope* taught me much that continues to influence my work to this day: that seemingly dry governmental files can vividly bring to life the struggles of individuals and their families, that policy planning can be a surprisingly helpful lens for uncovering the ideological underpinnings of an era, and that a focused historical case study can speak volumes to the gendered and economic inequalities that remain within our world today. I was also lucky to arrive in Melbourne just as *Drawing the Global Colour Line* was heading to press, and so benefited from many conversations with Marilyn about the importance of transnational history, a field in which she was quickly becoming a leading voice. That book has since become a staple on my British Empire syllabus, since it is unparalleled in its ability to bring to life the shifting currents of power and intellectual influence that crisscrossed the Anglophone world at the dawn of the twentieth century. The amount of ground that it covers—both geographically and conceptually—is breathtaking, and my students have consistently ranked it among their favorites from the semester, calling it provocative, eye-opening, and eminently readable. I've always thought that it is such a testament to Marilyn's extraordinary intellect that her work has transformed so many fields, from gender and whiteness studies, to immigration and transnational history, to the history of Indigenous activism. Yet it is also a testament to her generosity of spirit that she has dedicated countless hours to mentoring and supporting the rising generation of historians. She has certainly been a role model for me, showing me that it is possible to reach the heights of one's profession while also remaining a committed mother, teacher, and feminist. I never did get that ARC grant back in 2007, but I have benefited from years of lively conversation, unfailing encouragement, and wonderful friendship from Marilyn, for all of which I feel very fortunate indeed!

ABOUT THE EDITORS

Joy Damousi is Professor of History and ARC Laureate Fellow at the University of Melbourne. She has published widely on aspects of women's history, the aftermaths of war, and the history of migration and refugees. Her current research is on a history of child refugees and Australian internationalism during the twentieth century. She is President of the Australian Academy of the Humanities and President of the Australian Historical Association.

Judith Smart, Adjunct Professor at RMIT University, is Deputy Chair of the History Council of Victoria. She co-edits the *Victorian Historical Journal* with Richard Broome, co-authored with Marian Quartly *Respectable Radicals: A History of the National Council of Women of Australia 1896–2006*, and co-edited with Shurlee Swain *The Encyclopedia of Women and Leadership in Twentieth-Century Australia*.

LIST OF CONTRIBUTORS

Warwick Anderson, University of Sydney
Roland Burke, La Trobe University
Liz Conor, La Trobe University
Clare Corbould, Deakin University
Joy Damousi, University of Melbourne
Graeme Davison, Monash University
Stephen Garton, University of Sydney
Patricia Grimshaw, University of Melbourne
Victoria Haskins, University of Newcastle
Samia Khatun, University of Liberal Arts, Bangladesh
Kate Laing, La Trobe University
Sophie Loy-Wilson, University of Sydney
John Maynard, University of Newcastle
Mark McKenna, University of Sydney
Henry Reynolds, University of Tasmania
Tim Rowse, University of Western Sydney
Judith Smart, RMIT University
Ian Tyrrell, University of New South Wales

INDEX

Note: page locators in italics denote footnotes; bold indicates illustrations.

A

Aarons, Sam 102
Abbott, Tony, Anzac speech 2014 9, 10
Aboriginal activism 227, 244
   impact on historiography 219
Aboriginal activists 139, 145–7
   criticism of white feminists 57
   influence of black power movement on 226–8
   influence of Civil Rights Movement on 159
   intimidation and surveillance of 125
   self-determination 150
Aboriginal Affairs NSW 132
Aboriginal historiography, South Asian diaspora 162–3, 169
Aboriginal history 34
Aboriginal massacres 70
'The Aboriginal Mother in Western Australia' (Bennett, 1933) 138
Aboriginal people
   assimilation programs 124–5
   Cooper's classification of 147–8
   depictions during colonial period **69**, 70
   forced removal of children 128, 130–1
   identification with African American causes 221–3, 226
   1930s humanitarian discourses 144, 150
Aboriginal/Indigenous rights 156–7
   Bryces support of 103–4, 106
   challenges of campaign 159
   changing focus of race relations 1970s 160
   communist discourse 139–42
   impact of changing race relations on career 161
   international campaigns by women activists 33
   white women's activism 130
Aboriginal women
   activism for rights of 130
   feminist campaigns for women protectors 122, 142–4, 149
   oppression of 149–50
   and white feminists 236–7
Aborigines Protection Board (NSW) 118, 121–35, 145
   denial of permission for access to records 131–4
   enduring legacy of policies 123, 126–7, 129
   legal powers 124
   mass destruction of records and papers 127–8, 134–5
Aborigines' Protection Society 104, 142, 223
Aborigines Welfare Directorate 133
abortion laws 74
Achibald, J.F. 7
Adams, Herbert Baxter 211, 215
Afkhami, Mahnaz 81, 82
African Americans, identification and alliance with Indigenous Australians 221–3, 226 *See also* Black Power Movement; press (African American)
Ah Mouy, Louis 185
AIATSIS 123
Alexander, F.M. 207
Alexander, Sally 29, 33, 230–1
Allen, Judith 25–6, 39
Allen, Margaret 25
Allen & Unwin 29
Al-Tabari 171–2
Altman, Denis 1
American exceptionalism 193–4, 197, 199, 201
   myth of 211
   resilience of 202
American Historical Association 34
American Historical Review 30, 218

American historiography 218
American history writing
  nationalist tone 211–12
  transnational approaches 212–13
American Progressivism 196, 207, 209
Americanisation phenomenon 9
Anderson, Benedict 181
Anglo-Saxonism
  as substitute for 'white man' 214–16
  transnational approach 206
Anti-Slavery Society 104, 138, 142, 158, 223
Anzac Girls (ABC) 10
Anzacs 9–11, 13
  challenging myth 52
  historians reimagining myth 11–12, 15–16
  masculinisation 18, 19, 45
arbitration systems 192–3
archival material and research 110–11
  Australia returns documents to Japan 178–9
  difficulty accessing 129, 131–4
  historical methodology for South Asian 167
  inclusion of Asia-Pacific 177–8
Armenian refugees 99–101, 104
Armenian Relief Fund 103, 104–5
Asia Pacific Centre for Women and Development (APCWD) 81, 88–9
assimilation programs
  Aboriginal people 124–5
  half caste Aboriginals 143–4
  self-determination policies 150
Associated Negro Press 225
asylum seekers, Australia's treatment of 175–6
Auntie Barbara 126
Auslander, Leora 237, 238
'Australia in the World' lecture series (2013) vii–viii
Australia Peace Council 154–5
Australian Aboriginal Progressive Association (AAPA) 125, 145–7
Australian Aborigines' League (AAL) 141, 147
Australian Academy of the Humanities 36
Australian Catholic University 27
Australian Communist Party 154

Rights for Aborigines: Draft Program for the Struggle Against Slavery (1931) 125
Australian democracy 17
Australian Dictionary of Biography 26
Australian Federation of Women Voters 142
Australian Federation of Women's Societies for Equal Citizenship 142
Australian Feminism: A Companion (Caine, 1998) 40–1
Australian Feminist Studies 25
Australian Historical Association (AHA) vii, 26, 230, 233
  conference (Brisbane) 2014 16–17, 18
  conference (Sydney) 1998 217
  Lake's contribution to 240
  Lake's presidency 35
Australian Historical Studies 27, 191
  audience 31
  Historical Reconsiderations series 30
  Lake on board vii
Australian historiography 11–12, 218
  Anzac history 11–12
  Australian women 131
  departure from 8
  feminism between wars 137
  impact of Indigenous activism on 219
  nationalism 17
  soldier settlement 14
  South Asian diaspora 168–70
Australian Institute of Company Directors 75
Australian national identity 17 *See also* 'whiteness'
Australian National University vii, 107
  Inglis invites Lake to speak to PhD students 7, 94
  Women's Studies programs 24, 25
Australian nationalism 9
  alternative history of 16
  Lake's contribution to historiography 17
  Lake's critique of radical 17–20
  masculinisation 15
  See also Anzacs
Australian Nominating Committee 8
Australian Peace Congress 1950 155
Australian press, documentation of Armenian refugee plight 105–6

Australian Research Council
  Discovery grant 80
  Future Fellowship 68
  Linkage program 39
Australian Union of Women 47
Australian Women's History Network (AWHN) 28, 39
  See also International Federation for Research in Women's History (IFRWH)
Australian Women's Register website 42
Australian Women's Studies Association 25
Australian Women's Weekly 158
Australianama: The South Asian Odyssey in Australia (Khatun, forthcoming) 162, 172
Aveling, Marian *See* Quartly, Marian
ayahs 170

B

baby bonus 43–5, 147
  criticism by women doctors 44
  reaction of mothers to 45
  See also maternal feminism
Baer, Gertrud 58
Bailey, Rev 116
Baillie, Helen 142
Baldock, Darrell 1
Bale, Colin *11*
Ballantyne, Edith 60, 62
Bamblett, Lawrence 123
Bancroft, George 211
Bandler, Faith 13, 218
  appeal to cross-section of race and class 156–7
  book launch and HREOC award 33
  friendship with Street 155
  heritage and childhood 153
  impact of changing race relations on career 160, 227
  invitation to Lake to write biography 152–3
  involvement with Australia Peace Council 154–5
  as NSW FCAATSI state secretary 157
  parallels with Lake's childhood 154
  public appeal 155–6
  research for biography 35
  role in 1967 referendum 157–9

Bandler, Hans 156
Banivanua Mar, Tracey 34, 226
Bank of Sweden Tercentenary foundation 236
Barker, Lorena 123
Barrett, Dr Edith 43, 44
Barton, Edmund 183
Barton, Helen 14
Bashford, Alison 231–2
Bayley, W.A. 110
Bega Gazette 109
Behl, Aditya 167
Bengali sufi poetry book 164 *See also Kasasol Ambia* (Stories of the Prophets)
Bennett, Mary Montgomerie 33, 41, 137, 138, 142, 143, 144
Bevege, Margaret 27
Bhabha, Homi K. 214
birth control debates 45–6, 48–9, 54–5
  conservative WILPF members and 56
Black Panther Party 227
Black Power movement 226–8
black press *See* press (African American)
Blewett, Neal 1
Blom, Ida 32
"'Blood Votes and the 'Bestial Boche'" (Shute, 1976) 38
Bolloway, Dick 109
Bongiorno, Frank 10 *See also* 'Honest History' group
Boon, David 1
border politics 186, 189–90
Border Protection Bill 175
Borges, Jorge Louis 163
Boris, Eileen 232
Born in the Cattle (McGrath, 1987) 26
Boucher, Ellen 243–4
Boulding, Elise 57–8
boundary objects, 'whiteness' as 213–14
Bourne, Randolph 212
Boyce, James 1
'Briney' 109
British Commonwealth League (BCL) 33, 142, 143
British Medical Association (Australian branch) 44
Brock, Peggy 26
Broken Hill Historical Society 164
Broken Hill mosque 164
Brookings Institute 195

249

Brooks-Higginbotham, Evelyn 35
Brown, Bob 1
Brown, James 12
Bryce, Ernest 103, 104, 105–6
Bryce, James 184, 209
Bryce, Mary 103–6
Buesken, Petra 36
Bulletin 7, 183
Burbank, Victoria 136
Bureau of Labor Statistics 194
Burke, Don 73
Burton, Antoinette 28, 29, 33, 35, 211, 232–3
Butler, Judith 73

C

Caine, Barbara 29
Calvert, Ashton 2
Calvert, Christopher 2
Calvert, Hannah 2
Calvert, Marilyn *See* Lake, Marilyn
Calvert, Pamela 2
Calvert family 2, 6
Cambridge University Press 235
camel industry 164, 165, 168, 170
Camp, Kay 58
Camp, William 58
Campo, Natasha 28
Carnegie Endowment 195
Carter, Jimmy 92
Cassin, Rene 86
Chakrabarty, Dipesh 28, 233–4, 243
Charter feminists 42, 48
Chaudhuri, Nupur 34
Cheok, Hong Cheong 185
Chicago Defender 225
Chief Secretary Records Letters Received 132
Chifley, Ben 154
child refugees 98–9
    internationalism and transnationalism 96–7
Chinese Imperial Commissioners 189
The Chinese Question in Australia (1879) 185, 186–7
Christison of Lammermoor (Bennett, 1927) 144
Christopherson, Leonie 39
CISH *See* International Committee of Historical Sciences (CISH)

Citizenship: Intersections of Gender, Race and Ethnicity 31–2
Civil Rights Movement 159
Clark, Andrew Inglis 1
Clark, Manning 110
Clark, Victor Selden 191–203
    appraisal of New Zealand arbitration 192
    on Australia's racial exclusion 200, 201
    as Commissioner for Immigration, Labor and Statistics 200–1
Clarke, Uncle Tom 126
coalition politics 156–7
Collins, Felicity 113, 114
colonial education, British India 171
colonial masculinity 182
colour bar, White Australia Policy as 178–81
Commission on the Deportation of Armenian Women and Children 101
Commission on the Status of Women (CSW) 47
Commonwealth Conciliation and Arbitration Court 192
communism, humanitarian discourse on Aboriginality and level of rights 139–42, 146, 149
Communist Party of Australia (CPA) 141
    Draft Programme of Struggle Against Slavery 139–40
Companion to Feminist History (Crawford, 1998) 29
Companion to Tasmania History (Alexander, 2005) 2
comparative history 36, 191, 194, 201, 204, 205, 212–13
    distinct from transnational history 209
    popular topics 1990s 32
conferences
    AHA (Brisbane) 2014 16–17, 18
    AHA (Sydney) 1998 217
    American Historical Association conference 2007 34
    Berkshire History Conference 1990 31
    Berkshire History Conference 1996 28, 32
    'Beyond Freedom: New Direction in the Study of Emancipation' conference (US) 2011 219–20
    CISH (Madrid) 1990 28

Index

CISH (Montreal) 1995 28–9
CISH (Oslo) 2000 32
Commonwealth Labour Parties conference (Toronto) 1947 225
Conference (WCIWY) Mexico City 1975 87–8
'Crossing Borders: International Dialogues on Gender, citizenship and Social Politics' (Stockholm) 1994 236
First World Conference on Human Rights 1968 (Iran) 86
'Gendered Nations' (Berlin) 1995 234
'Historicising Whiteness: Transnational Perspectives on the Construction of an Identity' (Melbourne) 2006 162
IFRWH conference (Melbourne) 1998 33
Independent Scholars Conference (Sydney) 1998 152
maternity bonus 1923 44–5
nation-wide conference of women 1923 43–4
NCWA 1935 45–6
NCWA 1936 46
Second World Conference on Human Rights (Vienna) 1993 83
Social Sciences History Association Conference (Chicago) 1992 31
Stockholm University 1997–1999 32
Stout Research Centre for the Study of New Zealand Society, History and Culture 1988 28
UN Tribune satellite conference 61–2
WILPF (US) 1967 59
Women and Labour 6
Women and Labour (Sydney) 1978 23, 27, 36
Women and Labour (Melbourne) 1980 27
women's conference (Copenhagen) 1980 62
World Conference Beijing 1995 83
Congress for International Cooperation and Disarmament (CICD) 1964 53–4
Conlon, Anne 23, 39
connected histories 212–13
Connected Worlds: History in Transnational Perspective (Lake & Curthoys (eds), 2005) 95, 96, 238

Conor, Liz 28
Conrad 1
consciousness-raising groups 38
Contagious Diseases legislation 44
Convention on the Elimination of All Forms of Discrimination against Women 1983 71
Cooke, Constance Ternent 41, 142
Cooper, William 147, 149
Cootamundra Homes 134
Corkhill, William 118
Cornelius, Stella 59
Cott, Nancy 35, 234
Council for Aboriginal Rights 141
Council of the Australian Academy of the Humanities vii
Country Women's Association 60
Coward, Dan *38*
Crawford, Patricia 29
Creating a Nation (Grimshaw, Lake, McGrath & Quartly, 1994) 29–30, 39, 121–2, 217, 235, 238
Creed, Barbara 70
Cuba 196
Curthoys, Ann 23–4, 28, 34, 39, 207, 235
  participation in WLM 1970s 65
Curtin, John 154

D

Damned Whores and God's Police (Summers, 1975) 22
Damousi, Joy 10, *11*, 14, 30
Daniels, Kay 24, 38
  influence on Lake 3–4, 25, 208
D'Aprano, Zelda 27
Dart, Dr Ellice 46
Darwin Community College 239
Davey, Margaret 48–9, 50
Davidoff, Leonore 31
Davis, Natalie Zemon 30
Davison, Graeme 5, 7
Dawkins, John 67
Day of Mourning protest 1938 130
Deacon, Desley 25
Deakin, Alfred 16, 17, 180–1, 182, 184–5, 191, 209, 215
Deakin University 27
Deane, Sir William 33
Department of Aboriginal Affairs 129
Department of Health, establishment 207

Department of Youth and Community 133
'A Desire for a Yank' (Lake 1992) 237
diaspora
   Pacific Islanders 160–1
   Tasmanian 1
   See also South Asian diaspora
Dilke, Charles 16–17
A Divided Society: Tasmania During World War One (Lake, 1975) 4–5, 13–14, 37
Dixson, Miriam 13, 22, 39
Does Khaki Become You? The Militarisation of Women's Lives (Enloe, 1983) 63
Donaldson, David 127–8
Donaldson, George 127
Donaldson, Robert 127, 128
Donovan, John 125
Double Time: Women in Victoria, 150 years (Lake & Farley (eds), 1984) 5, 8, 27, 72
Doyle, Jim 125
Doyle, Robert 73
Draft Programme of Struggle Against Slavery 139–40
Drawing the Global Colour Line (Lake & Reynolds, 2008) 8, 35, 52, 95, 184, 210–11, 214, 235, 238, 241
   American review and reaction to 219
   impact on US historians 220
   importance of 232, 244
Du Bois, W.E.B. 162, 184, 210, 212, 213
Dudink, Stefan 32
Durand Line 168

E

Eade, Susan 23
Economic and Social Commission for Asia and the Pacific (ESCAP) 89
Edmonds, Penny 34
Elder, Catriona 28
Eley, Geoff 32
Emmett, Hilary 221, 227
The Encyclopedia of Aboriginal Australia (Howie-Willis, 1994) 123
The Encyclopedia of Women and Leadership in Twentieth Century Australia (2014) 42
Enloe, Cynthia 63
Eureka Youth League 155
Evans, Raymond *11*, 26
exceptionalism 193, 197 *See also* American exceptionalism

F

Faith: Faith Bandler, Gentle Activist (Lake, 2002) 122, 230
Fallaci, Oriana 91
Faludi, Susan 77
Farmers' Advocate 100
Faye, Esther 28
Federal Council for the Advancement of Aborigines and Torres Strait Islanders (FCAATSI) 155, 157
   Easter Conference 1970 160
   role in petition for referendum 158
Federal Council of Aboriginal Affairs 155, 157 *See also* Federal Council for the Advancement of Aborigines and Torres Strait Islanders (FCAATSI)
'Female Desires: The Meaning of World War II' (Lake, 2008) 34, 217
feminism 21–2
   first-wave 22
   maternal 43–7, 60, 63, 64, 149
   matricidal 65
   phases of 40–1, 42, 46–7, 64
   post-colonial 73
   second-wave 38, 40, 63, 86–7
   state 57, 80, 91
   White Australia Policy 181–3
Feminism and History (Scott (ed), 1996) 34
Feminism: The Public and the Private (Landes (ed), 1998) 34
Feminist Club 130
feminist history 13, 14, 24, 33, 51
   Aboriginal women and white feminists 32, 236–7
   Australian history 39
   half caste and full blood terminology 137–8, 149
   humanitarian discourse on Aboriginality and level of rights 138–9, 146, 149
   interrogations into Aboriginal history 26
   Lake's contribution to 190, 240–1
   links between personal and political 37, 38
feminist history circles 3
feminist internationalism 142–4
   criticism of removal of children 142–3
Feminist Studies 29

feminists
  Charter 42, 48
  mainstream 42, 47, 50
  online biographies of 42
  radical 41
femocrats 25, 57, 71
Ferree, Myra Marx 236
festschrift vii, 37
First Woman Presidential Candidate (FWPC) 74
Fischhof, Jennifer 60, 61
Fisher, Andrew 43
Flanagan, Richard 1
Flinders University, Women's Studies programs 25
Foley, Gary 227
Foner, Eric 220
For and Against Feminism (Curthoys, 1988) 24
Ford, Ruth 28
Foster, Stephen 5
'Foster Parents' Plan for Children in Spain' (PLAN) 102
Fox, Lindsay 10
Fox-Pitt, Commander 158
Frader, Laura 29, 35
Frankfurter, Felix 17
Franklin, Stella Miles 26
Fraser, Nancy 32
Fraser government 71
Freedom Bound II (Holmes & Lake, 1995) 144
Freedom Rides 227
Freedom Road (Fast, 1944) 155
Freeman, E.A. 209, 215
Fricker, David 179
Friedan, Betty 61
  on Iran speaking tour 1974 86, 87, 93, 93
frontier feminism 34, 122, 130
'Frontier Feminism and the Marauding White Man' (Lake, 1996) 122
frontier history 113 *See also* Wintle, Emily (née Gillespie)
Frost, Lucy 70
Fujikane, Candice 186
full blood terminology *See* half caste/full blood terminology

G

Gaitskell, Baroness Dora 86
Gal, Susan 236
Gale, Betty 54
Gallipoli (Nine Network) 10
Gandhi, Mohandas 210
Garran, Robert 182
Garvey, Marcus 145
'Gender, Race, Xenophobia and Nationalism' (2004) 32
Gender and History 31, 34
Gender and War (Damousi & Lake, 1996) 30, 94, 95
gender as analytical category 30, 31, 35
  Australian history 39
  interest in Scandinavia 31
  self-determination 150
  war history 38
gender bias, knowledge systems 72
gender inequities 75
gender pay gap 72, 75
Gender Studies 75
  under attack in US 79
  dismantling of 73, 76–7
Gendered Nations (Blom & Hagemann, 2000) 234
Gentle Invaders (Ryan and Conlon, 1975) 23
Getting Equal: The History of Feminism in Australia (Lake, 1999) 29, 40, 41, 42, 50, 152
Gibbs, Pearl 130, 149
Gilbert, Margaret 114
Gillespie, Emily *See* Wintle, Emily (née Gillespie)
Gillespie, John 120
Gillespie, Michael 115, 116, 119
Ginibi, Ruby Langford 170
Goldstein, Vida 14, 41, 55, 99
Gollan, Robin (Bob) 4, 18
Good and Mad Women (Matthews, 1984) 25
Goodall, Heather 26, 124, 132, 133, 134
Goodisson, Lillie 46
Goonrey, Christine 114
Gordon, Linda 35
Governor General's Centenary Medal for Service to History viii
Great War
  emergence of internationalism 51

impacts of 13, 14
revisionist state histories 37–8
as themes in Lake's work 14–15
See also Anzacs
Greek Civil War 98 *See also* Greek diaspora; *paidomazoma*
Greek diaspora 96, 97
paidomazoma 98
Greenwood, Irene 58, 61
Greer, Germaine 41, 61–2
on Iran speaking tour 1974 86, 87, 93
Griesemer, James R. 214
Griffis, William Eliot 199
Griffith University, Women's Studies programs 25
Grimshaw, Patricia 42, 94, 122, 240, 242
role in IFRWH 39
See also Melbourne Feminist History Group

H

Haebich, Anna 26
Hagemann, Karen 32, 33, 234
Haigh, Bruce 9
half caste / full blood terminology
communist humanitarian discourse 139–42, 146, 149
feminist historiography 137–8
feminist internationalism lens 143–4
as field of distinctions 148–9
as harmful way to categorise people 147
half-caste newborn murder case *See* Wintle, Emily (née Gillespie)
Halkes, Dr Catharina 63–4
Hall, Catherine 29, 31, 32, 33, 230, 235
Hall, Di 231
Harris, Sir John 138
Harvard Chair of Australian Studies 2001–2002 vii, 8, 35, 238
Harvard University Press 36
Harvester Judgment 192
Haskins, Victoria 34, 121, 129–35
Hasluck, Paul 158
Hawaii, settler-based labour policies 200–1
Heagney, Muriel 43
Hecate 38
HECS 67–8
Heiser, Victor G. 207
Hellman, Lilian 35
'Heroes and Heroines: Sexual Mythology in Australia 1914–1918' (Shute, 1975) 38
heteronormativity 73, 76
Higgins, Henry Bourne 16, 17, 191, 209
historical storytelling 162–3
Muslim 171–2, 173
Historical Studies, Lake and Davison's articles in 7
historicism 193–4, 198
historiography
European texts and origins 185
Muslim 171–2
See also Aboriginal historiography; Australian historiography; *ta'rikh*
history books
Bengali-language text of Sufi poetry 163–4
role of 162, 163, 173
'A History of Feminism in Australia' (essay, 1998) 29 *See also Getting Equal: The History of Feminism in Australia* (Lake, 1999)
The History of the Prophets and the Kings (Al-Tabari) 171–2
History Workshop Journal 34, 230
Hobart High 2
Hobart Mercury 2
Hobart Women's Action Group 23
Hobson, Barbara 29, 31–2, 235–7
Hofmeyr, Isobel 28
Hofstra University 32
Holland, Alison 144
Holmes, Katie 33, 71, 144
Holmes, Margaret 53, 57
'Honest History' group 10
Horne, Donald 12
How Empire Shaped Us (Burton & Kennedy (eds), 2016) 35
Howard, John 175
Howe, Adrian 70
Howe, Renate 27
Hudson, Peter 1
human rights, Chinese–Australian historical treatise 185, 186–7 *See also* Aboriginal/Indigenous rights; international human rights
humanitarianism 99–106
Aboriginal rights 103–6, 138–9
women as active humanitarians 101–6, 144
Hunt, Attlee 182
Hyslop, Jonathan 211

I

Imagined Communities (Anderson, 1983) 181
Immigration Restriction Act 1901 179–80, 183, 184
Independent 184
Indian Archipelago 165, 166, 170
Indigeneity, differentiated?? 136–7
Indigenous Australians *See* Aboriginal people; Pacific Islanders/Torres Strait Islanders
Inglis, Ken 7, 94
International Committee of Historical Sciences (CISH), conferences 28–9, 32
International Council of Women 33, 40
International Federation for Research in Women's History (IFRWH) 28, 39
 conference 1998 33
 tribute 232
international human rights 80, 187, 230
International Labour Organization (ILO) 142
International Woman Suffrage Alliance 33, 41
International Women's Year 1975–1985 22, 53, 61, 63, 87
 research project 3–4, 24
International Year of the Child National Committee 50
internationalism 51–2
 role of women in 99–106
 women's history 21
 See also feminist internationalism
intersectionality 73, 233
Invasion to Embassy (Goodall, 1996) 26
'The Inviolable Woman: Feminist Conceptions of Citizenship, 1900–1940' (Lake, 1998) 34
Iran 80–93
 First World Conference on Human Rights 1968 86
 human rights and women's rights paradoxes 83, 90–1
 Reid on institutional sponsored reforms 89–90
 SAVAK (secret police) 91, *93*
 second-wave feminism speaking tour 1974 86–7, 93
 Shah regime 84–90
 Shah regime collapse 93
 state sponsored feminism 91
 UNESCO Congress on the Eradication of Illiteracy 85
 White Revolution reforms 84, 91
 women's rights activism in 83–4
Iran–United Nations enterprise 80
Isaac, Rhys 218
Isbister, Dr Claire 48, 49, 50
isnad (truth-chains) 172

J

Jackson, Jay 224
Jackson, Rex 134
Jalland, Pat *11*
James, Margaret 27
Janene (Felicity Collins' sister) 113
Japan, Australia returns archival documents to 178–9
Jarrett, Colin 126–7
Jennings, Kate 56
Jeppe, Karen 101
jingoism 10, 11
John, Cecilia 99
Johnson, Dick 125
Johnston, Susan 133
Jones, Edith 142
Journal of American History 212
Journal of Political Economy 202
Journal of the History of Sexuality 34
Journal of Women's History, Lake on board vii
Joyce, Eileen 1

K

Kasasol Ambia (Stories of the Prophets) 163–4, 170–4
 elaborate metaphors in 167, 171
 journey to Broken Hill 168–70
 mislabelling of 165
Kavanaugh, Brett 74
Kearney, Marjorie 14
Kelly, Farley 27
Kelly, Ray 123
Kennedy, Dane 35, 237
Kennet government (Vic) 78
Kerber, Linda 29, 34, 237–8
Kessler-Harris, Alice 29, 35, 239
Khan, Anno 168–9
Khan, Mirza 168
Khan, Sher 169

Kidd, Benjamin 199
Kinchela Homes 134
Kingsley-Strack, Joan (Ming) 125, 129–30
Kingston, Beverley 13, 23, 24, 39
Kirkby, Diane 27
knowledge systems, gender bias 72
knowledge-relations 163, 167
Koch, Christopher 1
Kramer, Paul A. 215–16

L

La Trobe University vii, 5, 27, 208
  Lake as founding director of Women's Studies 27–8, 70–1
  Women's Studies programs 66
Labour History, Lake on board vii
Labour History, Women at Work (Curthoys, Eade & Spearritt, 1975) 23
The Labour Movement in Australasia: A Study in Social Democracy (Clark, 1906) 191
  criticisms of 198
Lacey, Tom 125, 226
Ladies' Home Journal 1975 87
Laidlaw, Zoe 70
Lake, Jess 5, 27
Lake, Katherine 5, 23, 27
Lake, Marilyn 1, 10, 144
  achievements, contributions and awards vii–viii, 8
  biography skills 152–3
  birth of Kath and Jess 5, 27
  early years in Tasmania 2–3
  editorial boardships vii, 236
  evolving research trajectory 207–9
  as Fellow of Australian Academy of the Humanities 36
  as founding director of La Trobe Women's Studies 27–8, 70–1
  on Freeman's theories 215
  Harvard Chair of Australian Studies 2001–2002 vii, 8, 35, 238
  influence and mentorship 68, 231, 242, 244
  influential figures in early academia 2–4, 19–20
  marriage to Sam Lake 5
  '1914: Death of a Nation' AHA address (2014) 16–17
  parallels with Bandler's childhood 154
  as president of AHA 36
  Visiting Professorial Fellowships vii
  See also Melbourne Feminist History Group; 'The War Girls'
Lake, Marilyn—books *See Creating a Nation* (Grimshaw, Lake, McGrath & Quartly, 1994); *A Divided Society: Tasmania During World War One* (Lake, 1975); *Double Time: Women in Victoria, 150 years* (Lake & Farley (eds), 1984); *Drawing the Global Colour Line* (Lake & Reynolds, 2008); *Faith: Faith Bandler, Gentle Activist* (Lake, 2002); *Gender and War* (Damousi & Lake, 1996); *Getting Equal: The History of Feminism in Australia* (Lake, 1999); *The Limits of Hope: Soldier Settlements in Victoria 1915–38* (Lake, 1987); *What's Wrong with Anzac?* (Lake, Reynolds, McKenna & Damousi (eds), 2010); *Women's Rights and Human Rights: International Perspectives* (Grimshaw, Holmes & Lake (eds), 2001)
Lake, Marilyn—collaborations
  Lake and Curthoys collaboration 95, 96, 211, 238
  Lake and Damousi collaboration 30, 94, 95
  Lake and Reynolds collaboration 17, 35, 95–6, 210–11, 234, 235, 238
  transnational studies of white men 214, 219
  See also Drawing the Global Colour Line (Lake & Reynolds, 2008)
Lake, Marilyn—published articles and essays 7, 15, 30, 31, 32, 33, 34, 36, 122, 181, 217, 230, 231, 237, 241
Lake, Sam 5
Lambie, Jacqui 1
Landes, Joan 34
Lane, William 7
Lang, Jack 146
Langdon-Davies, John 102
Larsson, Marina *11*, 14
lascars 168
Latham, John 100
Lawson, Louisa 7
League of Nations 33, 40, 51, 99
League of Nations Union 99

Liberaction (newsletter) 23
Lilith 231
The Limits of Hope: Soldier Settlements in Victoria 1915–38 (Lake, 1987) 6–7, 8, 13, 14, 30, 39, 94
   influence of 243–4
Lipset, Seymour Martin 197
Littlejohn, Linda 41
Looking for Blackfellas' Point (McKenna, 2012) 107, 112, 113
Lothian, Kathy 226
Lowe, Alice 128, 129
Lowe, Kong Meng 185, 186, 210
Lyons, Enid 1
Lyons, Joseph 1, 146, 147

M

Macaulay, Thomas Babington 171
Macdonald, Charlotte 28
Mackinnon, Alison 25
Macquarie University 26
   Women and Labour conference 1978 23, 27, 36
Magarey, Susan 24–5, 39 *See also* Eade, Susan
mainstream feminists 42, 47, 50
Man Made Language (Spender) 66
Managing Gender (Deacon, 1989) 25
Mares, Peter 241
maritime frontier 198
Martel, Gordon 34
masculinisation
   and Anzacs 18, 19, 45
   Australian nationalism 15, 18
Masculinities in Politics and War (Dudink & Hagemann, 2004) 234
masculinity 7, 30, 240
   Anzac mateship 18
   critiques of 73, 76
   as social construct 182
   white 210–11, 213, 235
'Masculinity as Practice and Representation' 32
maternal feminism 43, 47, 60, 63, 64, 149
Maternal Thinking (Ruddick, 1990) 63
maternity allowance/bonus 148, 180
Maternity Allowance (1912) 43
matricidal feminism 65
Matthews, Freya 71
Matthews, Jill Julius 25, 67

Maynard, Fred 125, 145, 146, 147, 149
Maynard, John 121, 122, 123–9, 145, 226
McClintock, Anne 213
McGrath, Ann 26, 29, 34, 39, 122
   Senate Committee on Stolen Wages 2004 submission 131–2
   tribute 239–41
McGuire, Eddie 74
McIntosh, Betty 58
McKenna. Mark 10
McKeown, Adam 35
McLachlan, Craig 73
McRae, Malcolm 4, 19, 208
Melbourne Feminist History Group 39, 94, 242 *See also* Australian Women's History Network (AWHN)
Melbourne University Press 4–5
Memory and Migration in the Shadow of War (Damousi, 2015) 97
Menzies government 54
Methodist Church of Australia 49
MeToo movement 72, 78
Michel, Sonya 29, 31, 33, 236
Midgely, Clare 34
militarisation of history 15
Millet, Kate 93
minimum wage 180, 192
Minister for Youth and Community Services 133–4
Ministry of Aboriginal Affairs 133, 134
Minute Books 1911–1969 132
Minute on Education 1835 171
'Mission Impossible: How Men Gave Birth to the Australian Nation—Nationalism, Gender and other Seminal Acts' (Lake, 1992) 15, 181, 217, 231
Mitchell, Thomas 69–70, 165, 170
   map of 'Indian Archipelago' **166**
Mitchell Library 133
Monash University 208, 239
   Department of Zoology 5
   scholarship to Lake 5
   tutorship 27
Montessori, Maria 79
Moore, William Harrison 99
Morley, William 104
Morning Post 180–1
Moses, Claire 29
Moss, May 46

mothercraft nursing 45, 46
'Mothers' Rights and Children's Needs: Maternal Citizenship in a Comparative and TransPacific Frame' (Lake, 2018) 36
Muggeridge, Eric 102
'multiple points of identification' *See* intersectionality
Murnane, Mary 24
Murray, Ben 169
Murray, Sir George 70
Murray, Suellen 59
Museums Victoria viii
Muslim historical storytelling 171–2, 173
Muslim historiography 171–2
   truth-chains (*isnad*) 172
Mussingkon, Wacvie 227
MV *Tampa* 175, 189
My Wife, My Daughter, and Poor Mary Ann (Kingston, 1975) 23

N

National Anzac Centre 9
National Council of Women NSW (NCWNSW) 44, 48, 50 *See also* Isbister, Dr Claire
National Council of Women of Australia (NCWA) 39–40, 41, 60
   conferences 1935& 1936 45–6
   fight to retain integrity of family unit 48–9
   medical control and expertise emphasis 44–5
National Council of Women Qld (NCWQ), birth control measures 46
National Council of Women SA (NCWSA) 48–9
National Council of Women Victoria (NCWV) 43–4, 100
   birth control debates 46
National Foundation for Australian Women 42
National History Curriculum viii
National Joint Committee for Spanish Relief 102
National Library 39, 110
National Library of Australia 185
National Life and Character: A Forecast (Pearson, 1893) 183, 185

nation-building
   challenging mainstream theories 15–16, 182, 205, 237
   role of Chinese–Australians in 186
NCWA *See* National Council of Women of Australia (NCWA)
Neale, Kerry *11*
Needham, Rev. J.S. 146
Negro World 145, 226
neoliberalism's impact on tertiary education 67, 77
New Deal for the Aborigines (Wright, 1938) 140
New Deal for the Aborigines (Wright, 1944) 141
new imperial history 29, 206, 209, 216
new social history 13
New Zealand arbitration system 192
Newman family 1
newspaper articles 35
Ngai, Mae 241–2
Nine Australian Progressives (Roe, 1984) 3
1967 referendum campaign
   role of Bandler in 157–9
   role of Street in 158
Noonuccal, Oodgeroo 157
'NSW Aborigines Protection/Welfare Board 1883–1969: A History' (Haskins & Maynard, forthcoming) 121
NSW Government, Anzac Advisory Council 10–11
NSW Police Force 123
NSW Racial Hygiene Association 46
NSW RSL 12
NSW Trades and Labour Council 140
NSW Welfare Board 123, 124, 132–3
   See also Aborigines Protection Board (NSW)

O

O'Connor, Lizzie *See* Conor, Liz
Odgers, Esme 101–3
O'Farrell, Barry 10
Office of the Status of Women 71
Officer of the Order of Australia (AO) viii
Oliver, Bobbie *11*
online exhibitions 42
Oppenheimer, Melanie *11*
oral history 114

Index

Aboriginal community testimonies 126–7, 135
Aboriginal historiographical traditions 169
settler 114
See also Wintle, Emily (née Gillespie)
Orloff, Ann 236
Orr, Sydney Sparkes 4
Outback Ghettos (Brock, 1993) 26
Outlook 196
overlapping fields of power *See* intersectionality
Oxford Handbook on Gender, War and the Western World Since 1600 (Hagemann & Dudink) 32, 234
Oxford University Press
  Australian Feminism: A Companion (Caine, 1998) 40–1
  Companion to Feminist History (Crawford, 1998) 29
  The Limits of Hope: Soldier Settlements in Victoria 1915–38 (Lake, 1987) 7, 27
  'Reading in Feminism' series 34
  Social Politics: International Studies in Gender State and Society 236

P

Pacific Islanders / Torres Strait Islanders
  deportation from plantations 180
  identification with African American causes 221–3, 226
  role in sugar industry 153, 160–1
Pacific Islanders Labourers Act 180
Pahlavi, Princess Ashraf 81, 85–6, 87
  seeks Reid to direct APCWD 88–9
Pahlavi, Shah Mohammed Reza 84
paidomazoma 98
Paisley, Fiona 28, 34
pan-Aboriginalism 137
Pan-Pacific Women's Congress 33
Pascoe, Carla 36
patriarchy
  authority over Aboriginal women 138
  gendered oppression and 63–4, 65
  ways to challenge and question 72
peace activism 53, 60, 65
Pearson, Charles 183, 184–5, 187, 209, 230
Pedersen, Susan 35
Penguin
  Double Time: Women in Victoria, 150 years (Lake & Farley (ed), 1984) 27
Perkins, Charles 227
petitions for 1967 referendum campaigns 158
Picot, Anne 24
Pierson, Ruth 34
Pink, Olive 130, 143
'The Politics of Respectability: Identifying the Masculinist Context' (Lake, 1986) 7, 30, 31, 231
Ponting, Ricky 1
Porto Rico and Its Problems (Clark, 1930) 195
post-colonial feminism 73
post-Greek migration 96
Poulson, Bruce 2
Powell, J.M. 14
Presbyterian Women's Association 49
press, reporting of Aboriginal issues 142
press (African American)
  accounts of white Australians 224–5
  circulation numbers 223
  reporting conditions of oppressed and colonised people 222–3
  reporting slavery conditions in Australia 1930s 223–4
pre-war progressivism 45
Progressive Era 192, 193, 197, 199
Progressive New World: How Settler Colonialism and Trans-Pacific Exchange Shaped American Reform (Lake, forthcoming) 3, 36
Progressive reform 190–1, 194
  themes 200
public lecture series vii–viii
Public Record Office Victoria 186
Pyne, Rob 74

Q

Quartly, Marian 5, 29–30, 39–40, 94, 122, 240, 242 *See also* Melbourne Feminist History Group
'Queen Narelle' 118, **119**

R

race politics 176–7, 181, 182
Racial Discrimination Act 1975 76
racism
  against Chinese in nineteenth century 183, 188–9, 210

259

as defense measure 176–7
　Victorian legislation provisions 179–80
radical activism 22 *See also* feminism
radical nationalism, Lake's critique of 17–20
rallies and petitions, effectiveness of 78–9, 158
Ravenscroft, Alison 71
Read, Peter 133–4, 135
The Real Matilda (Dixson, 1976) 22
Recognition Struggles and Social Movements: Contested Identities, Power and Agency (Hobson (ed), 2003) 32, 236
Red Cross 14
refugee rights, women's role in advocacy 99–106
Reid, Elizabeth 41, 61, 62, 80
　Australian delegation to WCIWY 87
　as director of APCWD 81, 88–9
　persistence and tenacity in compromised political situation 92–3
　reflection on institutional sponsored reforms 89–90, 92
　See also Asia Pacific Centre for Women and Development (APCWD)
Reiger, Kerreen 27
Research Centre for Women's Studies (SA) 25
Respectable Rascals: A History of the National Council of Women of Australia 1896–2006 (Quartly & Smart, 2015) 39, 42–3, 46–7, 50
'Rethinking Labour Rights through the "Coolie" Question' (Lake, 2015) 241
Reynolds, Henry 1–2, 10, 121, 240 *See also Drawing the Global Colour Line* (Lake & Reynolds, 2008); Lake, Marilyn—collaborations
Reynolds, Rev E.B. 104
Rezaulla, Munshi 163, 164, 167, 171
Rickard, John 5
Ridgeway, Sid 125
Rights for Aborigines: Draft Program for the Struggle Against Slavery (1931) 125
Rinnan, Arne 175
Rischbieth, Bessie 41, 47, 138, 142, 144
RMIT lectureship 27
Robertson, Mavis 61
Robson, Lloyd 1, 4–5

Rockefeller Center (Italy) 31, 235
Rockefeller Foundation 207
Roe, Jill 26
Roe, Michael *1*, 3, 4, 19
　influence on Lake 207–8
Roosevelt, Theodore 183–4, 192–3, 196, 199, 200, 201, 215
　Progressive reforms 207, 209
Rose, Jacqueline 76, 77
Ross, Dorothy 198, 211
Rothfield, Evelyn 62
Rothfield, Phillipa 71
Rowley, Hazel 35
Royce, Josiah 17, 182
Ruddick, Sara 63
Russell, Penny 242–3
Rutgers University 31
Ruttley, Val 112, 119
Ryan, Edna 23, 39
Ryan, Lyndall 25

S

Sainsbury, Daine 236
Sattar, Abdul 169
Saunders, Kay 26
SAVAK 91
Save Our Sons 54
Save the Children Fund 99
Scates, Bruce *11*
Schenk, Rod 144
scholarships 5
Schomburg Center for Research in Black Culture 222
Scott, Joan 30, 34
Scott, Rose 26, 41
Sculthorpe, Peter 1
segregation programs, full blood Aboriginals 144
self-determination 227
　Indigenous 136, 150, 159
　Indigenous critique 151
Senate Committee on Stolen Wages 2004 131–2
Serle, Geoffrey 5, 9
settler colonialism 34, 219
settler oral history 114 *See also* Wintle, Emily (née Gillespie)
Sewanee Review 183–4
Sex Discrimination Act 1984 71
sexism 55, 62, 74

Shah Mohammed Reza Pahlavi 84–90
    Friedan on 93
Shaw, Alan 2, 5, 6
Sheet Metal Workers' Union 140
Shiels, William 187
Shute, Carmel 27, 38 See also 'The War Girls'
Sisterhood of International Peace 56
slavery discourse 228
    Bandler's identification with 227
Sluga, Glenda 243
Smart, Judith *11*, 27, 39–40 See also 'The War Girls'
So Much Hard Work: Women and Prostitution in Australian History (Daniels (ed), 1984) 25
social and labour reform 196–7
Social Contract (Rousseau, 1762) 78
social democrats, Victorian British 16–17
Social Politics: International Studies in Gender State and Society 31
    'Citizenship: Intersections in Gender, Race and Ethnicity' 236
    Lake on board vii, 236
soldier settlement 13, 14
"The Souls of White Folk' (Du Bois, 1920) 184
South Asian diaspora 165, 173
    Aboriginal historiography 162–3, 169
    Australian historiography 168–70
    ayahs (female domestic servants) 170
    pioneers vs aliens literature on 165–7
    See also camel industry
Spanish Civil War 101, 102
Spearritt, Peter 23
Spence, Catherine 25, 41
Spender, Dale 66
SS Darius 168
Stanley, Peter 10 See also 'Honest History' group
Star, Susan Leigh 214
State Archives of New South Wales 123, 133
state feminism 57, 80, 91 See also Iran
State Library of New South Wales 33, 110, 123
'Statement by Feminist Scholars on the Election of Donald Trump' 77–8
'Stirrers with Style' online exhibition 42
Stockholm University vii

Advanced Research School in Comparative Gender Studies 32
Stolen Generations, archival material and research 133–4
Stoler, Ann Laura 212–13
storytelling *See* historical storytelling
Street, Jessie 41, 47, 141, 157
    friendship with Bandler 155
    role in 1967 referendum 158
Subrahmanyam, Sanjay 212, 213
sugar industry 153, 195
    deportation of Pacific Islanders 180
    role of Pacific Islanders 153, 160–1
Sullivan's Cove Waterfront Authority viii
Summers, Anne 13, 22, 39, 41, 55
Sun (newspaper) 105–6
Suter, Dr Keith 58
Swain, Shurlee 27
'Sydney and the Bush' (Davison, 1978) 7
Sydney Central Criminal Court 108
Sydney Morning Herald 110
Sykes, Bobbi 156

T

Taffe, Sue 144
Tampa (ship) 175, 189
Tampa election 175–6
ta'rikh 171
Tarlinton, Alexander 108
Tarlinton, Elizabeth 108, 111, 113, 114
Tarlinton, James 108
Tarlinton, Margaret 108, 111, 112
Tarlinton, Mrs 108, 111, 118
Tarlinton, Thomas 108
Tarlinton, William 108
'Tarnished Memory: "Emily's Story" and My Family Tree' (Collins, 2013) 113
Tasmania
    high achievers and diaspora 1
    influential figures in Lake's early years 2–3
    1967 bushfires 6
    pioneering feminists 38
Taylor, Charles 32
Ten Books that Shaped the British Empire: Creating an Imperial Commons (Burton & Hofmeyr (eds), 2014) 28
tertiary institutions
    dismantling of Women's and Gender Studies 73, 76

impact of neoliberalism on 67, 77
For Their Own Good (Haebich, 1988) 26
Thelen, David 212
Theobald, Marjorie 27
Thompson, Peter 133
Tims, Margaret 57
Tocqueville, Alexis de 193
Tosh, John 32
'Towards Equal Citizenship for Aborigines' petition (1962) 158
transgender women 76
transnational history 96, 98, 234
   approaches to US history 204–5
   from Australian perspective 204–16
   distinct from comparative history 209
   Lake's contribution to 122, 190, 210–11, 234
   United States history 204–5
transnationalism
   as framework for history 96
   Greek diaspora 97–8
   role of women in 106
   White Australia Policy 183–5
   'whiteness' as 95–6, 176–7, 210
   women's history 21
Tree, Marietta 86
Tregear, Edward 194
Treloar, Bob 11
tributes from afar 229–44
   Alexander, Sally 230–1
   Bashford, Alison 231–2
   Boris, Eileen 232
   Burton, Antoinette 232–3
   Chakrabarty, Dipesh 233–4
   Cott, Nancy 234
   Hagemann, Karen 234
   Hall, Catherine 235
   Hobson, Barbara 235–7
   Kennedy, Dane 237
   Kerber, Linda 237–8
   Kessler-Harris, Alice 239
   McGrath, Ann 239–41
   Ngai, Mae 241–2
   Russell, Penny 242–3
   Sluga, Glenda 243
trolling 74
Trove 110, 119
Troy, Jaky 123
Trumpism 72, 74, 77
Turner, Frederick Jackson 197, 211
Turner, Ian 4, 5
Tyrrell, Ian 211–12, 218, 228

U

Ulrich, Laurel Thatcher 35
UNESCO Congress on the Eradication of Illiteracy 85
Union of Australian Women 65
United Associations of Women (UAW) 130
United Nations 33, 40, 51
   Commission on the Status of Women (CSW) 47, 84–5
   Decade for Women 1975–1985 53, 61, 63
   Group of 77 coalition 86
   Tribune satellite conference 61–2, 88
   Universal Declaration of Human Rights 80, 157
   See also International Women's Year 1975–1985
United States
   annexations 192, 194
   Anthracite Strike 1902 192
   attack of Gender Studies 79
   Department of Commerce and Labor 195, 198
   Federal Equal Rights Amendment 83
   Progressive reform 190–1
   social and labour reform 196–7
   Women's Marches 78
United States history
   from Australian perspective 220–1
   impact of Australian settler colonialism on 218–19
   transnational history approach 204–5
Universal Negro Improvement Association (UNIA) 145, 226
University of Adelaide 2–3, 25
University of Chicago 237
University of Maryland vii
University of Melbourne
   Ashworth lectureship 27
   'Australian Mothering in Historical and Contemporary Perspective' conference 2018 36
   Lake's festschrift vii, 37
   'Historicising Whiteness: Transnational Perspectives on the Construction of an Identity' conference 2006 162

University of New South Wales 24
University of Sussex 2–3
University of Sydney vii, 18, 56
University of Tasmania 3
    academic scandal case 4
    Lake's participation in women's groups 23
University of Technology, Women's Studies 24
University of Western Australia vii
Uphill all the Way (Daniels, 1980) 3

V

Veysey, Laurence 211
Vicinus, Martha 29
Victoria University (NZ), 5th Annual Conference 1988 28
Victorian Honour Roll of Women viii
Victorian Women's Trust viii
Vietnam War 53–6
violence against women 74–5
vitalists 207 *See also* American Progressivism

W

Walker, Kath 157 *See also* Noonuccal, Oodgeroo
Walkowitz, Judy 33
'The War Girls' 38
Ward, Dolly 117
Ward, Edwin 117
Ward, Russel 4, 18, 208
Ward Registers 1916–1928 132, 133, 134
Warren, Elizabeth 74
Waterson, Duncan 5
Watt, Elizabeth 136
Webb, Jessie 99–101
Webb, Sidney 16
websites 42
Welfare Board legislation 1940 124
What's Wrong with Anzac? (Lake, Reynolds, McKenna & Damousi (eds), 2010) 10, 15, 95, 240
White, Richard 5
White, Shane 218, 228
'A White Australia' (Lake, 2004) 230
White Australia Policy
    African American press condemnation 225
    Clark's views on 200, 201
    as colour bar 178–81
    through feminist theory 181–3
    impact on proposed children refugee adoptions 103
    literacy test 180
    through transnational frame 183–5
'white labour' 199–201
'white man'
    Anglo-Saxonism as substitute for 214–16
    transnational 214
'The "White Man", Race and Imperial War during the Long Nineteenth Century' (Lake, 2016) 32
white masculinity 210–11, 213, 235
'white men's countries', transnational history 205–6, 219
Whitehouse, Mary 48
'whiteness' 216
    as act of self-preservation 182–3
    as Australian national identity 17
    as boundary object 213–14
    as transnational phenomenon 95–6, 176–7, 210
Whitlam, Gough 81
Whitlam government 48, 61, 82, 89
WIDF 62
Wilkins, Roy 86
Williams. Fiona 236
Wilson, Caroline 74
Windschuttle, Keith 134
Winter, Elizabeth 115
Wintle, Alf 117
Wintle, David 114–15, 117
Wintle, Elizabeth 116
Wintle, Emily (née Gillespie) 107–20
    memoir 118
Wintle, Jack 117
Wintle, Jane 112, 117
Wintle, Walter 114, 116
Wolfe, Patrick 218, 221
Woman's Right to Choose Bill 74
women
    marginalisation in Australian nationalism 18
    violence against 74–5
    See also Aboriginal women
'Women, Black, Indigenous: Recognition Struggles in Dialogue' (Lake, 2003) 32

Women, Class and History (Windschuttle (ed), 1982) 23
Women for Peace 54
Women in Australia: An Annotated Guide to Records (Daniels, Murnane & Picot, 1977) 3, 24
Women of Today 101
Women's Electoral Lobby 22, 23, 47–8, 60, 90
women's history 21–36
   internationalism 21, 28–9
   Lake's role in transforming 21–2
   prominent feminist historians 24–7
   research project 24
   transnationalism 21, 29
Women's History Review 34
   Lake's article on Mary Bennett (1993) 33
Women's International Democratic Federation (WIDF) 62
Women's International League for Peace and Freedom (WILPF) 33, 52–3
   anti-Vietnam War protests 53–6
   engagement with WIDF 62
   evolution and adaptation of ideas 53, 63–4
   interaction with WLM 56–64
   membership 1970s 56, 60
   reassertion as peace organisation 57–8, 62–3
   reluctance in involvement with WLM 59, 60
   triennial congress 1986 Netherlands 63
   WA branch 58–9
Women's International Peace Congress 1919 99
women's labour movement 181–2
Women's Land Army 154
Women's Liberation Movement (WLM) 21–2, 23, 25, 41, 47, 49, 56
   interaction with WILPF 56–64
   transnational focus 57
women's movements
   1950s and 1960s 54–5
   1970s 55–6
   emergence of internationalism 51
   impact on women's history 21–2
   labour 181–2
   See also Women's Liberation Movement (WLM)

Women's Organization of Iran (WOI) 81, 82, 83, 90, 91
Women's Peace Army 55
Women's Rights and Human Rights: International Perspectives (Grimshaw, Holmes & Lake (eds), 2001) 33
Women's Studies 24, 25, 66
   dismantling of 73, 76–7
   effect of funding slashing 67
   interdisciplinary subjects 70–1
   Lake as founding director 27–8, 70–1
   rebadging as Gender Studies 73, 76–7
women's work 23, 25, 71–2
workshops 28, 31
world history 205
The World War Two Reader (Martel (ed), 2004) 34
World's Work 196
Worsley, Peter 141
Wright, Carroll D. 192
Wright, Richard 35
Wright, Tom 140, 141, 143, 149

Y

Yale University 'Beyond Freedom: New Direction in the Study of Emancipation' conference 2011 219
Young Communist League 101
YWCA 33, 48

Z

Zainu'ddin, Ailsa 27
Ziino, Bart *11*, 14